Global Poverty

Around 1.4 billion people presently live in extreme poverty, and yet despite this vast scale, the issue of global poverty had a relatively low international profile until the end of the twentieth century. In this important new work, Hulme charts the rise of global poverty as a priority global issue, and its subsequent marginalization as old themes edged it aside (trade policy, financial stability and peace-making in regions of geo-political importance) and new issues were added (terrorism, global climate change and access to natural resources).

Providing a concise and detailed overview of both the history and the current debates that surround this key issue, the book:

- outlines how the notion of global poverty eradication has evolved
- evaluates the institutional landscape and its ability to attack global poverty
- analyzes the conceptual and technical frameworks that lie behind the contemporary understanding of global poverty (including human development, dollar-a-day poverty and results-based management)
- explores the roles that major institutions have played in promoting and/ or obstructing the advancement of actions to reduce poverty
- discusses the emerging issues that are re-shaping thinking, and the future prospects for global poverty eradication.

The first book to tackle the issue of global poverty through the lens of global institutions, this volume provides an important resource for all students and scholars of international relations, development studies and international political economy.

David Hulme is Professor of Development Studies and Head of the Institute for Development Policy and Management at the University of Manchester. He is Director of the Brooks World Poverty Institute and the Chronic Poverty Research Centre at the University of Manchester.

Routledge Global Institutions

Edited by Thomas G. Weiss

The CUNY Graduate Center, New York, USA

and Rorden Wilkinson

University of Manchester, UK

About the series

The "Global Institutions Series" is designed to provide readers with comprehensive, accessible, and informative guides to the history, structure, and activities of key international organizations as well as books that deal with topics of key importance in contemporary global governance. Every volume stands on its own as a thorough and insightful treatment of a particular topic, but the series as a whole contributes to a coherent and complementary portrait of the phenomenon of global institutions at the dawn of the millennium.

Books are written by recognized experts, conform to a similar structure, and cover a range of themes and debates common to the series. These areas of shared concern include the general purpose and rationale for organizations, developments over time, membership, structure, decision-making procedures, and key functions. Moreover, current debates are placed in historical perspective alongside informed analysis and critique. Each book also contains an annotated bibliography and guide to electronic information as well as any annexes appropriate to the subject matter at hand.

The volumes currently published are:

44 Global Poverty
How global governance is failing the poor (2010)
by David Hulme (University of Manchester)

43 Global Governance, Poverty, and Inequality (2010)
edited by Jennifer Clapp (University of Waterloo) and Rorden Wilkinson (University of Manchester)

42 Multilateral Counter-terrorism (2010)
by Peter Romaniuk (John Jay College of Criminal Justice, CUNY)

The volumes currently under contract include:

The Regional Development Banks
Lending with a Regional Flavor
by Jonathan R. Strand (University of Nevada)

Millennium Development Goals (MDGs)
For a People-Centered Development Agenda?
by Sakiko Fukada-Parr (The New School)

Peacebuilding
From Concept to Commission
by Robert Jenkins (The CUNY Graduate Center)

Human Security
by Don Hubert (University of Ottawa)

UNESCO
by J. P. Singh (Georgetown University)

UNICEF
by Richard Jolly (University of Sussex)

FIFA
by Alan Tomlinson (University of Brighton)

International Law, International Relations, and Global Governance
by Charlotte Ku (University of Illinois)

Humanitarianism Contested
by Michael Barnett (University of Minnesota) and Thomas G. Weiss (The CUNY Graduate Center)

The Bank for International Settlements
The Politics of Global Financial Supervision in the Age of High Finance
by Kevin Ozgercin (SUNY College at Old Westbury)

International Migration
by Khalid Koser (Geneva Centre for Security Policy)

Global Health Governance
by Sophie Harman (City University, London)

The Council of Europe
by Martyn Bond (University of London)

Human Development
by Richard Ponzio (US Department of State)

The United Nations Development Programme (UNDP)
by Stephen Browne (The International Trade Centre, Geneva)

Religious Institutions and Global Politics
by Katherine Marshall (Georgetown University)

South Asian Association for Regional Cooperation (SAARC)
by Lawrence Saez (University of London)

The International Trade Centre
by Stephen Browne (The Future of the UN Development System (FUNDS) Project, Geneva) and Samuel Laird (University of Nottingham)

The Group of Twenty (G20)
by Andrew F. Cooper (Centre for International Governance Innovation, Ontario) and Ramesh Thakur (Balsillie School of International Affairs, Ontario)

The UN Human Rights Council
by Bertrand G. Ramcharan (Geneva Graduate Institute of International and Development Studies)

For further information regarding the series, please contact:

Craig Fowlie, Senior Publisher, Politics & International Studies
Taylor & Francis
2 Park Square, Milton Park, Abingdon
Oxford OX14 4RN, UK

+44 (0)207 842 2057 Tel
+44 (0)207 842 2302 Fax

Craig.Fowlie@tandf.co.uk
www.routledge.com

To Mum and Dad who saw the beginning of this book but not its completion.

To my amazing children – Edward, Jasmine and Saffron – for limitless guidance on IT, indie music, horse-trading and much more.

To Georgina who keeps our show on the road and makes life so much fun.

Global Poverty

How global governance is failing
the poor

David Hulme

Routledge
Taylor & Francis Group

LONDON AND NEW YORK

First published 2010 by Routledge
2 Park Square, Milton Park, Abingdon, Oxon, OX14 4RN

Simultaneously published in the USA and Canada
by Routledge
270 Madison Avenue, New York, NY 10016

Reprinted 2010

Routledge is an imprint of the Taylor & Francis Group, an informa business

© 2010 David Hulme

Typeset in Times New Roman by
Pindar NZ, Auckland, New Zealand
Printed and bound in Great Britain by
CPI Antony Rowe, Chippenham, Wiltshire

British Library Cataloguing in Publication Data
A catalogue record for this book is available from the British Library

Library of Congress Cataloging in Publication Data
Hulme, David.
Global poverty : how global governance is failing the poor / David Hulme.
    p. cm. — (Routledge global institutions)
    ISBN 978-0-415-49077-1 — ISBN 978-0-415-49078-8 — ISBN 978-0-
203-84476-2 1. Poverty—International cooperation. 2. Poverty—Government
policy. 3. International agencies—Evaluation. 4. International organization.
I. Title.
    HC79.P6H86 2010
    362.5'526—dc22   2010007741

ISBN 13: 978-0-415-49077-1(hbk)
ISBN 13: 978-0-415-49078-8 (pbk)
ISBN 13: 978-0-203-84476-2 (ebk)

Contents

Illustrations

Boxes

Figures

Tables

Foreword by the series editors

The current volume is the forty-second in what has now become recognized as a dynamic and well-regarded series on "global institutions." The series strives to provide readers with definitive guides to the most visible aspects of what we know as "global governance" as well as forensic accounts of the issues and debates in which they are embroiled. Remarkable as it may seem (particularly as the situation has not changed in the half decade since the publication of our first volume), there exist relatively few books that offer in-depth treatments of prominent global bodies, processes, and associated issues – much less an entire series of concise and complementary volumes. Those that do exist are either out of date, inaccessible to the non-specialist reader, or seek to develop a specialized understanding of particular aspects of an institution or process rather than offer an overall account of its functioning. Similarly, existing books have often been written in highly technical language or have been crafted "in-house" and are notoriously self-serving and narrow.

The advent of electronic media has helped by making information, documents, and resolutions of international organizations more widely available, but it has also complicated matters. The growing reliance on the Internet and other electronic methods of finding information about key international organizations and processes has served, ironically, to limit the educational materials to which most readers have ready access – namely, books. Public relations documents, raw data, and loosely refereed websites do not amount to intelligent analysis. Independent analyses compete with a vast amount of electronically available information, much of which is suspect because of its ideological or self-promoting slant but which is free. Paradoxically then, a growing range of purportedly independent websites offering analyses of the activities of particular organizations has emerged, but one inadvertent consequence has been to frustrate access to basic, authoritative, critical, and well-researched texts. The market for such has actually been reduced by the ready availability of varying quality electronic materials.

For those of us who teach, research, and work in the area, the access to up-to-date and authoritative information has been particularly frustrating. We were delighted when Routledge saw the value of a series that bucks trends and provides key reference points to the most significant global institutions and the evolution of the issues that they face. Routledge knows that serious students and professionals want serious analyses, and they are willing to pay reasonable prices to have that access. We have assembled a first-rate line-up of authors to address that market. Our intention is to provide one-stop shopping for all readers – students (both undergraduate and postgraduate), interested negotiators, diplomats, practitioners from non-governmental and intergovernmental organizations, and interested parties alike – seeking information about most prominent institutional aspects of global governance.

Global Poverty

David Hulme's book could not have arrived at a more compelling and appropriate time. Almost half the world's population lives in poverty – mostly in the Global South, but often in hidden and forgotten enclaves in the industrial North. Yet the enduring nature of poverty, and the afflictions it gives rise to, seldom make front-page headlines or the evening news. Indeed, poverty only really comes to public attention during moments of acute crisis and hardship, but, all too quickly, its causes, consequences, and prevalence, fall quickly from public view. Two recent events illustrate this dynamic well. First, reporting of the 2008/9 financial crisis, known almost universally as the "credit crunch," drew attention only momentarily to the house repossessions of those that had been offered mortgages at unsustainable rates. But this attention highlighted not the difficulties and hardships of the less well off, or the reasons for or consequences of their financial situation; rather, it dwelt on the follies of a global banking system that lent to those less likely to be able to repay the debt. And, as the credit crunch snowballed into a crisis of the global financial system, attention moved swiftly away from the destitute towards the sizable bailouts offered to banking institutions and the immorality of a financial bonus culture. Almost forgotten were those hit hardest by the financial crisis. Completely obscured from view remained the absolutely destitute, those that were never in a position to have been offered credit in the first place.

A second example relates to the January 2010 earthquake in Haiti. The deaths of some 230,000 people, and the injuries to some 300,000 more, drew attention to the desperately poor of Haiti and initially resulted in news coverage of the lives of many of the poorest residents there. However, once the relief effort was fully underway, media attention quickly turned away from issues of destitution to focus on the difficulties of getting logistical support to the country and the nefarious attempts to "adopt" children in the quake's wake. Just a few weeks later, the poor of Haiti had slipped from public consciousness, leaving poverty on that island a persistent and enduring fact of life. And while it is the case that the on-going relief effort will target some of the poor, a concerted poverty eradication effort remains conspicuous in its absence.

What makes the lack of a concerted effort to eradicate poverty, in both Haiti as well as across the world, all the more worrisome is the fact that international institutions – since they became a formalized feature of global politics – have always been involved in issues of poverty and development.[1] And while it is the case that some advances have been made, widespread and enduring poverty persists. So what is to be done?

David Hulme's book is the first to tackle the issue of global poverty through the lens of global institutions. His purpose is to review the ways in which international institutions have been involved in poverty reduction strategies and to assess the successes. There is much to cheer about in David's book. His argument is that we have reached a point in time where a consensus on the necessity for a concerted attempt at eradicating poverty has crystallized. Less pleasing, however, is that the emergence of this consensus has not been accompanied by an equally serious concerted effort. What we have, as a consequence, is a mismatch between words and deeds.

The prevalence of global poverty, its enduring character, and the variety of institutions formally and indirectly involved in its eradication[2] ensured that we could not have a series on Global Institutions without an authoritative account on this topic.[3] In other words, the topic spoke for itself. And once we had decided to contract a book on the topic, it was very clear to us that we wanted David Hulme to write it for us.

David is currently Professor of Development Studies and Executive Director of the Brooks World Poverty Institute at the University of Manchester. He is one of the world's foremost authorities in poverty, having influenced policy and thinking in ways few scholars can claim. David counts among his areas of expertise rural and development policy and planning; poverty reduction strategies; micro-credit and micro-finance; the sociology of development; the role of civil society and NGOs; technical assistance; environmental management; public sector reform; and global poverty reduction strategies. And he has written and edited more than 15 books[4] and more than 80 articles, book chapters, and other pieces in the area.

David's expertise is very much in evidence in the pages that follow. He has produced one of the most cogent and compelling accounts of global poverty available. It bristles with insight, encourages the reader to turn the page, and continually highlights the need to treat issues of poverty with a greater seriousness. David's book will no doubt find a willing and receptive audience. It is as useful to undergraduate and graduate students as it is to practitioners and policymakers. It will also appeal to the lay public in ways that few academic books can. We heartily recommend it. And as always, we welcome comments from our readers.

Thomas G. Weiss, the CUNY Graduate Center, New York, USA
Rorden Wilkinson, University of Manchester, UK
March 2010

Notes

1 See Craig Murphy, *The United Nations Development Programme – A Better Way?* (Cambridge: Cambridge University Press, 2006); and Richard Jolly, Louis Emmerij, and Thomas G. Weiss, *UN Ideas That Changed the World* (Bloomington: Indiana University Press, 2009).

2 Other titles in this series of relevance include: Katherine Marshall, *The World Bank* (2008); Bernard M. Hoekman, *The World Trade Organization* (2007); Ian Taylor, *UN Conference on Trade and Development* (2007); and James Raymond Vreeland, *The International Monetary Fund* (2007). Forthcoming books of relevance in the series include Steve Hughes, *The International Labour Organization*; J.P. Singh, *UNESCO*; Richard Jolly, *UNICEF*; and Stephen Browne, *The United Nations Development Programme*.

3 See, also, Jennifer Clapp and Rorden Wilkinson, eds., *Global Governance, Poverty and Inequality* (New York: Routledge, 2010), especially the chapter by Eric Helleiner, "Global Governance Meets Development: A Brief History of an Innovation in World Politics."

4 See, among others, David Hulme, Joe Hanlon and Armando Barrientos, *Just Give Money to the Poor*, (West Hartford, CT: Kumarian Press, 2010); David Hulme, Tony Addison, and Ravi Kanbur, *Poverty Dynamics: Interdisciplinary Perspectives* (Oxford: Oxford University Press, 2009); David Hulme and Armando Barrientos, *Social Protection for the Poor and Poorest* (New York: Palgrave, 2009); and David Hulme, Alastair Greig, and Mark Turner, *Challenging Global Inequality: The Theory and Practice of Development in the Twenty-First Century* (New York: Palgrave, 2006).

Foreword by Richard Jolly

The year 2015 is the target year for the MDGs – the Millennium Development Goals for halving poverty worldwide and improving the human condition of people in all parts of the world. The goals were agreed by 147 heads of state and representatives of most other governments, at a summit meeting held at the United Nations in New York in September 2000. The goals were part of a broader Millennium Declaration also agreed by the heads of state.

This book provides the most careful and comprehensive description and analysis to date of the process leading to the setting of these goals and to the Declaration. Against this background, it also distils a set of challenges for the future.

The whole process which led to the MDGs was unprecedented, both for the number of countries formally endorsing the goals and, equally significant, for the formal support from the three major international institutions which backed them – the UN itself, the Bretton Woods Institutions and the OECD. By 2000, the UN already had a forty year record of formulating development goals. This began in 1960 when UNESCO set goals for expanding education from 1960 to 1980 and when a year later, the UN's General Assembly launched a "Development Decade" with goals for accelerating economic growth in developing countries over the 1960s. The UN had also fixed targets for flows of aid and private capital from developed countries to support more rapid economic growth. But these and later UN goals never received formal endorsement from the Bretton Woods Institutions, nor from OECD. Thus universal acceptance of the MDGs in the year 2000 was a first.

In spite of this unprecedented level of support, Hulme's analysis brings out a range of difficulties and contradictions:

- His detailed account and careful analysis of how the MDGs were framed and evolved reveals the tensions and contradictions with two parallel processes – the evolution of the human development paradigm and the adoption of a results-based management system, with both of which the

UN and UNDP in particular were involved and to which, in principle, they were committed.

- In addition, all three – the MDGs, human development and results based management – presented problems and difficulties of implementation for countries and for international bureaucracy. Most notably, this was because many countries were still locked into policies framed by neo-liberal economic orthodoxy. Indeed such policies were still being strongly promoted by the IMF and sometimes by the World Bank, as conditions of loans and certificates of good economic housekeeping.

- Perhaps most important and original, Hulme identifies the mixed motivations of the various governments and other parties even while formally backing the MDGs. Among the self-interested reasons motivating the various governments and agencies, Hulme lists the following: "the creation of an account showing that the spread of capitalism would benefit all of the world's people (and so economic globalization should continue); policies and programmes that might reduce flows of illegal immigrants from poorer into richer countries; programs that would discourage the recruitment of young men into "terrorist" organizations; images of compassion that improved a country's or organization's standing in international circles; stabilized aid flows so that aid agencies did not have to downsize; and many other self-interested reasons.

Hulme does not ignore the compassion and moral visions behind many of those involved in pursuing the MDGs and the Millennium Declaration: a genuine desire to improve the lives of very poor people; a belief in the need to reduce social and economic inequality; a commitment to reduce the impact of climate change; and wider concerns with bequeathing to future generations a better world.

However, the contradictions and difficulties need to be faced – and faced well before 2015. Leaving the issues until 2015 or shortly before, will lose the opportunity for learning lessons from progress and problems so far, for making course-corrections and for carefully considering what should follow the MDGs. Just as serious, leaving the difficulties and contradictions to continue without careful review, runs serious risks of public disillusionment if and when it becomes clear that many of the goals will not be achieved – and were perhaps misleading and many even unachievable when they were first proposed.

Although sharply critical at times, Hulme's analysis sustains a continually positive and constructive concern. He is highly aware of the frailty of government commitments and sometimes even the hypocrisy behind the global goals of poverty reduction. But he never risks throwing out the baby with the bath water, of letting human opportunity disappear in a flood of cynicism.

Indeed, in the final chapter he identifies in specific terms what needs to be done by whom and how. The book concludes with challenges to each party to take the actions required.

No one can be expected to agree with every word or nuance of Hulme's analysis and interpretation – though I broadly agree with his main interpretation. If I have any reservation it is his underplaying of the experience of one UN agency in the 1980s which did show with remarkable success how goals could be used for worldwide mobilization. This was the experience of UNICEF pursuing the goal of reducing child mortality. This positive and largely successful experience undoubtedly served as a key example of how global goals could be used for country-by-country mobilization, even when many of the countries in Africa and Latin America were highly constrained by the economics of structural adjustment during what became known as the "lost decade of development".

UNICEF's experience brings out several critical elements of the process:

- The power of political and social mobilization
- The catalytic role which a UN agency can play if all its staff and financial resources are mobilized behind a global goal applied at country level
- The need for global goals to be adopted and adapted by each country – and the important part which a UN agency can play in helping this to be done
- The critical role which bold international leadership can play at the top of an international organization. Jim Grant, UNICEF's Executive Director at the time, was such a leader and mobilized the whole of its staff and resources to the effort which became known as a Child Survival and Development Revolution.

Some of this vision and focus was subsequently captured in results-based management, which since the 1990s has been widely promoted and adopted in the UN and in a number of donor agencies. But, as Hulme brings out, results-based management has often operated in contradiction to the spirit of the MDGs, emphasizing goals, incentives and management but in a way which has often missed out the vision and passion of leadership and the release of popular energy through political and social mobilization for children and people.

The third element in Hulme's analysis is human development – putting people at the centre of development strategy, as formally endorsed at the World Summit for Social Development in 1995. Hulme rightly identifies the path-breaking contribution of UNDP in creating the Human Development Report in 1990 – producing a succession of innovative and well analyzed subsequent reports on different themes. Much of the credit for creating these reports must go to Mahbub ul Haq and to the Nobel prize-winning economist, Amartya Sen. Human development has the potential for providing a broader and more human focused agenda for national and international development than neo-liberal economics. It incorporates as integral elements human rights, gender equality, environmental sustainability and a concern for equity and, at the same time, is fully consistent with the MDGs. But human development has never achieved the central international position as have the MDGs.

David Hulme places the blame for this failure on several groups:

- on academics for failing to develop human development as a epistemic community
- on NGOs for failing to make human development a global movement
- on governments, for failing to make human development central to their economic policies

I would add to this the failure of the UN institutions as a whole to adopt human development as an integrating frame for all their development programmes and actions. Too often, the Human Development Report has been treated, often with jealousy, as little more than an annual PR document report which brilliantly gathers headlines for UNDP in the world's press.

Human development, in fact, already means much more than this. Globally, the human development paradigm and the annual report continue to gather interest and support. At country level, over 600 national human development reports have by now been produced, applying the paradigm to the specifics of some 140 countries and all the main regions of the world. Meanwhile, the global economic crisis has shown with devastating clarity the inadequacies and costs of neo-liberal analysis and policy. The shameless neglect of any semblance of morality or equity by many bankers and hedge fund managers has stirred public outrage at some of the groups who have obviously benefited.

In chapter 8, David Hulme sets out the challenges for the future. In his words, the Millennium Moment may have passed but there is still time to pursue poverty reduction as a serious global goal. It will require a renewed alliance between the heads of international institutions and governments – especially those with leadership roles and in position to define agency position and set policies. Such persons – and the staff members who support them – need to maintain pressure on rich country governments to honour their MDG commitments. Global reporting needs to keep political parties and their leaders accountable for the promises they made. At the same time, pressure needs to be maintained on developing countries to improve domestic governance and to plan and implement national strategies directed to poverty reduction. All this can be linked to reforms for strengthening global governance and giving it a sharper focus on poverty reduction and social protection worldwide.

Hulme introduces some innovative ideas for giving more political appeal to such actions: linking poverty reduction initiatives to more favoured global issues – such as climate change, actions directed to international or national security and recovery from economic crisis; raising public awareness in education; and reporting more clearly and regularly in the media on progress.

Ultimately, political support for the MDGs will rest on a multitude of individual commitments. David Hulme gives examples of how such commitments can start small and local – and build up to making a difference on a national and global scale. Debt relief is one example, fair trade another, environmental action a third. The MDGs came into existence in part through such a process – when many individuals and non-government groups called for action to end poverty. This process began well and achieved unexpected and unprecedented success at the Millennium Summit. The process is still underway but it needs to be revitalized through the mobilization and renewed commitment of leaders, agencies, governments and millions of individuals if momentum is to be maintained and the goals achieved.

Richard Jolly

Acknowledgments

This is my first sole-authored book. To achieve this a cast of thousands has been necessary to support, guide, advise and motivate me. Below are the names of those who have provided particular inputs but there are many others who have assisted who are not identified: to all of you I offer my sincere thanks.

To start I must thank the Leverhulme Trust who provided a Major Research Fellowship Grant that allowed me to focus on this topic over the 2006 to 2009 period and to shift my interests from poverty at the 'micro' level to poverty at the 'macro' level. The referees for that proposal – John Harriss, Ravi Kanbur and John Toye – must also be thanked for their encouragement and guidance at an early stage, as must Maia Green for helping me think through the early concept. Especial thanks go to Karen Moore – who turned my hand-written notes into a successful fellowship proposal (I was in Bangladesh at the time of submission). Few research officers can have provided such high levels of intellectual and practical support for their PIs.

Many academic and professional colleagues have provided advice on the book and have commented on chapters or read earlier manuscripts. Rorden Wilkinson and Tom Weiss, the editors of the Global Institutions series, have taken an active role in shaping the content and argument of the book and encouraging me to complete it. I was fortunate to win a Johann Skytte Award from the Department of Government at Uppsala University that supported a workshop to review the first draft of this book. The participants at this workshop showed me how to strengthen my ideas and structure the argument more clearly. Many thanks to Li Bennich-Björkman who hosted and led the workshop, assisted by Malin Holm, and to Armando Barrientos, Hans Blomkvist, Sakiko Fukuda-Parr, Anirudh Krishna, Branka Likic-Brboric, Paul Mosley, James Scott, Kunal Sen, K.C. Suri, Tom Weiss and Rorden Wilkinson for giving me so much of your time and advice. Late on in the writing process a number of other kind colleagues looked at the manuscript and provided the encouragement to reach the finishing line – Tony German, Alastair Greig, Sam Hickey, Stuart Rutherford and Mark Turner.

During the course of researching and writing the book I interviewed and met with many people who advised me on analytical framework, key ideas and/or provided empirical materials. These include:

Tony Addison, Masood Ahmed, Zulfiqar Ali, Sabina Alkire, Thankom Arun, Stephanie Barrientos, Bob Baulch, Debapriya Bhattacharya, Colin Bradford, Lael Brainard, Karen Brooks, Rory Brooks, Jose Antonio Campo, Michael Carter, Robert Chambers, Ha-Joon Chang, Marty Chen, Vasudha Chhotray, Admos Chimhowu, Jennifer Clapp, John Clark, Michael Clemens, Barbara Crossette, Janek Cukcrowski, Arjaan de Haan, Stefan Dercon, Stephen Deveureux, Michael Edwards, Phil Evans, Ros Eyben, Chico Ferreira, Paul Francis, Bridget Fury, Newai Gabre-Ab, Harry Hagan, Brian Hammond, Barbara Harriss-White, Syed Hashemi, Eric Helleiner, Eveline Herfkens, John Hobcraft, Graham Hulme, Laurie Hulme, Solava Ibrahim, Nasrul Islam, Selim Jahan, Hilde Johnson, Richard Jolly, Margaret Kakande, Aasha Kapur Mehta, William Kingsmill, Stephan Klasen, Sarah Kline, Uma Kothari, Jomo Kwame Sundaram, Paul Ladd, Carol Lancaster, Ruth Levine, Charles Lwange-Ntale, Wahiddudin Mahmud, Tim Mahoney, Richard Manning, Catherine Marshall, Richard Marshall, Imran Matin, Simon Maxwell, Desmond McNeil, Stephan Meyer, Branko Milanovic, Thandika Mkandawire, Jonathan Morduch, Francoise Moreau, Caroline Moser, Lauchlan Munro, Craig Murphy, Deepa Naryan, Miguel Nino-Zarazua, Akbar Noman, Andy Norton, Alice O'Connor, John Page, Robert Picciotto, Seeta Prabhu, Biju Rao, Martin Ravallion, David Roodman, Rathin Roy, Takayuki Sahara, Pablo Sanchez, Nimal Sanderatne, Guido Schmidt-Traub, Binayak Sen, John Sewell, Andrew Shepherd, Salil Shetty, Go Shimada, Clare Short, Paul Spray, Asuncion St.Clair, Howard Stein, Nicholas Stern, Frances Stewart, Joe Stiglitz, Jan Vandermoortele, Rob Vos, Robert Wade, Bernard Walters, Michael Walton, Andrew Watson, Adrian Wood, Ngaire Woods, Michael Woolcock, A. Sylvester Young, John Young, Meles Zenawi and Sajjad Zohir.

Throughout the writing of the book I have been supported by excellent research officers. Karen Moore kicked the project into play and provided advice throughout; David Clark provided support in the early phases; and James Scott provided top class support and brought the project to completion. At the University of Manchester many people provided direct and indirect assistance. My personal assistant, Denise Redston, did a million different jobs to ensure I finished this project and was supported by the excellent administration team at the Brooks World Poverty Institute led by Ros McDonnell. Clive Agnew, the Head of the School of Environment and Development and Jayne Hindle were particularly helpful in keeping me clear of University administration tasks and creating a supportive environment across the School. Nick Scarle and colleagues in the School of Environment and Development Cartography Unit kindly prepared maps.

Finally, my gratitude to all other folk who have helped me to complete this book.

David Hulme
Manchester
February 2010

Abbreviations

AU	African Union
BRICs	Brazil, Russia, India, and China
BWIs	Bretton Woods Institutions (IMF and World Bank)
CDF	Comprehensive Development Framework (World Bank)
CDI	Commitment to Development Index
CE	Common Era
CSOs	Civil society organizations
DAC	Development Assistance Committee (of the OECD)
DFID	Department for International Development (UK)
DRC	Democratic Republic of the Congo
ECOSOC	The Economic and Social Council (UN)
ESAF	Enhanced Structural Adjustment Facility (of the IMF)
EU	European Union
FAO	Food and Agriculture Organization (UN)
FFD	Finance for Development
GATT	General Agreement on Tariffs and Trade
GAVI	The Global Alliance for Vaccination and Immunization
GCAP	Global Call to Action Against Poverty
GDP	Gross domestic product
GNI	Gross national income
GNP	Gross national product
GTZ	Deutsche Gesellschaft für Technische Zusammenarbeit
HDI	Human Development Index
HIPC	Heavily indebted poor countries
HPI	Human Poverty Index
IBRD	International Bank of Reconstruction and Development (World Bank)
ICISD	International Centre for Settlement of Investment Disputes
ICTs	Information and communication technologies
IDA	International Development Association (World Bank)

IDB	Islamic Development Bank
IDGs	International Development Goals (OECD-DAC)
IFC	International Finance Corporation (World Bank)
ILO	International Labour Organization (UN)
IMF	International Monetary Fund
IPRSP	Interim Poverty Reduction Strategy Papers
JSA	Joint Staff Appraisal (of the World Bank and IMF)
LDCs	Least developed countries
MDGs	Millennium Development Goals
MIGA	Multilateral Investment Guarantee Agency (World Bank)
MNCs	Multinational corporations
MTEF	Medium Term Expenditure Framework
NEPAD	New Partnership for Africa's Development
NGOs	Non-governmental organizations
NIEO	New International Economic Order
ODA	Official development assistance
OECD	Organisation for Economic Cooperation and Development
PEAP	Poverty Eradication Action Plan (Uganda)
PFPs	Policy Framework Papers
PPA	Participatory Poverty Assessment
PPP	Purchasing Power Parity
PRGF	Poverty Reduction and Growth Facility (IMF)
PRS	Poverty Reduction Strategy
PRSCs	Poverty Reduction Support Credits (World Bank)
PRSP	Poverty Reduction Strategy Paper
RBM	Results based management
SADC	Southern African Development Community
SAARC	South Asian Association for Regional Cooperation
SDI	Shack/Slum Dwellers International
TRIPs	Trade Related Intellectual Property Rights
UDHR	Universal Declaration of Human Rights
UN	United Nations
UNAIDS	United Nations Joint Programme on HIV/AIDS
UNICEF	United Nations Children's Fund
UNCTAD	United Nations Conference on Trade and Development
UNDESA	United Nations Department of Economic and Social Affairs
UNDP	United Nations Development Programme
UNEP	United Nations Environmental Programme
UNESCO	United Nations Educational, Scientific and Cultural Organization
UNFPA	United Nations Population Fund
UNIFEM	United Nations Development Fund for Women

USSR	Union of Soviet Socialist Republics
WB	World Bank
WDR	World Development Report
WEF	World Economic Forum
WHO	World Health Organization
WSF	World Social Forum
WSSD	World Summit on Sustainable Development
WTO	World Trade Organization (UN)

Introduction

"... it makes no moral difference whether the person I help is a neighbor's child ten yards from me or a Bengali whose name I shall never know, ten thousand miles away."

(Peter Singer, 1972)[1]

"We will spare no effort to free our fellow men, women and children from the abject and dehumanizing conditions of extreme poverty, to which more than a billion of them are currently subjected. We are committed to making the right to development a reality for everyone and to freeing the entire human race from want."

(UN General Assembly Millennium Declaration 2000: 4)

Today, as on all the previous days of the twenty-first century, almost one billion people will go hungry, 20,000 children will die from easily preventable health problems, 1,400 women will die from causes associated with maternity that are easy to diagnose and treat, and more than 100 million primary age children will not attend school. Every day, in this affluent world, hundreds of millions of people experience extreme forms of deprivation that inflict suffering and reduce or terminate their future prospects of having a good life and being productive. Our grandparents could claim that global poverty was inevitable – there were simply not enough resources, nor the technology to transform resources, to meet the needs of all of the world's people. They may or may not have been correct, but this is not a claim that we can make. Today the world has enough food for everyone to be fed. The resources and technology to provide basic services – primary education, health services and even cash transfers – are available. The problem is that our world is organized in such a way that around 1.5 to 2.5 billion people (depending on how you define poverty) have little or no access to the most basic of human needs. This can be seen as a problem of global governance.

In recent times the rich and powerful have made big promises about "ending poverty." At the Millennium Summit in September 2000, 189 nations, and no fewer than 149 national leaders, met in New York and committed themselves to ". . . freeing the entire human race from want." They signed the Millennium Declaration, identifying a set of goals that promised to halve extreme poverty across the world by 2015. That year, 2015, is to be a sort of "half way house" on the road to totally eradicating poverty. Freeing humanity from poverty is no longer an aspiration for moral philosophers or the odd visionary leader – it is to be a mega-project to which all the nations and peoples of the world are committed. After decades of half-hearted public hand-wringing the goal of global poverty eradication is, apparently, at the centre of the international agenda.

Back in 2000, as world leaders smiled for group photographs, patted backs and congratulated each other, there was a strong case that such an endeavor was long overdue. In a world of unprecedented affluence, why had it taken so long for leaders to agree to meet the most basic needs of so many fellow human beings living in extreme poverty? Why were so many people in rich countries struggling with obesity and suffering from "affluenza" while 31 percent of the world's children were moderately or severely stunted and a woman in Mali was 155 times more likely to die during pregnancy than a woman in the United Kingdom?

As this book reveals, the Millennium Declaration is not the first time that people have talked about eradicating global poverty. What is unique, however, is that this is a global consensus, that quantitative targets were agreed and that commitments were made by heads of government that all countries would contribute to this task through mixes of extra finance, domestic and international policy reforms and practical action. This commitment was confirmed in the Monterrey Consensus of March 2002 when the rich countries of the world promised to significantly increase their financial support for the achievement of the Millennium Development Goals (MDGs) while the poorer countries promised to improve their governance and reduce corruption. The stage seemed set for an unprecedented assault on global poverty . . . and then things began to falter as the new millennium lost its novelty, commitment faded, promises were neglected or forgotten and other international issues were given a higher priority.

The graduation of global poverty onto the international agenda might be seen as evidence of progressive social change on the grandest scale. Alternatively, it could be seen as the world's most successful confidence trick – with rich nations, powerful organizations and global elites (in rich and poor countries) retaining the existing structures of power and resource access while maintaining their legitimacy – and at next to no cost for themselves. This book seeks to shed light on the ways in which mixes of compassion for poor people and self-interest, altruism and selfishness, have re-defined international development as global poverty eradication. It provides an analysis of the institutions, political forces and ideas that led to the framing of the world's major social challenge as global poverty – a worldwide problem requiring a global partnership of countries, citizens, businesses and civil societies to agree targets, reform policies, specify mechanisms and allocate finance for its eradication. The findings are complex – the main actors are not simply good or bad nor right or wrong – the account reveals many mixed motives, unlikely coalitions and strategic compromises.

The book describes and analyzes:

- How the idea of global poverty eradication has evolved;
- The history and geography of global poverty;
- The institutional landscape for attacking global poverty;
- The "nuts and bolts" of how attempts to tackle global poverty are organized (goals, plans, finance and technical measures);
- The major debates that surround actions to reduce global poverty;
- The emerging issues that are re-shaping thinking about how to reduce and/or eradicate global poverty; and
- Future prospects for the idea of global poverty eradication, and the policies and practices that are meant to tackle it.

Why worry about global poverty?

Exactly what the term "poverty" means is highly contested.[2] At a very general level there is recognition that poverty is the "want of the necessities of life."[3] The poor are those who lack these necessities and their situation contrasts with the non-poor who, at the very least, can meet their most basic needs. Global poverty, or world poverty, implies that such deprivation cannot be adequately understood at a local, community or even national level. It must be conceptualized at the global level if one seeks to seriously understand why poverty occurs and/or take action against poverty. In the late 1990s the idea of globalization became central to much intellectual activity and everything became "global" – we lived in a global village with a global economy based on global communications . . . we suffered from inadequate global governance and some hypothesized that we were moving towards a global culture. Conceptualizing poverty at a global level might therefore seem like lazy thinking, but that is not so: the invention of global poverty was more than simply following a fashion. Three particular arguments fostered the advance of this idea.

The most commonly heard reason for being concerned about global poverty is a moral case derived from normative reasoning. This argues that all human beings should seek to reduce the suffering of other human beings and, in particular, that those whose basic needs are secure should assist those whose basic needs are not met. This is not simply about helping relatives, friends and neighbors but, as Singer argues in the quote at the opening to this chapter, it applies to the distant needy – people who may be ". . . ten thousand miles away." The pursuit of social justice requires that the poor in any part of the world should be assisted by those with the means to assist them. From this perspective such actions are not simply charity – they are a responsibility, for individuals and states, to assist the poor wherever they are.[4] This argument has deep roots in moral philosophy and religious thought but can also be formulated in more popular constructs, ranging from the pop music of "feed the world" to the fashionable wristbands of "make poverty history."

The second argument arises out of causal ideas and is based more on the value of self-interest than altruism. It argues that those whose basic needs are met (the non-poor) should assist the poor, if they want to maintain and improve their own (i.e. the non-poor's) well-being. The relatively better-off should be good neighbors and assist poor people who live near them, to improve local and national social cohesion and to reduce the incentives for excluded social groups to threaten social and economic stability. But, this also applies to non-neighbors. If the distant needy have no prospects for improvement then some of them might be more likely to support violent political groups, at the extreme support "terrorists," and/or seek to illegally migrate to more affluent countries. So, helping the distant needy may reduce social and political problems in the rich world. This has been a commonly made point in the US since 9/11, although the evidence to support it is very mixed.[5] There is also a liberal economic strand to this argument. It posits that the more that poor people around the world increase their incomes and assets then the greater will be global demand and the greater will be the economic opportunities of the better-off as well as the poor. This position focuses on economic growth, the promotion of trade and integrating the poor into global markets, rather than international transfers (aid and debt forgiveness), social policy or social activism.

The third argument derives from causal analysis and holds that the developed countries have a duty to assist in tackling global poverty because they are responsible for the economic and political structures that have created and maintain extreme poverty.[6] In effect, this is a critique of globalization as it views such processes as a major cause, in some cases *the* cause, of poverty. The unfairness of the world trade regime, the dominance of multinational corporations (MNCs) based in rich countries, rich country control over finance and technology, structural adjustment and other factors are alleged to actively keep poor people poor. In recent years a second strand of argument, the problem of climate change, has greatly strengthened this position. The world's most economically advanced countries and wealthiest people have pumped CO_2 into the atmosphere for more than a hundred years and this is now undermining the livelihoods of poor people in poor countries through climate variability (floods, droughts, cyclones, etc.), sea-level rises and long-term climate change. From this perspective the causes of poverty are global and so the solutions must be conceptualized in global terms. Local and national action can do little to make trade fair, re-shape international finance or mitigate climate change. Poverty may be experienced at the individual level but it must be conceptualized and tackled as global poverty.

In recent years such debates have moved to the core of my academic and professional work on international development. I became particularly interested in the contrasting responses that I encountered to the idea and practices of global poverty eradication in my teaching and research. Many of my students enthusiastically embraced the idea of tackling global poverty as a great advance over the pre-existing notion of international development. At elite levels, politicians I met, such as Clare Short and Gordon Brown, were (and remain) genuinely fired up by the idea; the leaders of global agencies, such as Kofi Annan (UN) and Jim Wolfensohn (World Bank), argued that devices such as the MDGs provided an unprecedented opportunity for mobilizing resources and making action more effective. The shift to global poverty eradication certainly attracted more media attention than had international development, and celebrities, such as Bob Geldof and Bono, promoted popular support for an assault on global poverty through concerts, mass mobilizations and well-staged trips to Africa with vast media coverage (as well as holding private meetings with world leaders).

On the other hand were those who saw promises and plans for global poverty eradication negatively. Some of my students were very cynical, believing that such promises and plans were rich world posturing and/or an attempt to impose new forms of control and conditionality on the policies of developing countries. There are several different aspects of this critique: as a false promise that enhances the image and legitimacy of wealthy countries and powerful organizations but which they do not intend to keep; as a compromise that means that developing countries are discouraged from pursuing genuinely alternative national development strategies; or, as a sell-out that weakens efforts to achieve human rights around the world and/or replace capitalism with a more egalitarian and socially just alternative.[7]

In between these two contrasting positions were many who do not see the impact of the idea of global poverty in such black and white terms. They believe that the idea of global poverty eradication may support some desirable actions (more predictable and better coordinated aid flows) but might hamper others (the need for fundamental reforms to global institutions). I started my research for this book from this hybrid position believing that the results of a strategic shift to "global poverty eradication" could not be judged theoretically. Empirical study was needed to understand where this idea came from and how it impacted on the policies and practices of different actors over time.

These different positions, as the book shows, reflect ethical concerns about the values that should be pursued; technical analyses and judgments about the best ways of tackling global poverty; and, the self-interest of individuals, groups, organizations and nations. The smiling faces of the world's leaders at the Millennium Summit hid a world of complex posturing, negotiation, competition, collaboration and at times intrigue that underpinned the processes leading up to the event and the subsequent processes associated with "implementing" global poverty eradication in the early twenty-first century.

I must identify my own normative agenda from the outset. I think the existence of extreme poverty in an affluent world is morally unacceptable and I am keen to persuade others to think about this issue and to take action. While I enthusiastically support the reduction of economic and social inequality within countries and between countries, and the honoring of human rights around the world (and recognize these as elements of the fight against poverty), I believe that eradicating extreme poverty takes priority. This is because of the ways in which extreme poverty obstructs human flourishing: it means that people are hungry and live in pain and anguish; it stops children from being educated; it means that people cannot develop their cognitive and physical capabilities (they grow up physically stunted and have reduced reasoning ability); it allows others to exploit the labor and bodies of the poor; and it makes poor people feel shame and indignity for conditions they cannot control. At the extreme, and at a rate of more than 1,000 deaths per hour, it means that people die from easily preventable causes – deaths that could have been avoided by access to a few dollars' worth of medicines or health services. Promoting human rights and reducing inequality can help tackle extreme poverty, but the priority is poverty reduction.

My academic and professional work over the years leads me to believe that different mixes of policy and action are needed to assist poor people in different contexts. For most of my career this work has been at the "micro" level: analyzing rural development projects, small farmer agricultural services, micro-finance, non-governmental organization (NGO) operations and household poverty dynamics. These experiences demonstrated that neither the market nor the state is the solution to the "problem" of poverty. Both private action and public action are needed to produce economic growth and effectively tackle poverty, although the exact mix varies with specific contexts and needs to change over time. My recent interests in "macro" level processes, the topic of this book, have confirmed this heterodox position.

Encouraging better-off people to feel morally indignant about extreme poverty is probably the easiest part of an attempt to assist extremely poor people. However, for well-meaning people to take effective action to support the efforts of poor people to improve their lives and the prospects for their children, the concerned (development professionals, social activists, students and "ordinary citizens") need to have an understanding of why people remain poor in an affluent world and what they might do to help tackle the causes of poverty. By examining how and why international development became global poverty eradication, and exploring the implications of this shift, this book aspires to be one small part of this quest for understanding. If it helps existing and aspiring colleagues in the professional field of international development and/or poverty reduction to understand the ways in which our efforts are framed then I shall have succeeded. If it helps to encourage students and a wider public to think about extreme poverty, and perhaps take action, then it may have merited the resources with which I have been entrusted.

The book has Gramscian underpinnings and, just as importantly, it is guided by Gramsci's notion of "pessimism of the intellect and optimism of the will." While much of the analysis reveals the duplicity of those with economic and political power (promising to "end poverty" and then going on with business as usual) and the difficulties of changing power relations (for example, most people acknowledge that the governance structures of the World Bank and International Monetary Fund (IMF) lack legitimacy in the contemporary world, but systematically changing them seems nigh impossible) I believe that change is possible and will occur. The key issue is accelerating the speed of progressive social change by identifying effective strategies and tactics. Central to these efforts are creating and promoting ideas that change attitudes, norms, policies and behaviors in ways that assist poor people to improve their lives and their prospects in the ways that they seek – ideas matter.

The book's approach

This book takes a global political economy perspective weaving together concepts, methods and materials drawn from economics, politics, sociology, geography and other social sciences. It views the evolution of the idea of global poverty, and policies and practices to tackle global poverty, as the outcome of a complex and changing configuration of forces: what Robert Cox conceptualizes as a historical structure (Figure I.1).[8] Three categories of forces interact in such a structure: *material capabilities*, technological and organizational capabilities with productive and destructive potentials; *ideas*, including intersubjective meanings, around which there is widespread

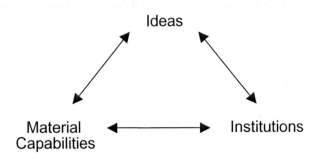

Figure I.1 Cox's framework

Source: Robert Cox (see Note 9 of this chapter for reference).

agreement across a society, and "collective images of social order," which are often several and opposed; and *institutions*, amalgams of ideas and material power that are a means of stabilizing and perpetuating a particular social order. Institutions reflect the power relations prevailing at the time of their origin and are often formalized as organizations.

The influences of these three types of forces on each other are reciprocal and the directions and strength of influence vary over time and with each particular case.

As is discussed in later chapters, for global poverty the material capabilities that are most important lie in the staggering contrast between the material, technological and organizational wealth of the rich world (the G7, especially the United States, other Organization for Economic Cooperation and Development (OECD) countries, and now the BRICs – Brazil, Russia, India and China) and the more limited material capabilities of the poor world (especially those classed as least developed countries or LDCs).[9] Within countries, whether rich or poor, there are also vast differences between the command over material resources, technology and labor that different segments of the population can exert.

Behind the idea of global poverty eradication lies the belief that the contemporary world has the aggregate material capabilities to ensure that no human being experiences extreme poverty. However, those who control such capabilities (national governments and leaders, businessmen, financiers, corporations, political elites and middle classes in rich and poor countries) seek to maintain their command over resources, technologies and organizations in ways that directly or indirectly deny poor people access to the most basic of human needs. At times countries may act as unitary states pursuing a known national interest based on a clear understanding of their present and future material capabilities. But, commonly, there are networks and coalitions of sub-national interest groups (sometimes loose and temporary and sometimes tight and long-lasting) shaping political debates and actions domestically and internationally. For example, farmers' associations in many rich countries manage to block liberalization in agricultural trade in ways that damage the prospects of poor farmers in developing countries. Throughout the book the ways in which those who control material capabilities are able to influence and often dominate the framing of issues and the behaviors of institutions are analyzed.

Tens of thousands of institutions have been (and are) engaged in shaping thinking about global poverty in recent decades, mobilizing resources (for themselves and in support of poverty reduction policies) and taking action. These range from the usual suspects – the World Bank, IMF, UN General Assembly, UN Secretariat, specialized UN agencies, OECD's Development Assistance Committee (DAC), national governments, bilateral aid agencies and major development NGOs – to actors whose role is seen as more recent, or was neglected in earlier analyses – social movements (especially the women's and environmental movements), the media, civil society, faiths and faith-based organizations, philanthrocapitalists, and celebrities. To function, these institutions and actors have to draw on material capabilities (from the assets they already control, public taxes, business profits, donations and voluntary labor or charging for their services) so that they can mount operations and promote and challenge ideas. These institutions, or parts of them, often coalesce into loose networks or formal coalitions to achieve common goals and/or strengthen their influence over the news media.

In terms of ideas, the clash between neo-liberal capitalism and alternative development strategies – historically, socialism and communism, but more recently, basic needs, human development, human rights, and reducing inequality – has framed thinking on, and action against, global poverty.[10] Neo-liberalism highlights growth and markets while the alternatives focus on "means not ends" and posit a major role for the state and often for international public action. Related to this are the contests about "how" global poverty can be explained – is this through the positivist, measurement-based exercises favored by orthodox economists focused on individual behavior or the social structural analyses of political economists, anthropologists and sociologists? Many other ideas have shaped the ways in which global poverty is imagined and treated – results-based management, reproductive health, sustainable development, gender equality, philanthropy, public opinion and partnerships. All of these have contributed to the recent re-framing of international development and national development in poor countries as global poverty eradication. Boas and McNeill view such acts of "framing" as having great practical significance.

The exercise of framing is composed of two parts: one, drawing attention to a specific issue . . . two, determining how such an issue is viewed.
A successful framing exercise will both cause an issue to be seen by
those who matter, and ensure that they see it in a specific way. And this
is achieved with the minimum of conflict or pressure . . . an effective
"frame" is one which makes favored ideas seem like common sense.[11]

While framing the goal and task of assisting people whose most basic needs
are not met as global poverty eradication may sound like a logical goal for
people who are public spirited, this is not the only concept available for framing how disadvantaged people might be supported. It is useful to consider
what is gained and what is lost by framing analysis and action on human
deprivation as an attack on extreme poverty across the world. Certainly,
this advantages certain institutions – the UN, World Bank, IMF and others – as "global problems" generate activities and responsibilities for global
institutions.

First, some thought is required as to how the goal of tackling poverty
should be expressed. There are three main terms that are used to label such
efforts – poverty alleviation, poverty reduction and poverty eradication.
While some analysts use these synonymously the three terms have distinct
meanings. *Poverty alleviation* suggests lessening the intensity of some of the
poverty that some people experience. The term's associations with medicine
suggest that it is about palliative actions – dealing with the symptoms but
not the causes of poverty. As a result, the term fell out of favor in the 1990s
and is not widely used. Nowadays, when it is used, this is sometimes in a
pejorative sense – implying that a policy or program is tokenistic.

Poverty eradication is at the other end of the spectrum. It connotes
analyses and efforts to end poverty – dealing not only with the symptoms
but also with the causes of poverty and, for its achievement, removing all
of those causes for all poor people. This is the grandest goal from a poverty
viewpoint. But, it is such a grand goal that many engaged in policy formulation and practical action have felt that it is too great a promise to make.
They step back from expressing their goal in this way because they imagine
that even in a just world there would be some residual extreme poverty and/
or they see poverty in relative terms . . . tackling poverty could never be a
completed task, it will always be work in progress. For such folk, poverty
realists and poverty relativists, the goal is usually framed as *poverty reduction*. The causes of poverty must be attacked, not just the symptoms, but the
main issue is the speed of poverty reduction – which should be as rapid as
possible. These discussions influenced debates about poverty around the millennium so that the 1995 UN Social Summit aspiration "to eradicate absolute
poverty by a date to be set by each country" was moderated into the MDG

target of "halving extreme poverty by 2015." Poverty reduction was to be understood as a staging post on the way to poverty eradication . . . at some yet to be determined future date.

Many of the complex questions about what goals should be pursued to assist poor people and/or reduce human suffering can be captured by a comparative analysis of three distinct ways of conceptualizing and tackling the problem. The problem may be framed as *reducing global poverty*[12] or *realizing human rights*[13] or *reducing global inequality*.[14] (Here I make the assumption that the goals have to be viewed as ends and not means. Economic growth may be central to human advancement but as a means and not an end – in its own right growth has no intrinsic value[15].) While these three concepts have many similarities in terms of the actions they might promote they lead to the identification of different forms of analysis and different priorities.

Reducing global poverty – this concept has been shaped by micro-economic and human development concepts. It is implemented by a variety of technical specialists (economists, health professionals, nutritionists, educationalists, environmental scientists, etc.). It seeks to define extreme poverty, identify the extreme poor and target resources and policy changes on the poorest countries and poorest people so that they achieve, at least, minimum levels of access to basic goods and services. While this is a long-term task it has a relatively clear conclusion – once extreme poverty is eliminated the job is complete.

Realizing human rights – the origins of this concept lie in legal studies and philosophy and this is implemented by lawyers and social/political activists. It seeks to define human rights and then ensure that all people achieve their rights. Importantly, it allocates responsibility to those who have a duty to ensure rights. It does not explicitly target "beneficiaries," as all of humanity should achieve their human rights. However, it requires that those who obstruct human rights be confronted and, if necessary, be publicly sanctioned for their failures to meet obligations and/or violate human rights. Realizing human rights is usually seen as an on-going task that applies to all countries (poor and rich) and has no clear end point.

Reducing global inequality – this concept has been dominated by political scientists and other social scientists (including economists on income inequality). It has never been officially declared a global goal. At the national level efforts to reduce inequality have been associated with excellent social and economic results (as for example in Scandinavia) and sometimes with appalling ones (as in Cambodia under Pol Pot). While the measurement of global inequality has focused on income, the proponents of this concept seek political and social equality between nations and peoples. The targets of this approach include less well-off countries and people, who need to control more income or assets or power, and better-off countries and people, who need to have less income or assets or power (through voluntary or involuntary redistribution). This is usually seen as an on-going task without a clear end point.

The relative attractiveness of these different approaches for framing efforts to assist poor people has changed over time. The human rights approach, in the form of the Universal Declaration of Human Rights (UDHR), was the initial front runner in the late 1940s. However its prominence waned with the rise of modernization theory, the ascendancy of economics as the leading policy-relevant social science and the focus on pursuing economic growth over the 1950s and 1960s. It was posited that the "trickle down" from growth would raise the incomes of the poor and rapidly reduce poverty. Subsequent dissatisfaction with the achievements of modernization strategies led to a variety of counter-proposals in the 1970s. From Washington, DC, via the World Bank, came the call, and substantial funding, for a direct focus on poverty reduction through rural development in the poorest countries. From the "Third World," via the UN[16] in New York, came calls for a new international economic order (NIEO) that would focus on reducing economic and political inequality between nations so that global public policy would no longer be determined by the maneuvering of the Cold War powers. These counter-proposals were swept aside by the rise of neo-liberalism in the late 1970s and its focus on market-based growth and minimizing the role of the state. It was not until the 1990s that growth, as the priority global goal, was challenged. During the 1990s both poverty reduction (the Copenhagen Social Summit and the OECD's International Development Goals) and human rights (the Vienna Human Rights Summit and the promotion of "rights-based approaches to development") gained higher profiles. However, when political agreement had to be reached over what goals would appear in the Millennium Declaration, global poverty reduction was the compromise that was settled on. Human rights remained in all the main declarations and were identified as fundamental for the achievement of the MDGs, but the immediate goals for policymakers to pursue were clearly specified as targeted poverty reduction.[17]

The structure of the book

Following this introduction the first chapter examines the history and geography of global poverty. It provides an overview of what is known about the very gradual improvements in the human condition over the period 1CE to around 1820CE and the subsequent acceleration of poverty reduction that has occurred in the last 200 years. The contemporary geography of poverty is described and, while this chapter concurs with the orthodoxy – that the deepest and most multi-dimensional poverty is concentrated in sub-Saharan Africa – it also argues that there is a large and contiguous region of poverty in sub-Siberian Asia.

In Chapter 2 the conceptual debates that surround the idea of poverty are examined in detail. These are of central importance to this book, as the meaning that is invested in "poverty" has profound implications for the understanding of why poverty occurs and for prescriptions about what needs to be done and who needs to do it. Those who have studied poverty concepts can skip this section. The second part of this chapter examines the major frameworks for understanding poverty through an exploration of the recent literature covering both the polemics, which might be found on an airport newsstand,[18] and more nuanced and reflective analyses.

Chapter 3 explores the institutional landscape for global poverty reduction. This is complex terrain: it covers official multilateral organizations (the UN, World Bank, IMF and others); the various multilateral associations of states; national and sub-national governments; the non-state institutions that have risen into prominence over the last 20 years (social movements, NGOs, faiths and the private sector); public-private partnerships; and the recent prominence of exceptionally influential individuals such as Bill Gates and Bono (philanthrocapitalists and celebrities). These institutions and actors often associate in formal partnerships and networks but there are also many informal networks that link different actors, interests and ideas together.

Chapter 4 looks at the nuts and bolts of global poverty eradication – the ways in which it is measured, programmed, planned, financed and delivered. The chapter charts the invention of the $1-a-day poverty measure (now $1.25-a-day measure) that has been so significant in persuading politicians and publics that the global poor exist (if it can be counted it counts); the evolution of the MDGs; efforts to globally mobilize more resources to tackle poverty through the Finance for Development Summit and other initiatives; the UN's Millennium Project and Millennium Campaign that were launched to implement the MDGs; Poverty Reduction Strategies that are intended to ensure that poor countries effectively pursue poverty reduction targets; the national and local implementation activities that are so vital to deliver poverty reduction goods and services (but are so often neglected in official accounts); and, poverty reduction monitoring and accountability processes. It finds that there is an "all change – no change" paradox. While most of the mechanisms are "new" – introduced around the turn of the millennium and claiming to be based on different values and ideas than their antecedents – the structures of power that guide what actually happens (or does not happen) "on the ground" have changed very little. This is because national governments and multilateral institutions, and their leaders, can make promises about poverty reduction targets and actions and know that they are unlikely to be held to account by their citizens or governing bodies.

Chapter 5 extends this analysis and examines the main strategic choices that face efforts at global poverty eradication. Is the economic growth that can reduce poverty best achieved by orthodox, neo-classical policies focused on markets, or more heterodox policies that recognize a role for the state and believe that different countries need different mixes of policy? What are the best trade policies for poverty reduction – free trade or fair trade or something more nuanced? What is the role of foreign aid – does it reduce poverty or cause poverty (or are the outcomes complex)? And, is the problem of poverty largely about state fragility and violent conflict and, if so, what can be done? The conclusion of this chapter argues that the continued inability to reform the structures and processes of global governance undermines international, national and local efforts to reduce poverty.

Chapter 6 looks to the future and identifies four issues that are transforming the context for global poverty eradication. It asks how the new global geography of wealth and power, with the economic rise of China and India, will affect global poverty. What impacts will climate change have on the prospects for global poverty reduction (will this be a disaster or will this lead to an unrivalled era of global collective action)? As global poverty becomes increasingly concentrated in urban areas will the knowledge base that we have, grounded on the understanding of rural poverty, be adequate? Finally, this chapter examines the prospects for the evolution of an international social norm that finds extreme poverty morally unacceptable in the affluent world of the twenty-first century. Changing social norms saw slavery abolished in the nineteenth century and apartheid discredited in the twentieth century – are they the answer to the scourge of global poverty in the twenty-first century?

The main findings of the book are drawn together in Chapter 7. This argues that the opportunity created by the "millennium moment" for a truly concerted, global effort to reduce poverty has been lost: it was always only an outside possibility given the political economy of our times and the low priority that those of us doing well – the elites and middle classes of rich and poor countries – place on the welfare of the "distant needy." The result is neither a glass half empty nor half full – the glass has a little more in, but that is not good enough. Global poverty is now on the international agenda, but generally as a footnote to the issues that are genuinely gaining the attention of those with power and influence at the global level – terrorism, access to natural resources, financial stability, trade and growth, and climate change.[19]

Does this marginalization of global poverty mean that we should despair and give up? No, but it does mean that those seeking to improve the position and prospects of the world's poorest people will need to think both practically and strategically. Chapter 8 looks at "What can be done?" Practically, with an eye on the short term, concerned professionals and citizens must strive for incremental improvements in policies and resourcing for poverty reduction – increases in aid, more effective aid, making trade a little fairer, implementation of anti-corruption measures, strengthened social protection policies and better public services in poorer countries. With an eye on the longer term and the grander goal, they must strategize on how to advance the diffusion of eradicating poverty as a global norm – through promoting ideas, gaining media and political attention, encouraging and supporting norm entrepreneurs and other activities. Their hope, our hope, must be that eventually extreme poverty in an affluent world will be seen as morally unacceptable by the vast majority of world citizens and in all societies – like slavery, apartheid and not letting women vote.

Notes

1 Peter Singer, "Famine, Affluence, and Morality," *Philosophy and Public Affairs* 1, no. 3 (1972): 231–232.
2 See Chapter 2.
3 Henry Watson Fowler, Francis George Fowler and Della Thompson, *The Concise Oxford Dictionary* (Oxford: Oxford University Press, 1995), 1071.
4 This case is made very forcefully by Peter Singer in *The Life You Can Save: Acting Now to End World Poverty* (London: Picador, 2009). See also Deen K. Chatterjee, ed., *The Ethics of Assistance: Morality and the Distant Needy* (Cambridge: Cambridge University Press, 2004).
5 The 9/11 suicide bombers were from Saudi Arabia (a high income country), none of them came from backgrounds of extreme poverty and they were financed by wealthy people.
6 See Thomas Pogge, *World Poverty and Human Rights* (Cambridge: Polity Press, 2008); and Irene Khan, *The Unheard Truth: Poverty and Human Rights* (New York and London: W.W. Norton, 2009).
7 See Ashwani Saith, "From Universal Values to Millennium Development Goals: Lost in Translation," *Development and Change* 37, no. 6 (2006); Focus on the Global South, ed., *Anti Poverty or Anti Poor? The Millennium Development Goals and the Eradication of Extreme Poverty and Hunger* (Bangkok: Focus on the Global South, 2003).
8 Robert W. Cox, "Social Forces, States and World Orders: Beyond International Relations Theory," in *Approaches to World Order*, ed. Robert W. Cox and Timothy J. Sinclair (Cambridge: Cambridge University Press, 2002), 85–123.
9 The UN classes 50 countries as least developed. This is based on three criteria: low income, human resource weaknesses and economic vulnerability. See http://www.un.org/special-rep/ohrlls/ldc/ldc%20criteria.htm
10 In Chapter 2 these ideas are examined in more detail.
11 Morten Boas and Desmond McNeill, *Multilateral Institutions: A Critical Introduction* (London; Sterling, Va.: Pluto Press, 2003), 1.

12 As we shall see, in global public policy statements elements of these different conceptual positions can be woven together. For example, the MDGs include elements of human rights and inequality reduction (through the focus on gender equality and women's rights) and economic growth (through the income target).

13 While some human rights proponents are textualists, treating the UDHR as revelatory and repeating its normative case, others are much more political and see it as an ideological device for political mobilization.

14 For a comprehensive examination of trends in global inequality see Branko Milanovic, *Worlds Apart: Measuring International and Global Inequality* (Princeton: Princeton University Press, 2005).

15 But see Paul Collier and Stefan Dercon, "The Complementarities of Poverty Reduction, Equity and Growth: A Perspective on the World Development Report 2006," *Economic Development and Cultural Change* 55, no. 1 (2006) for the argument that a focus on such normative issues neglects the centrality of growth in poor countries and may misdirect policy (as well as being anti-democratic).

16 In the 1970s the ILO led a call for a focus on "basic needs" that was grounded in the concept of extreme poverty reduction.

17 The one exception was MDG 3 pursuing gender equality.

18 The rise of the idea of global poverty eradication is evidenced by the copies of *The End of Poverty*, *The Bottom Billion*, *Dead Aid* and *White Man's Burden* I have seen on sale at Dhaka, Dubai, Dulles, Heathrow, Nairobi and Schipol airports.

19 The evidence for this continues to mount. At the December 2008 Doha meeting on "Finance for Development," the follow-up conference to the Monterrey meeting of March 2002, only one OECD and BRIC leader turned up – Nicholas Sarkozy on behalf of the EU. The heads of the World Bank and IMF (who have publicly pledged to eradicate poverty) were too busy to attend the meeting. Media coverage of the event was minimal and the stage looks set for rich countries to reduce commitments to foreign aid and debt forgiveness. The Doha "development round" on trade policies has stalled and rich countries are reneging on promises to reform policies so that they are not anti-poor. At the climate change summit in Copenhagen in December 2009 the rich world (and emerging powers) rhetoric about assisting poor countries and poor people to adapt to global warming was not matched by commitments.

1 The history and geography of global poverty

"[f]or ye have the poor always with you."

(Gospel of Saint Matthew 26: 11)

"The problem is not that we have tried to eradicate global poverty and failed;
the problem is that no serious and concerted attempt has ever been made."

(James Grant, Executive Director of UNICEF, 1993)[1]

For most of the last 2,000 years the economic and social condition of humanity has improved at a slow, sometimes imperceptible, pace. But this changed around the early nineteenth century and since then there has been a dramatic reduction (in historical terms) in the proportion of the human population experiencing poverty and deprivation. This chapter tracks the improvements in economic and social conditions over the last two millennia, charts the emergence of ideas about "ending poverty" in recent centuries, explores the growing significance of these ideas in the last 20 years and maps the contemporary geography of global poverty.

Global poverty: pre-history to 1820

The idea that the most basic needs – food, clean water, clothing, shelter, basic health services – can be provided to all of humanity is relatively recent. For most of human history the vast majority of people have been materially poor. Hunger and food insecurity have been a norm, famines have been common, life expectancy has been short, epidemic disease levels and mortality have been high and exposure to the elements (through lack of clothing or shelter) a daily experience. Despite extraordinary technological breakthroughs – plant and animal domestication, irrigation, the design of tools and implements, the wheel and the manufacture of materials (bronze, iron, pottery and thread)

– early human populations increased almost imperceptibly as life expectancy was low and resources-technology interactions were insufficient to support larger numbers.

Things changed little over the first millennium of the Common Era (CE). Human population grew by only around one-sixth in a thousand years (0.02 percent per annum) and by 1000CE ". . . the average infant could expect to live about 24 years. A third would die in the first year of life, hunger and epidemic disease would ravage the survivors."[2] The reduction of poverty was hampered by very low economic growth rates, reflecting dependence on agriculture with very limited technical change. Over the period 1CE to 1000CE world per capita growth rates are estimated to have been zero or even fractionally negative for some areas, including Western Europe.[3] In such circumstances any significant reduction in the rate and depth of poverty would have been highly difficult. The rate of improvement in the human condition may have risen a little over the early and middle centuries of the second millennium, particularly in Western Europe, although the Black Death led to dramatic reductions in population that took decades to recover. Paradoxically, the plague may have led to increased wages for peasant farmers and agricultural laborers in areas such as Western Europe and China. With land and physical capital unaffected by the disease, the loss of a section of the labor force meant that those who survived were more productive, leading to significant improvements in the real wage for agricultural laborers.[4] Higher wages led to higher purchasing power, and increasing numbers of people began to consume luxury items such as Northern furs and Eastern spices. The evidence therefore suggests that the period around 1350–1500 saw an initially smaller but substantially better-off population in Europe.[5] The effects of the plague elsewhere, however, were more unequivocally negative than in Western Europe. In the Islamic world the ravages of the plague led to economic decline, greater political instability and a probable increase in poverty. The reasons for this contrast with the experiences of Western Europe lie in differences in political and economic systems between the two regions. In the Middle East, the response to the economic disruption caused by the plague was for the elite to further squeeze the peasantry, who suffered increased taxes and oppression rather than seeing their relative wealth increase as was the case in Western Europe. Economic decline in the Islamic world also led to increased military conflict with surrounding groups. The net result was that in Egypt, for instance, the population fell by around 50 percent, while agricultural output fell by as much as 68 percent, implying lower productivity and most likely declining real wages, and therefore higher poverty.[6]

Around the middle of the second millennium CE, governments in some of the emerging states of Europe began to make public policy interventions to alleviate hunger and reduce poverty. In the sixteenth century the Elizabethan Poor Laws started to operate in England requiring that parishes had to provide support for their poor (although it may have taken another 50 years to get these laws fully implemented). The French state focused on food security and in the eighteenth century its civil servants began to count the poor and indigent, and identify ways of stopping temporary crises (crop failure and a collapse in demand for agricultural labor) pushing the transient poor into chronic poverty.[7] In the late eighteenth century the nascent US government debated whether it had international responsibilities – if foreign sailors were washed ashore was caring for their welfare a US responsibility or could states only legitimately try to protect their own citizens? In contrast, other policies actively intensified human suffering. Most obviously the promotion of the slave trade by the British, Portuguese, Spanish and other European powers killed millions in the "middle passage," left millions in chains in the New World, and economically and socially disrupted many African societies (creating a legacy that hampers development in Africa to this day). Maddison estimates that between 1000 and 1820 global life expectancy rose from only 24 to 26 years and per capita income (in 1990 US$) from $453 to $667 (Figure 1.1).[8] This, however, represents an annual economic growth rate of only 0.05 percent, which, though an improvement on that of the first millennium CE, was still too low to bring about a significant alteration in the general human condition.

Although GDP per capita and life expectancy rose only slowly, profound changes took place in the middle of the second millennium CE. After the population collapse brought about by successive waves of the plague, a population explosion took place after 1500 driven by the discovery of the New World by Christopher Columbus in 1492 and the transfer of high-yield crops from the Americas to Europe, Africa and Asia. As Alfred Crosby puts it: "while men who stormed Tenochtitlán with Cortes still lived, peanuts were swelling in the sandy loams near Shanghai; maize was turning fields green in south China, and the sweet potato was on its way to becoming the poor man's staple in Fukien."[9] These crops thrived in the Old World and improved the nutritional intake available to its people, helping to push back the Malthusian population restraints. By contrast, the biological transfer from the Old World to the New following the discovery of America was unambiguously negative for the Amerindians. With no immunity to Old World diseases their populations collapsed, with perhaps as much as 95 percent of the indigenous population falling victim to the pathogens brought by the settlers.[10]

Throughout the period examined here, poverty remained high and improvements in social indicators and GDP per capita were slow to non-existent. Nonetheless, behind the scenes, as it were, a gradual process of technological and cultural change was occurring in Western Europe that would bring

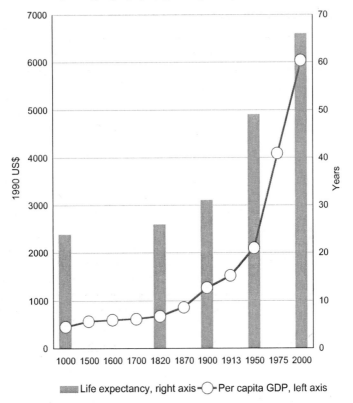

Figure 1.1 Global GDP per capita and life expectancy, 1000–2000

Source: Angus Maddison, *The World Economy: A Millennium Perspective* (Paris: Development Centre of the Organisation for Economic Co-operation and Development, 2001)

about a sea-change in the human condition. The slow accumulation of ideas and technological progress, coupled with rising literacy and the rapid diffusion of knowledge through the printing press, all combined with a culture that was increasingly obsessed with technology and empirical investigation, culminated in the scientific and industrial revolutions.[11] With these twin developments and the integration of the world economy through sailing ships in the first period of globalization, a step change in growth rates came about and the burden of poverty began to fall substantially, though highly unevenly. The European powers controlling these technological changes were able to capture the bulk of the gains through imperial and colonial strategies. The institutions they created – modern states, navies, insurance, bills for trade, international treaties – may not have kept Western Europe peaceful but they did permit it to dominate global trade and politics.

Global poverty: around 1820 to 1950

Since around 1820[12] the human condition, in relative historical terms, has been transformed: average life expectancy rose from 26 years to 66 years and average per capita income from $667 to $5,709 by 2000 (Maddison 2001: 31, 264). Although detailed statistics are not available it seems certain that over this period many other social indicators – infant mortality, literacy, nutrition and morbidity – have improved spectacularly. But, as the processes of world development have shifted from being "extensive" (settling new lands and extending agriculture) to "intensive" (urbanization, industrial agriculture and non-agricultural economic activities) advances in the human condition have become very unevenly spread. In the countries that industrialized early on, what Maddison calls Group A countries (Western Europe, the United States, Canada, Australia, New Zealand and Japan), by 2000 life expectancy had risen to 78 years and average per capita income to $21,470.[13] By contrast, in Maddison's Group B countries (those in Africa, Asia excluding Japan, Latin America, Eastern Europe and Russia) life expectancy had reached only 64 years and per capita income only $3,102. While in almost all countries economic and social conditions had improved significantly over the period 1820–2000 there were enormous differences between countries and some-times within countries. From a world in which absolute poverty was the norm we had moved to one in which levels of absolute poverty were very low in some places (for example across Scandinavia) while they remained a majority condition in other regions (for example most of Central Africa).

Such dramatic improvements in human lives and capabilities are both a product of the human imagination while also re-shaping that imagination. Around the time that the underlying conditions for these advances were emerging, the well-established idea that "the poor will always be with you"[14] came under challenge in Europe and North America. As Stedman Jones elaborates, in the late eighteenth and early nineteenth centuries social think-ers, such as de Condorcet and Paine, began to imagine and promote the idea of "an end to poverty."[15] For de Condorcet in 1795, the gap between the rich and the poor was not a natural aspect of "civilization [but] . . . was largely to be ascribed to 'the present imperfections of the social art.'"[16] A set of ideas, often very contested, began to emerge about poverty alleviation and even poverty eradication. For de Condorcet (and others), "ending poverty" was about social transformation and the creation of ". . . real equality . . . the abolition of inequality between nations . . . [and] . . . the progress of equality within each nation."[17]

For other writers, such as Burke and Malthus, this was not merely a foolish misunderstanding of why people were poor, but a dangerous attack on the institutional foundations of European prosperity, the monarchy, the Christian

Church and the entire social order. The laboring and/or undeserving poor needed to work harder, have fewer children and cease their vices (laziness, drunkenness and fornication). The deserving poor – widows, orphans and the disabled – could be supported by the (Christian) charity of the wealthy. During this era the basic concepts of the debates that underpin contemporary analyses[18] of global poverty and global poverty eradication were established.

Over the nineteenth century Maddison's Group A countries experienced rapid economic growth as they industrialized, urbanized and engaged in international trade. Alongside this they experienced major improvements in social indicators as food security improved and simple advances in public health – clean drinking water, sanitation and basic hygiene – reduced infectious disease levels and mortality. While the condition of the working classes in the cities of many Group A countries was appalling in the early phases of industrialization and the shift to factory work,[19] conditions improved over time. Some of these industrializing states began to introduce "modern" social policies to reduce the vulnerability and improve the welfare of their populations. The most obvious example is Germany under Bismarck: in the 1880s he introduced health, accident, old age and disability insurance and laid the foundations for the country's twentieth-century welfare system.

While the economies and societies of many Group B countries were transformed by the colonial powers, there is little evidence of fundamental economic or social improvement for their populations. Life expectancy in Group B countries increased by only two years, from 24 to 26, over 1820 to 1900[20] and "native" incomes improved little. While there is much evidence of the economic exploitation of Group B populations, and neo-Marxist analysts argue that the "Third World" was actively immiserized by colonialism, writers such as Findlay and O'Rourke argue that some improvements occurred through increased demand for commodities and infrastructural development.[21] Whatever the balance sheet on colonialism,[22] it is clear that India was wracked by colonially administered, some would argue colonially created, famines;[23] the economic and social foundations of the inhumanity that has characterized life in the Belgian Congo, now the Democratic Republic of the Congo (DRC), were laid;[24] and, Britain was prepared to go to war to promote opium addiction in China.

Over the period 1900 to 1950 the patterns became more complex. While economic growth and social indicator improvements continued in Group A countries (but were disrupted by two world wars and the Great Depression) in many Group B countries social indicators, such as reduced infant mortality and higher life expectancy, improved rapidly. For example, life expectancy in Group B leapt from 26 to 44 years in the early twentieth century as basic public health measures were introduced. However, with the exception of some Latin American countries, economic growth in the developing countries was relatively slow and, where it occurred (for example, South Africa, Chile and Malaya) the benefits were highly concentrated in a small segment of the national population. Per capita income in Africa continued to grow, though not as fast as other regions, while that of Asia (excluding Japan) declined by an average of 0.02 percent a year. Over this period China suffered from political instability culminating in the civil war that stretched between 1927 and 1950, and its GDP per capita declined significantly, from $552 in 1913 to $439 in 1950.[25] The Indian sub-continent was re-industrializing after the forced de-industrialization that had occurred in the early years of British rule, but this did not reverse a yearly GDP per capita decline of an average of 0.22 percent for the period 1913–1950.[26]

Alongside changes in material capabilities, changes in ideas were also taking place. At the time when the United States was considering whether it would engage in World War II, President Franklin D. Roosevelt delivered an important speech that would have significance for the founding of the institutions of the UN and for the idea of tackling global poverty. In his "Four Freedoms" speech of January 6, 1941 he identified freedom from want as a global priority: "The third freedom is freedom from want – which translated into universal terms, means economic understandings which will secure to every nation a healthy peacetime life for its inhabitants – everywhere in the world." As World War II concluded, the stage was set for the creation of the UN, for re-building war-ravaged Europe and Asia and for rapid decolonization around the world with its promise of "development."

Global poverty: the early development decades (1950–1990)

While World War II imposed a tremendous cost on humanity – with millions killed and maimed and the populations of Europe, Japan, South-east Asia and other regions deeply impoverished – its conclusion was followed by a series of potentially progressive changes. Principal among these were the impetus that the war had given to the founding of more effective international organizations and the process of decolonization.

The founding of the UN in 1945 was promoted by several different goals – to ensure peace and stop international warfare, to create economic stability and, more broadly, to promote human betterment. Its agencies were to lead on the global diffusion of improvements in agriculture, health, education, science and technology. In 1947, it produced the first "global consensus"[27] on eradicating poverty – the Universal Declaration of Human Rights (UDHR). This was approved by the UN's 51 original members and by all countries that have subsequently joined the UN. The key articles in relation to poverty are 25 and 28:

Everyone has the right to a standard of living adequate for the health and well-being of his family, including food, clothing, housing and medical care . . . Everyone is entitled to a social and international order in which the rights and freedoms set forth in this Declaration can be fully realised.

(*UDHR*, Articles 25 and 28)

The second impetus for poverty eradication came from decolonization, commencing with independence for the Indian sub-continent in 1948, as the European powers realized they could no longer hang on to their colonies. World War II had weakened their military grip over colonies and had challenged ideas of white superiority. In addition, the educated elites in many colonies – India, Ghana, Indonesia and others – were making well-reasoned cases for independence and for the existence of a class of national leaders. Many of these emerging leaders appear to have believed that the national plan they would launch shortly after independence would lead almost automatically to material prosperity for all within a decade or two. Nehru told the people of India that

. . . development ha[s] become a sort of mathematical problem which can be worked out scientifically . . . [men] of science, planners, experts who approach our problems from a purely scientific point of view . . . agree, broadly, that given certain preconditions of development, industrialization and all that, certain exact conclusions follow almost as a matter of course.[28]

In the late 1940s and 1950s the vision that most leaders had for their countries was not of poverty reduction or meeting basic needs, it was much grander – national development, rapid economic and social progress, industrialization and mass consumption. Modernization was just around the corner and developing countries would rapidly catch up with industrialized countries.[29] Poverty would be eradicated by rapid "trickle down" as the benefits of economic growth and increased incomes created modern jobs and wealth spread through national populations. The financial and technological gaps in the "Third World" could rapidly be plugged through foreign aid and technology transfer.

Despite unanimous acclamation of the UDHR at the UN, with strong US leadership from Eleanor Roosevelt (the president's wife), no concrete plans were laid to implement their promise of meeting basic needs for all. Similarly, while the industrialized nations encouraged national planning in newly independent countries, their support (and foreign aid) for development rarely went beyond an analysis of their foreign policy and domestic political interests. Throughout the 1950s development, human rights and the nascent idea of alleviating poverty were sidelined at international meetings and at the UN as the specter of the Cold War dominated global policy debates.[30]

The environment changed dramatically, but briefly, in the 1960s when Kennedy came to power and the United States again took on the leadership of the UN's development efforts.[31] Both Kennedy and his Republican opponent Richard Nixon saw foreign aid and the idea of development as a significant component of their anti-communist strategies. With Kennedy in power the rapid speed with which development goals were pursued within the UN system surprised most UN officials and observers. By December 1961 he had persuaded UN member states to unanimously agree its first "Decade of Development" and set targets to achieve this. These were: (i) 5 percent annual growth in GNP in developing countries and; (ii) the provision of 1 percent of their GNP by industrialized countries as financial flows to developing countries each year. These were crude targets but, alongside UN targets for disease eradication and universal primary education, they set the stage for future international efforts.

However, the Bay of Pigs fiasco and the Cuban Missile Crisis soon diverted Kennedy's attention from development and for many years it was left to academics and social activists to raise public awareness of global poverty and encourage national and international action. In the United States and Europe these included Andrew Shonfield (1960) *The Attack on World Poverty*, Gunnar Myrdal (1970) *The Challenge of World Poverty: A World Anti-Poverty Programme in Outline* and J.K. Galbraith (1979) *The Nature of Mass Poverty*. Writers from the newly independent countries provided more political accounts of why their peoples were poor as typified by Frantz Fanon's (1961) *The Wretched of the Earth* and Walter Rodney's (1973) *How Europe Underdeveloped Africa*. They looked not for "plans" to escape poverty but for revolution and the overturning of the capitalist system that exploited their economies. Structural economic analysis in Latin America, allied with neo-Marxist thinking in Europe in the late 1960s and early 1970s, amplified the calls for radical transformation.

The post-war era of decolonization coincided with what Maddison calls the twentieth century's "golden age" for economic growth, 1950 to 1973.[32] While the bulk of this growth was in the industrialized world there was progress also for the developing world. Average GDP per capita in Africa, Asia and Latin America increased (Figure 1.2) and alongside this there were significant improvements in life expectancy (Table 1.1) and other social indicators such as access to education. But the patterns were complex and the processes underlying them very different from the rapid and smooth transition to "ultimate prosperity" that modernization theory promised. By the mid-1960s India was portrayed in the West as facing a neo-Malthusian future of high fertility, famine and premature death;[33] Malaysia and Indonesia were seen as moving into civil wars; Indochina was falling apart; and in 1973, Kissinger declared Bangladesh to be a permanent "basket case." The picture in Africa, initially seen as having a secure future because of its lower population to resources ratios, was not looking good: growth was sluggish[34] and morbidity and mortality remained very high (Figure 1.3). Nigeria had been torn apart by a vicious civil war and Uganda, "the pearl of Africa," was controlled by a "mad man" (Idi Amin). In China, Mao's "Great Leap Forward" had led to between 20 and 43 million people starving to death and had set back social and economic progress. All of the grand competing strategies for human betterment – capitalist growth, mixed economy modernization, Soviet-style industrialization or peasant revolution – appeared to be failing the poor.

Dissatisfaction with the progress of the developing countries meant that by the late 1960s modernization, as an academic theory and as a development strategy, was falling out of favor in the West. From the World Bank, Hollis Chenery argued for a strategy of "Redistribution with Growth" suggesting that catching up was not sufficient: inequality needed to be reduced and the rich world would have to redistribute some of its wealth.[35] While this

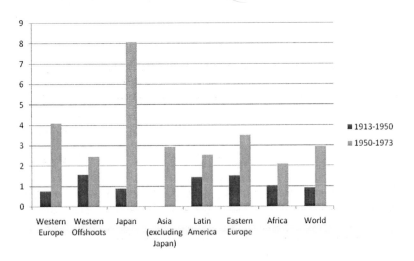

Figure 1.2 Annual growth in GDP per capita, 1931–1950 and 1950–1973

Source: Angus Maddison, *The World Economy: A Millennium Perspective* (Paris: Development Centre of the Organisation for Economic Co-operation and Development, 2001), 126.

Note: The figure for Asia (excluding Japan) for 1913–1950 is –0.02.

Table 1.1 World and group life expectancy, 1950 and 1999

Country group	Average life expectancy		Rate of growth of life expectancy (annual average compound growth rate)
	1950	*1999*	
Group A	66	78	0.34
Group B	44	64	0.77
World	49	66	0.61

Source: Angus Maddison, *The World Economy: A Millennium Perspective* (Paris: Development Centre of the Organisation for Economic Co-operation and Development, 2001), 31.

Notes:
Group A: Western Europe, United States, Canada, Australia, New Zealand and Japan.
Group B: Africa, Asia excluding Japan, Latin America, Eastern Europe and Russia.

was not radical in terms of the ideas of Frantz Fanon, Walter Rodney and Andre Gunder Frank, it was radical for an institution in Washington, DC. However, the redistributive element of Chenery's thinking soon faded in the World Bank as Robert McNamara shifted its policies to a direct assault on poverty and a focus on rural development rather than industrialization.[36] While developing countries began increasingly to take their policy lead from the World Bank, and shifted into the cul-de-sac of Integrated Rural Development Projects,[37] politically many of them attempted to promote a New International Economic Order or NIEO (see below) that would be fairer to the South. For the rich countries of the North there were other more

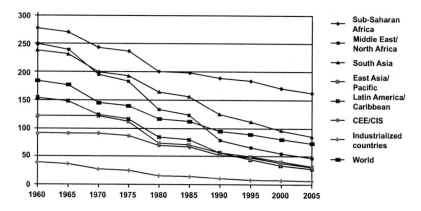

Figure 1.3 Trends in child mortality rates 1960–2005 (under-five mortality rate per 1,000 live births)

Source: UNICEF, *Progress for Children: A World Fit for Children Statistical Review No. 6* (New York, UNICEF, 2007), 18.

pressing problems than development: coping with the oil price hikes of the 1970s, and associated economic problems; dealing with the United States' defeat in Vietnam; and, for the United States and Union of Soviet Socialist Republics (USSR), competing in a global arms race.

A major attempt to attract attention to the problems of poorer countries and poor people, linked to the idea of the NIEO, was made by the Brandt Commission and their report *North-South: A Programme for Survival*.[38] Despite the international credibility of its chairman and members, and its warning that "[t]here is a real danger that in the year 2000 a large part of the world's population will still be living in poverty," the impact of the Report was very limited.[39] Its timing was unfortunate, coming after the 1979 oil price rise when the North feared recession, and with the election of conservative governments in the United States, United Kingdom, Japan and West Germany. Both Thatcher and Reagan attended the 1981 Cancun meeting to discuss the Report. Thatcher was doubly pleased at the results of her participation. She was able to scupper "[t]he whole concept of 'North-South' dialogue . . . [which] was in my view wrong-headed . . . [and Cancun was] the last of such gatherings."[40]

Around 1980, with the arrival of Reagan and Thatcher, the intellectual ascendancy of neo-liberal ideas, and the informal shifting of intellectual authority for development from the UN to the IMF and World Bank[41] (often referred to as the Bretton Woods Institutions or BWIs), the idea of a concerted international effort at global poverty reduction stalled. The BWIs demanded that developing countries, many of which were now deeply indebted and dependent on IMF loans and approval, pursue structural adjustment policies. These neo-liberal policies assumed that if the state was "rolled back," through deregulation and privatization, and the market allowed to determine most resource allocations then rapid economic growth would ensue. Poverty reduction was not a direct goal for these policies: once "the prices are right" then poverty would automatically reduce as the benefits of growth trickled down. The influence of the Washington Consensus (stabilize, privatize, liberalize) dominated structural adjustment thinking in the 1980s and early 1990s. It is widely judged to have produced "a lost decade" for Africa and developing countries more generally.[42] Growth did not ensue, regressive policies such as user fees for education and health blocked access to essential services for poor people and state structures and national political stability were eroded.[43] Fortunately, this powerful counter-revolution in development thinking and policy did not stamp out all alternatives. China had commenced its reform program autonomously and, by the late 1980s, senior figures in the UN system were laying plans for a new push that would re-focus development policy on the poor and disadvantaged.

Global poverty: recent history (1990–2010)

In many ways the year 1990 marked a tipping point in the evolution of ideas about poverty and poverty reduction. Against the backdrop of the end of the Cold War and growing doubts about the results of structural adjustment, the World Bank's *World Development Report 1990* chose poverty as its theme and acknowledged the need for economic reform to be accompanied by social policies.[44] The report presented the first serious attempt to count the world's poor using a common measure. It introduced the "dollar-a-day" headcount measure of global poverty and estimated that around 1.1 billion people lived in extreme poverty.[45] Perhaps even more significantly, the first *Human Development Report* was published by the United Nations Development Program (UNDP) in 1990. This promoted the idea of human development[46] as an alternative to neo-liberal economic growth and made the idea accessible to a wider group of professionals and to the serious media. It gave left of center social activists a relatively coherent framework from which to argue for policy change although it must be noted it gave them limited guidance for challenging macro-economic policy orthodoxy. 1990 was also the year of the World Summit for Children in New York, back to which the processes leading to the creation of the Millennium Development Goals (MDGs) can be traced.

The World Summit for Children achieved its identified goals, of mobilizing political commitment and setting concrete targets to improve the prospects of the world's children. In addition, it established the notion that "global summits," that is large meetings of national leaders, could motivate processes leading to real improvements in human welfare. While some summits and UN conferences might be caricatured as glorified talking shops, Jim Grant's leadership of the Children's Summit, and the implementation of plans to achieve its goals, showed that this did not have to be the case. Norm entrepreneurs throughout the UN and civil society were on a roll in the early 1990s and other major UN conferences followed on Environment and Development (Rio in 1992), Human Rights (Vienna in 1993), and Population and Development (Cairo in 1994).[47] This burst of official activity was amplified by the growth of lobbying and advocacy by NGOs and social movements following the end of the Cold War.[48]

The peak year for UN summitry was 1995 with the World Summit on Social Development (WSSD) in Copenhagen and the UN Fourth World Conference on Women in Beijing six months later. The Social Summit was crucial for the evolution of a new approach to tackling poverty. It was at Copenhagen that a form of global consensus was first reached that poverty reduction was the priority goal for development.[49] The WSSD approved the target of eradicating dollar-a-day poverty and re-affirmed the declarations made at New York, Rio and Cairo. Implicitly it drew on the idea of human development and viewed poverty as being multi-dimensional. While the radical left saw Copenhagen as a sell-out[50] – an acceptance of global capitalism – for the center left, center and center right this was a "consensus." The agreement at Copenhagen had particular legitimacy as 117 heads of state and government attended it – the largest meeting of heads there had ever been.[51]

In the same year the UN Women's Conference at Beijing – driven to a great degree by the women's movement – re-affirmed the goals of gender equality and women's empowerment. Many delegates saw the time as ripe for ambitious, post-Cold War global strategies of empowerment and social transformation rather than the technicist and managerial approach of Copenhagen.[52] However, the energy and drive of the conference was not matched by its impact on global policy making. Being the second conference that year proved disastrous: only two heads of state attended Beijing giving it little political leverage in the international arena.

In 1996 the Food Summit convened in Rome by the UN's Food and Agriculture Organization (FAO) declared the goal of halving the number of people experiencing poverty and hunger. This would eventually become Goal 1 of the MDGs. UN conferences continued in the latter half of the 1990s but many observers report "conference fatigue" setting in. The forum for shaping the global agenda on poverty reduction was about to shift from these vast and diverse UN jamborees to much smaller formalized meetings centered on Paris – mainly of men from industrialized countries.

The debates and declarations of these UN global conferences and summits were impressive. They led to increased media coverage of the issues and raised public awareness. But, with the notable exception of the Child Summit, implementation after these events was relatively limited. The annual budgets and policies of developing countries did not systematically shift towards declared goals and, despite the public promises, levels of official development assistance (ODA) from rich countries to poor countries as a share of GDP continued their long-term decline. With the Cold War over, OECD countries, with the notable exception of Japan, had decided that foreign aid merited a lower priority – increased interest in the moral case for aid was not sufficient to compensate for the weakening of the foreign policy case. With the Soviet Union no longer a threat, buying allies in the poor world with foreign aid was now less important for the Western powers. Anyway, they had other priorities, and ODA was shifted from developing countries to support economic and political liberalization in the middle income countries of Eastern and Central Europe.

For the donor club, the OECD's Development Assistance Committee (DAC), this created great unease and stimulated their listing seven International Development Goals (IDGs)[53] in 1996 in an attempt to generate public support

Table 1.2 The International Development Goals (IDGs)

1. Economic well-being: The proportion of people living in extreme poverty in developing countries should be reduced by at least one-half by 2015.

2. Social development: There should be substantial progress in primary education, gender equality, basic health care and family planning, as follows:
   a. There should be universal primary education in all countries by 2015.
   b. Progress toward gender equality and the empowerment of women should be demonstrated by eliminating gender disparity in primary and secondary education by 2005.
   c. The death rate for infants and children under the age of five years should be reduced by two-thirds the 1990 level by 2015. The rate of maternal mortality should be reduced by three-fourths during this same period.
   d. Access should be available through the primary health-care system to reproductive health services for all individuals of appropriate ages, including safe and reliable family planning methods, as soon as possible and no later than the year 2015.

3. Environmental sustainability and regeneration: There should be a current national strategy for sustainable development, in the process of implementation, in every country by 2005, so as to ensure that current trends in the loss of environmental resources – forests, fisheries, fresh water, climate, soils, biodiversity, stratospheric ozone, the accumulation of hazardous substances and other major indicators – are effectively reversed at both global and national levels by 2015.

Source: Development Assistance Committee, "Shaping the 21st century: the contribution of development cooperation" (Paris: OECD, 1996).

for foreign aid (Table 1.2). These goals brought together components from the declarations of the recent summits and conferences, although the Copenhagen commitment to eradicate poverty by an unspecified date was converted into reducing extreme poverty by half by 2015. The IDGs achieved political traction in some OECD countries, especially through the efforts of Clare Short in the United Kingdom and her three colleagues in the Utstein Group (the Ministers for International Development of Germany, the Netherlands and Norway) but they had little impact over powerful donors, such as the United States and France, and the BWIs.

In developing countries the IDGs achieved little or no resonance. This list came from a document produced entirely by rich countries and promises of "partnership" sounded like well-worn aid agency rhetoric. Besides, the most powerful agencies poorer countries had to engage with were the World Bank and IMF, not bilateral donors. However, as discussed below, this IDG list was set to make a come-back.

In 1998 control of the global poverty agenda returned to the UN as planning for the Millennium Assembly of the United Nations, to be held at

New York in September 2000, commenced. The UN's new Secretary-General, Kofi Annan, was keen to make global poverty reduction central to the UN agenda and to avoid being driven along by peace-keeping, security and emergency issues as had his predecessors.[54] In May 1999 he identified four main themes for the Millennium Assembly. The second was "development, including poverty eradication." The shift in development thinking that had emerged at Copenhagen was now being institutionalized. Development was no longer about national development (economic growth and generalized improvements in welfare); rather it was synonymous with targeted poverty eradication (or reduction).

Negotiations, at the UN and many other venues, eventually led to Kofi Annan approving two documents to prepare the General Assembly for the Millennium Declaration. The first, *We the Peoples: The Role of the United Nations in the 21st Century*, was launched on April 3, 2000.[55] Poverty eradication was the leading issue for the Report, but it had a quite different set of poverty reduction goals than the OECD-DAC's IDGs. The pressures of the UN membership had led *We the Peoples* to have less of a human development focus than the IDGs. The capabilities of child, maternal and reproductive health and gender equality were much less evident while issues such as "bridging the digital divide," making information and communication technologies (ICTs) more accessible gained a high profile.

Annan's second document sought to demonstrate that the UN was coordinating its global poverty reduction activities with the other big players – the World Bank, IMF and the OECD-DAC – and was co-authored with the leaders of these agencies. These three agencies felt that the IDG listing had distinct advantages over *We the Peoples*. As a result, in June 2000 when Annan stood beside his three colleagues and launched *A Better World for All: Progress towards the International Development Goals*,[56] this document re-iterated the DAC's 1996 IDGs almost exactly. It re-affirmed the primacy of the results-based management thinking favored by OECD countries and the BWIs. It led to Annan coming in for heavy criticism from civil society groups such as the World Council of Churches which were horrified to see him agreeing with the IMF and World Bank.[57] Most significantly, the goals in *A Better World for All* included reproductive rights and reductions in child and maternal mortality – human development goals that *We the Peoples* had omitted. Beyond its content *A Better World for All* revealed an important aspect of the global poverty reduction goal setting process – it was a twin track process. The aid donors of the OECD were continuing to pursue their preferences and had support from the BWIs. In parallel, the UN was mounting a similar exercise to produce a list for the Millennium Summit – but that list had to satisfy a larger constituency with different interests, the UN General Assembly's 189 member states.

Over summer 2000 there were frantic negotiations about what should finally go into the Millennium Declaration.[58] With around 150 heads of government or state due to attend, and Annan seeking a mandate for UN reform, the Millennium Summit had to be a success. As the big day approached a compromise was reached that included goals for rich countries (aid, debt, trade and policy reforms) and strengthened the goals related to gender equality and child and maternal mortality. These additions, deletions and compromises worked – the Millennium Declaration was unanimously approved at the UN General Assembly on September 8, 2000.

The next formal stage of the process was for the Secretary-General to draw up a "road map" showing how the world would achieve its global poverty reduction commitments. But, before the UN could develop a plan for implementing the Millennium Declaration it needed final agreement on what the exact goals and targets were. Negotiations over 2001 eventually led to a task force comprised of officials from the DAC (representing OECD), World Bank, IMF and UNDP. It was this task force that finalized the MDGs[59] in what was claimed to be a purely technical exercise (Table 1.3). The MDGs were unveiled in Annan's *Road map towards the implementation of the United Nations Millennium Declaration* but, this authoritative listing was carefully qualified: "The list of millennium development goals does not undercut in any way agreements on other goals and targets reached at the global conferences of the 1990s."[60]

It is clear from the final form of the MDGs that the OECD-DAC's IDGs, as presented in *A Better World for All*, were taken as the primary document – the more powerful actors in these negotiations, both politically (the OECD's membership) and technically (the World Bank and the IMF), preferred the IDGs. Nevertheless, the negotiations had substance and there were two big decisions about what to drop and what to include in the MDGs. *Reproductive health* was dropped. This was an explicit goal in the IDGs, and central to the

Table 1.3 The Millennium Development Goals (MDGs)

Goal 1: Eradicate extreme poverty and hunger

Goal 2: Achieve universal primary education

Goal 3: Promote gender equality and empower women

Goal 4: Reduce child mortality

Goal 5: Improve maternal health

Goal 6: Combat HIV/AIDS, malaria and other diseases

Goal 7: Ensure environmental sustainability

Goal 8: Develop a global partnership for development

Note: See Appendix 1 for a full listing of MDG goals, targets, and indicators.

idea of human development, but the UN could not entertain this because of the objections of a small group of conservative Islamic states at the G77 (the association of developing country UN member states) in an "unholy alliance" with the Holy See.[61] The main addition was MDG Goal 8: *a global partnership for development*. This was imported from the Millennium Declaration and attempted to set targets for rich countries. The UN's developing countries were not going to accept a set of goals that applied only to them. However, there is a qualitative difference between Goals 1 to 7 and Goal 8. While Goals 1 to 7 were time-bound there were no concrete dates set for any Goal 8 indicators and most of the indicators lacked a quantitative target.[62] This reflected the power relations of the situation – the OECD's members were prepared to agree the directions they should move in but they were not prepared to set quantitative targets or agree dates for achievement.

Parallel with the processes surrounding the MDGs, the World Bank and IMF had established a national planning level mechanism that it was claimed would promote poverty reduction – Poverty Reduction Strategy Papers (PRSPs).[63] Originally, these were only to be prepared by countries seeking HIPC funding but they soon became a requirement for all countries seeking foreign aid.

The data available at the turn of the millennium confirmed the enormous scale of global poverty. The *World Development Report 2000/2001* elaborated that

> . . . [t]he world has deep poverty amid plenty. Of the world's 6 billion people, 2.8 billion . . . live on less than $2 a day, and 1.2 billion[64] . . . live on less than $1 a day. In rich countries fewer than 1 child in 100 does not reach its fifth birthday, while in poorer countries as many as a fifth do not. And while in rich countries fewer than 5 percent of all children under five are malnourished, in poor countries as many as 50 percent are.[65]

While average world per capita income had risen by 40 percent in the last quarter of the twentieth century average income per capita in Africa had not changed (Table 1.4). Many countries in sub-Saharan Africa, for example Nigeria, South Africa and Uganda, and some in Asia (such as Afghanistan) had seen average incomes decline since the 1970s. Staggeringly, average per capita income in the Democratic Republic of the Congo (DRC, formerly Zaire) dropped from $730 in 1973 to $220 in 1998 – extreme poverty had become a national norm. Social indicators were also a cause for alarm in sub-Saharan Africa with the HIV/AIDS pandemic and structural adjustment policies. Life expectancy reduced in many countries (Table 1.5) and literacy, nutrition, child and maternal mortality made little or no progress. As the new

Table 1.4 Changes in GDP per capita 1950–1998 for selected countries and regions (1990 international $)

Country/region	GDP pc in 1950	GDP pc in 1973	GDP pc in 1998
Afghanistan	645	684	514 Con Fleur
Australia	7493	12759	20390
Bangladesh	540	497	813 ?
Brazil	1672	3882	5459
Bolivia	1919	2357	2459
China	439	839	3117
DRC (formerly Zaire)	497	730	220
Egypt	718	1022	2128
India	619	853	1746
Indonesia	840	1504	3070
Iraq	1364	3753	1131 Connect
Italy	3502	10643	17759
Japan	1926	11439	20084
Malaysia	1559	2560	7100
Nigeria	753	1442	1232
Russian Federation	n/a	6577	4523
Saudi Arabia	2231	11040	8225
South Africa	2535	4175	3858
Uganda	687	838	725
United Kingdom	6907	12022	18714
United States	9561	16689	27331
West Europe	5013	12159	18742
LAC	2554	4531	5795
Asia (excl. Japan)	635	1231	2936
Africa	852	1365	1368
USSR (former)	2834	6058	3893

Source: Angus Maddison, *The World Economy: A Millennial Perspective* (Paris: Development Centre of the Organisation for Economic Co-operation and Development, 2001), 185, 195, 203, 206, 215, 224.

millennium commenced a clear pattern of extreme human deprivation could be identified. Sub-Saharan Africa experienced the most extreme, multi-dimensional, chronic poverty while South Asia had the largest numbers of people trapped in poverty (Figures 1.4 and 1.5).

But, dire need was not matched by dramatic action (as is examined in later chapters). Unfortunately, over the year during which the MDGs were being negotiated, prospects for a concerted push against global poverty weakened. In part this was, perhaps, inevitable: the millennium fever that had fuelled global promise-making was over and the main process for planning poverty reduction, PRSPs, was controlled by the BWIs. The World Bank was actively ambivalent to the MDGs but the IMF paid them only lip service.[66] Even more significant was the change of president in the United States. Clinton had been unwilling to take a lead in UN or OECD processes about global poverty

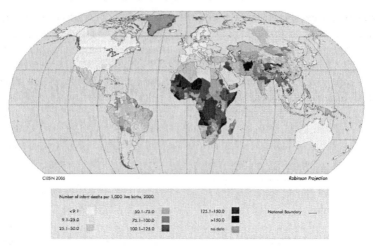

Figure 1.4 The global distribution of infant mortality

Source: *Where the Poor Are: An Atlas of Poverty*, Center for International Earth Science Information Network (Palisades, NY: Columbia University, 2006), 4, available at http://sedac.ciesin.columbia.edu/povmap/atlasMedia.jsp

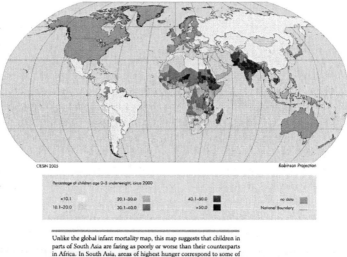

Unlike the global infant mortality map, this map suggests that children in parts of South Asia are faring as poorly or worse than their counterparts in Africa. In South Asia, areas of highest hunger correspond to some of the areas of highest population density. However, nowhere in the Americas comes close to the highest levels of hunger in the Eastern hemisphere, at least at the levels mapped.

Figure 1.5 The global distribution of hunger

Source: *Where the Poor Are: An Atlas of Poverty*, Center for International Earth Science Information Network (Palisades, NY: Columbia University, 2006), 5, available at http://sedac.ciesin.columbia.edu/povmap/atlasMedia.jsp

reduction because of domestic political opposition. Now power rested with a Republican president guided by a small group of neo-conservative advisors who were very suspicious of the UN and dismissive of foreign aid. This was highly inauspicious for the approaching UN Finance for Development (FFD) Conference, originally planned for 2001 but now delayed until March 2002. At the FFD it was expected that UN members, and particularly rich countries, would make pledges to raise the level of resources available to achieve the MDGs. It seemed likely that Bush would not attend the FFD Summit and possible that the United States would detach itself from the MDG process altogether. That would open the door for other countries to let global poverty reduction slide off the international agenda.

Two factors changed this. The 9/11 attacks led the Bush administration to think a little more than it had previously about "soft power" approaches to foreign policy. It showed more interest in the role of US foreign aid as an adjunct to the "war on terror." Second was that the FFD meeting was in Monterrey and the Mexican president, Vicente Fox, was convener. Bush had already declared that Mexico was the United States' most important foreign partner and in the media talked about his close personal relationship with Fox. This put pressure on Bush to accept the invitation and, once there he would have to show generosity. At Monterrey the United States pledged a further $5 billion per annum for poverty reduction – increasing its aid budget by half – and the EU an additional $13 billion a year.[67] This compared to estimates of an additional $50–100 billion per annum needed to achieve the MDGs – and many rich countries had caveats around their aid, trade and debt reforms. While the total commitments made at Monterrey were well below the levels hinted at in 2000, overall the FFD was viewed as a success. The MDGs were informally approved there (even if not formally ratified) and Bush indicated that the United States would be part of the evolving project for global poverty reduction that the MDGs represented.

At last the MDGs were ready for implementation. The UN established its Millennium Project, to pursue the MDGs practically, and the Millennium Campaign, to mobilize public support for the MDGs around the world.[68] The BWIs pushed all aid recipient countries into writing PRSPs, the DAC and its "like-minded" members encouraged all OECD countries to increase finance for poverty reduction, African leaders discussed plans to improve governance through the New Partnership for Africa's Development (NEPAD) and peer review mechanisms and celebrities and philanthrocapitalists lined up to support the goals. But, as is revealed in later chapters, keeping global poverty reduction on the international agenda post-2002 has been difficult. Other global priorities (terrorism, trade policy, climate change, energy security, financial crisis) have proved more pressing. National self-interest has continued to guide negotiating positions; and, the waning global superpower, the

Table 1.5 Life expectancy for selected countries and regions in 1950–1955, 1970–1975 and 2000–2005

Country/region	1950–1955	1970–1975	2000–2005
Afghanistan	31.9	39.7	46.0
Australia	69.6	71.7	80.2
Bangladesh	37.5	45.2	62.6
Brazil	50.9	59.5	70.3
Bolivia	40.4	46.7	63.9
China	40.8	63.2	71.5
DRC (formerly Zaire)	39.1	46.0	43.1
Egypt	42.4	52.1	69.6
India	38.7	50.3	63.1
Indonesia	37.5	49.2	66.5
Iraq	45.3	57.0	58.8
Italy	66.0	72.1	80.0
Japan	63.9	73.3	81.9
Malaysia	48.5	63.0	73.0
Nigeria	36.3	42.8	43.3
Russian Federation	64.5	69.7	65.4
Saudi Arabia	39.9	53.9	71.6
South Africa	45.0	53.7	49.0
Uganda	40.0	51.1	46.8
United Kingdom	69.2	72.0	78.3
United States	68.9	71.5	77.3
Western Europe	67.6	71.7	78.9
LAC	51.4	60.9	71.5
Asia	41.4	56.4	67.3
Africa	38.4	46.7	49.1
USSR (former)	–	–	–
More developed	66.1	71.4	75.6
Less developed	41.1	54.8	63.4
Least developed	36.1	44.2	51.0
World	46.6	58.1	65.4

Source: UN Population Division Database

United States, has remained ambivalent to the MDGs and many of its allies have followed. The Gleneagles G8 meeting of 2005 and the UN High Level Event of 2008, both led by the United Kingdom, have attempted to re-focus the rich world and the UN membership on global poverty eradication, but with only marginal effect.

The scale and geography of contemporary global poverty

The scale of poverty in the contemporary world is appalling (Table 1.6). The World Bank[69] estimates that 1.377 billion people live under the US$1.25-a-day extreme poverty line and 2.562 billion people under the US$2-a-day poverty (see Box 1.1 for an explanation of poverty lines). While this represents relative progress, with the proportion of extreme poor in the developing world over 1981–2005 down from 52 percent to 25 percent of population and the $2-a-day poor down from 69 percent to 47 percent, the absolute figures are unacceptable in a world with an average GDP per capita of $24.58-a-day. A redistribution of 0.33 percent (one-third of 1 percent) of global income to the poorest would eradicate extreme poverty, while a redistribution of 1.28 percent would eradicate $2-a-day poverty. Clearly at the global level the resources to eradicate poverty are not the over-riding constraint.

The recent economic crises (fuel, food and finance) have put poverty reduction into reverse. For example, the Food and Agriculture Organization (FAO) estimates that an additional 100 million people fell into hunger over 2008 and 2009 – so the number of hungry people will rise to 1.02 billion in 2010, well up from the 825 million in 1995.[70] The UN's *Millennium Development Goals Report 2009* records that an estimated 55 to 90 million people will fall into $1.25-a-day poverty in 2009 and that the achievement of many other poverty goals will slow down or reverse.[71] The cozy assumption of the early twenty-first century, that economic growth in China and India will ensure that aggregate global poverty figures will automatically decline, is being tested.

Table 1.6 The regional breakdown of $1.25- and $2-a-day poverty in 2005

Region	Millions of people below $1.25 a day (percentage of population)	Millions of people below $2 a day (percentage of population)
East Asia and Pacific	316.2 (16.8)	728.7 (38.7)
Of which China	207.7 (15.9)	473.3 (36.3)
Eastern Europe and Central Asia	17.3 (3.7)	41.9 (8.9)
Latin America and Caribbean	46.1 (8.4)	91.3 (16.6)
Middle East and North Africa	11.0 (3.6)	51.5 (16.9)
South Asia	595.6 (40.3)	1091.5 (73.9)
Of which India	455.8 (41.6)	827.7 (75.6)
sub-Saharan Africa	390.6 (51.2)	556.7 (73.0)
Total	1376.7 (25.2)	2561.5 (47.0)

Source: Shaohua Chen and Martin Ravallion, "The Developing World Is Poorer than We Thought, but No Less Successful in the Fight against Poverty," World Bank Policy Research Working Paper No. 4703 (Washington, DC: World Bank, 2008), 33–36.

Box 1.1 Global poverty lines and the incidence of poverty

Poverty lines attempt to define the economic resources needed to meet a person's minimum needs. In developing countries governments usually define an absolute poverty line. This is commonly done as the cost of a basic diet for an adult (providing 2,100–2,300 calories per day) plus the cost of a few essential non-food items, such as fuel, clothing and shelter. People whose consumption falls below this line are classed as poor and people above it are non-poor.

Until about 20 years ago these lines could only be applied at the national level. However, researchers at the World Bank have devised a method for making comparative estimates of poverty across the world. This has involved identifying global poverty lines and manipulating national level data so that it achieves "Purchasing Power Parity" (PPP). The original global poverty line was $1-a-day consumption at 1985 values. This has been updated and now several lines are used – recognizing that despite the scientific method behind poverty measurement the setting of a poverty line is always, in part, an arbitrary exercise. In 2008 the World Bank researchers highlighted the $1.25-a-day line as an extreme poverty line (it was the mean for the poorest 15 countries, in terms of per capita consumption, for which there is data) and the $2.00-a-day line for poverty (this was the median poverty line for all developing countries). For an idea of what life is like on $1.25-a-day see Box 1.2. PPP calculations attempt to adjust national level data so that $1 in one country would buy the same amount of goods as $1 in every other country: such conversions are technically demanding and although they have improved there are many remaining problems with them.

Most commonly the findings of such analyses are expressed in absolute terms (the number of people below the poverty line) and as *headcount ratios* (the percentage of a population below the poverty line). This is useful, but such measures say nothing about the depth of poverty (are most poor people just below the line or massively below it?) or the distribution of poverty (does part of the poor

(Box continued on next page)

population experience severe poverty?). To analyze these, the *poverty gap* (the average distance of the poor below the poverty line) and the *poverty gap-squared* (the weighted average of the squared distance of each poor person below the line expressed as a proportion of that line), are used.

The geography of global poverty depends on the choice of indicator – does one use the $1.25-a-day or $2-a-day measure or a composite measure, such as the Human Poverty Index (comprised of educational, health and life expectancy measures)? If one uses the $2-a-day line then sub-Saharan Africa and South Asia have almost identical incidences of head count poverty (73.0 percent against 73.9 percent). However, if one uses the $1.25 line then the incidence of poverty in sub-Saharan Africa is significantly higher than in South Asia (51.2 percent against 40.3 percent). This reflects the deeper consumption poverty in Africa: the "average" poor person in sub-Saharan Africa (for any poverty line) is deeper below the line than is the case for South Asia or other parts of the world.[72] For example, the average consumption of an extremely poor ($1.25-a-day) African is a horrifying $0.73 compared to $0.93 for a $1.25-a-day South Asian. Life on $1.25-a-day is hard but varies greatly with context and circumstances. There is no "average life" for extremely poor people. Box 1.2 provides an image of what life is like for someone in this position.

While the contemporary map of global poverty (Figure 1.6) indicates that income poverty is vast in both Africa and South Asia, the analysis of global poverty has increasingly shifted to a focus on sub-Saharan Africa. Given the continent's lost decade of the 1980s, followed by the lost decade of the 1990s with stagnant economic growth and the HIV/AIDS pandemic driving down life expectancy and causing appalling suffering, the highlighting of Africa's problems is no surprise. The international agenda has certainly focused on Africa: since the late 1990s the G7/8 has regularly had Africa as an agenda item; the Millennium Declaration devoted a separate chapter to "meeting the special needs of Africa"; and the United Kingdom's efforts to refocus the EU and G7/8 on the MDGs concentrated on the Report of the Africa Commission and the support it lent for increased aid and debt cancellation for Africa.

The idea that Africa is the locus for tackling global poverty has been reinforced by Paul Collier's influential book *The Bottom Billion*.[73] He argues that 70 percent of the world's bottom billion live in Africa and, on the assumption that economic growth in China and India will eventually eradicate poverty in Asia, that "Africa plus" (meaning sub-Saharan Africa plus countries such as Haiti, Bolivia, Turkmenistan, Laos, Burma and North Korea) is the future

Box 1.2 Extreme poverty: life on $1.25 a day

The use of the US$ as the currency unit for global poverty estimations gives people the feeling that they know what this means. But these measures are not about what you can buy with a dollar or two in New York or Nashville. Accounts of what poverty is like can be found in *The Chronic Poverty Report 2008–2009* and Collins *et al.* (2009) *Portfolios of the Poor*. These show how varied are the lives of poor people – there is no "average poor person." They also show that poverty is about more than just a lack of income – it is about being insecure and vulnerable, feeling that one lacks dignity and much more. From my conversations with poor people over the years one might expect the conditions described below.

Living on $1.25 a day. You are a member of a household dependent on casual laboring in South Asia or subsistence cropping on a small plot of rain fed land in Africa. When times are good you eat two meals a day of rice or maize flour with a little chili or vegetable. When times are bad you eat one meal a day. Sometimes, when there is no work or the rains fail, you do without food or make do with leaves from the bush or scavenging. Meat and fish are rarely eaten – only at celebrations and feasts. The children in your household probably do not attend school – if they do, they will probably have to drop out before completing primary level. If someone gets sick then usually you wait until they get better . . . and pray. If someone is really sick then you sell assets (the spade, pans, title to your home plot) or borrow money to pay for a hospital visit. At the hospital you are made to feel a non-entity – made to wait in long queues, treated as an idiot, nothing is explained to you. You are accustomed to death – brothers, sisters, cousins, parents died when you were young – it just happens. You get to vote every few years in the elections – but, you do not expect much of politicians. These people often pay violent gangs to help them get elected and they are known to be corrupt. What can you do? When you look out of the doorway in your leaky shack you worry about the unpaid rent and your outstanding emergency loans from relatives and traders. Your shack does not have electricity or sanitation – water comes

(Box continued on next page)

irregularly from a communal pump 200 meters away provided by an NGO. If you could just get a job (as a poorly paid maid or a security guard) or just get control of the land your father mortgaged to a moneylender or just marry a good man, life would be so different – a pair of shoes, clothes for the baby or a savings deposit so you could join a micro-credit group. In the distance you see the vehicles flashing past on the newly tarmaced road – lucky people in over-crowded buses, off to do poorly paid but regular work in factories and offices in town; and important people, in business or related to politicians, in air-conditioned BMWs and Mercedes – wearing flashy clothes, eating pizza . . . thinking of going on a diet.

geography of extreme poverty. This does not seem unreasonable given the high proportions of Africa's population that is \$1.25-a-day poor and the appallingly low social indicators in many African countries.

However, if one maps the data for Asia and disaggregates it for Indian states and Chinese provinces – which is not unreasonable given that most of these sub-national units have populations much bigger than those of the

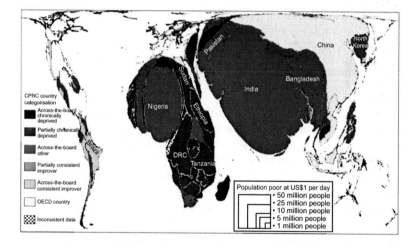

Figure 1.6 The global distribution of poverty (2008)

Source: Chronic Poverty Research Centre, Chronic Poverty Report 2008–2009 (Manchester, CPRC: University of Manchester, 2008). The area of each country is proportionate to the number of US\$1-a-day (extreme poor) people.

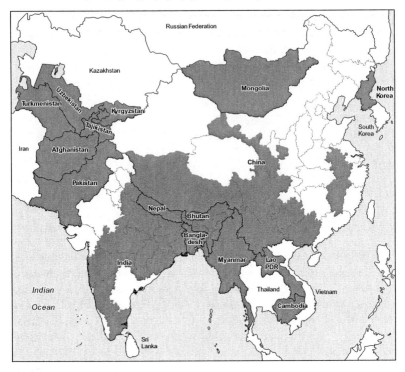

Figure 1.7 Poverty in Sub-Siberian Asia.

Note: The greyed area identifies countries, Indian states and Chinese provinces that suffer high levels of social and/or economic poverty. The resulting area of 'sub-Siberian Asia' should not, however, be considered to be definitive due to the poor quality of available data.

average African country – then a different geography emerges (Figure 1.7). A second poor continent can be identified – *sub-Siberian Asia*. This is a virtually contiguous area that stretches across northern India and Nepal to Bangladesh, Burma and Laos, takes in much of central and western China with Mongolia, includes Central Asia (Kazakhstan, Kyrgyzstan, Uzbekistan, Turkmenistan and Tajikistan) and completes in Afghanistan and Pakistan. Economic indicators of poverty (the $1.25-a-day headcount) and social indicators (illiteracy, maternal mortality, gender equality) for this continent are much higher than to the north in Russia, the west (Iran and Turkey), the south (southern India and Sri Lanka) and the east (Thailand and coastal China) (Table 1.4). While I argue that this is the world's second poor continent, it must be recognized that with the exception of Afghanistan, the depth of income poverty in sub-Siberian Asia is not at the extremely deep levels of sub-Saharan Africa. Research financed by NASA, using night-time lights as a surrogate for wealth, reaches similar conclusions – sub-Saharan Africa and sub-Siberian Asia are the two vast regions of the world where the populations are too poor to shine a light at night time.[74]

Proposing the recognition of sub-Siberian Asia is not to argue that Africa does not require special attention, analytically or in terms of assistance. What it does suggest is that the global geography of extreme poverty needs to be understood as "sub-Saharan Africa and sub-Siberian Asia plus some other countries." Assuming that poverty in China and India, and especially in India, will steadily fall because their average growth rates are high fails to recognize that these are continental scale countries: the lights in Bangalaru and Hangzhou may be shining 24/7 but it is hard to find the money to buy a candle in rural Tripura and Guizhou.

Conclusion

Over the last 200 years poverty has ceased to be the norm for humanity and, since around 1980, the global headcount index for income poverty has dropped at an unprecedented rate. Social indicators have also improved but they vary greatly between countries and regions. Famines have apparently been eradicated in Europe and Asia during the twentieth century and the three African famines of the twenty-first century (Ethiopia, Malawi and Niger) have all been on a small scale in comparative terms.[75] However, around 1.377 billion people (25.2 percent of the world's population) live in extreme consumption poverty ($1.25-a-day) and 2.562 billion people (47 percent of the world's population) survive on less than $2-a-day. In an affluent world this is morally unacceptable – a tiny re-allocation of global GDP would place all of these people over these poverty lines. While income poverty has reduced, complex patterns have emerged and there are very different levels of well-being (consumption, health status, literacy, security, life expectancy) in different parts of the world. The world's deepest economic poverty and worst levels of social deprivation are concentrated in sub-Saharan Africa. However, while some analysts now see the geography of global poverty as "Africa plus" (sub-Saharan Africa plus a mix of odd cases in Asia, the Caribbean and Latin America) this chapter reveals that global poverty is located in "sub-Saharan Africa and sub-Siberian Asia plus." Conditions in much of Asia have improved in recent times but the heartland of the Asian landmass still holds a vast number of very poor people. Understanding why so many people remain poor in an affluent world is the subject of the next chapter.

Notes

1 Quoted in Jan Vandemoortele, *Are We Really Reducing Global Poverty?* (New York: UNDP, Bureau for Development Policy, 2002), 4.

2 Angus Maddison, *The World Economy: A Millennial Perspective* (Paris: Development Centre of the Organisation for Economic Co-operation and Development, 2001), 17.

3 Maddison, *The World Economy*, 28.

4 Ronald Findlay and Kevin H. O'Rourke, *Power and Plenty: Trade, War, and the World Economy in the Second Millennium* (Princeton and Oxford: Princeton University Press, 2007), 112.

5 Findlay and O'Rourke, *Power and Plenty*, 120.

6 Findlay and O'Rourke, *Power and Plenty*, 127–133.

7 Olwen H. Hufton, *The Poor of Eighteenth-Century France, 1750–1789* (Oxford: Clarendon Press, 1974).

8 Maddison, *The World Economy*, 27–31. In this chapter the main indicators I use are life expectancy and GDP per capita (in 1990 US$). This is because historically these are the only reliable statistics available. In other chapters a broader set of economic and human development indicators is used.

9 Alfred W Crosby, *The Columbian Exchange: Biological and Cultural Consequences of 1492* (West Point, Conn. and London: Praeger, 2003), 199.

10 Findlay and O'Rourke, *Power and Plenty*, 160–161, citing Henry F. Dobyns, "Estimating Aboriginal Populations: An Appraisal of Techniques with a New Hemispheric Estimate," *Current Anthropology* 7, no. 4 (1966): 395–416. Note that the figure of 95 percent is highly contested.

11 Carlo M. Cipolla, *European Culture and Overseas Expansion* (Middlesex: Penguin, 1970).

12 I side with Maddison (Maddison, *The World Economy*, 45) in seeing 1820 as a good approximation of when economic conditions began to significantly change rather than the earlier orthodoxy of a sudden take-off, in Britain, around 1760.

13 Maddison, *The World Economy*.

14 Or, from the Gospel of Saint Matthew 26:11, "[f]or ye have the poor always with you."

15 Gareth Stedman Jones, *An End to Poverty? A Historical Debate* (London: Profile, 2004).

16 Jones, *An End*, 18.

17 Jones, *An End*.

18 And indeed the debates of Victorian times – see Gertrude Himmelfarb, *Poverty and Compassion: The Moral Imagination of the Late Victorians* (New York: Knopf, 1991).

19 See Friedrich Engels, *The Condition of the Working Class in England* (1844) for a description and analysis of living conditions in Manchester. I walk past the site of the appalling slum for Irish immigrants each day.

20 Maddison, *The World Economy*.

21 However, it should be noted that these "improvements" are compatible with impoverishment since they increased colonial control over subject populations and their economic activities.

22 For a detailed analysis of the colonial experience of the African poor see chapter 9 of John Iliffe, *The African Poor: A History* (Cambridge: Cambridge University Press, 1986).

23 Mike Davis, *Late Victorian Holocausts: El Nino Famines and the Making of the Third World* (London and New York: Verso, 2000).

24 See Adam Hochschild, *King Leopold's Ghost: A Story of Greed, Terror, and Heroism in Colonial Africa* (London: Pan, 2006).

25 Maddison, *The World Economy*, 215.

26 Maddison, *The World Economy*, 216.

27 I put this in quotation marks as in 1948 the majority of the world's peoples were not directly represented at the UN.

28 Cited in Bruce F. Johnston and William C. Clark, *Redesigning Rural Development: A Strategic Perspective* (Baltimore: Johns Hopkins University Press, 1982), 24.

29 There was no suggestion that "levelling down" might be needed and that the rich countries should redistribute their wealth and income.

30 US persecution of communist "subversives" in the UN Secretariat also soured US-UN relations.

31 John Toye and Richard Toye, "From Multilateralism to Modernisation: US Strategy on Trade, Finance and Development in the United Nations, 1945–63," *Forum for Development Studies*, no. 1 (2005): 140–144.

32 Maddison, *The World Economy*, 125.

33 As a 12 year old I remember watching a television program with my parents that convinced me that India was doomed to a Malthusian trap. My mother thought "we should send them food" while my father thought "they should all be sterilized."

34 Per capita GDP in Africa was only just keeping ahead of Asia (excluding Japan).

35 Hollis Chenery, Ian Bowen and Brian Jeffrey Svikhart, *Redistribution with Growth: Policies to Improve Income Distribution in Developing Countries in the Context of Economic Growth* (London: Oxford University Press for the World Bank and the Institute of Development Studies, University of Sussex, 1974).

36 It should also be noted that McNamara, just back from Vietnam, saw poverty reduction as part of a strategy to combat the spread of communism in the developing world.

37 In early career I researched Integrated Rural Development Projects. While the idea of integrated rural development had much to recommend it, the actual implementation of these projects made almost every mistake known to project management. They added to developing country debt without generating the promised growth and/or poverty reduction.

38 Independent Commission on International Development Issues, *North-South: A Programme for Survival* (London: Pan Books, 1980).

39 John Toye and Richard Toye, "From New Era to Neo-Liberalism: US Strategy on Trade, Finance and Development in the United Nations, 1964–82," *Forum for Development Studies*, no. 1 (2005): 176.

40 Margaret Thatcher, *The Downing Street Years* (London: HarperCollins, 1993), 168–170.

41 After World War II it appeared that the UN system would provide analysis and policy advice while the Fund and Bank would focus on providing finance for economic stability and development. In practice they competed to set the development agenda and the Fund and Bank's control over finance and backing from the US government gave them the upper hand.

42 John Williamson presents a more subtle interpretation of the Washington Consensus. However, the briefings to developing countries I witnessed in

Bangladesh, Kenya, Malawi and Sri Lanka in the early 1990s by World Bank advisors were very simple – stabilize, privatize, liberalize. While structural adjustment directly made millions poor, and may have weakened institutions, it must be noted that state action and public expenditure in many countries had to be reformed.

43 Paul Mosley, Jane Harrigan and John F.J. Toye, *Aid and Power: The World Bank and Policy-Based Lending* (London: Routledge, 1995).
44 The *World Development Reports* are not World Bank policy documents, but often they indicate the directions in which Bank policy will change in the future.
45 See Chapter 4 about the "$1-a-day" measure.
46 See Chapter 2 for a discussion of human development.
47 David Hulme, "Global Poverty Reduction and the Millennium Development Goals: A Short History of the World's Biggest Promise," Brooks World Poverty Institute Working Paper 100 (Manchester: University of Manchester, 2009).
48 See Michael Edwards and David Hulme, *Making a Difference: NGOs and Development in a Changing World* (London: Earthscan, 1992).
49 UNDP, *Human Development Report 1997: Human Development to Eradicate Poverty* (Oxford: Oxford University Press, 1997), 108.
50 Ashwani Saith, "From Universal Values to Millennium Development Goals: Lost in Translation," *Development and Change* 37, no. 6 (2006): 1167–1199; Sakiko Fukuda-Parr and David Hulme, "International Norm Dynamics and 'the End of Poverty': Understanding the Millennium Development Goals (MDGs)," BWPI Working Paper No. 96 (Manchester: University of Manchester, 2009).
51 A noticeable absentee was President Clinton. US reticence about the UN's social development agenda was not confined to Republican constituencies.
52 Rosalind Eyben, "The Road Not Taken: International Aid's Choice of Copenhagen over Beijing," *Third World Quarterly* 27, no. 4 (2006): 595–608.
53 There are only six bullet points as maternal and child mortality reductions are merged.
54 James Traub, *The Best Intentions: Kofi Annan and the UN in the Era of American World Power* (London: Bloomsbury, 2006), 147.
55 Kofi A. Annan, *We the Peoples: The Role of the United Nations in the 21st Century* (New York: United Nations Department of Public Information, 2000).
56 IMF, OECD, UN and World Bank, *A Better World for All* (Washington, DC: IMF, OECD, UN and World Bank, 2000).
57 See the World Council of Churches website for the sharp letter sent to Annan at http://www.wcc-coe.org/wcc/news/press/00/22pu.html. In some ways Annan's strategy marginalized civil society. The MD guided UN Secretariat member states agreements; BWFA guided UN-donor agreements; and, the "Global Compact" guided UN-business linkages on poverty. There was no corresponding activity or deal with NGOs and/or civil society.
58 The focus here is on the "development and poverty eradication" goals and not the entire document.
59 See Chapter 4 for a detailed examination of the MDGs.
60 UN, *Road Map towards the Implementation of the United Nations Millennium Declaration: Report of the Secretary-General* (New York: UN, 2001), 55.
61 See David Hulme, "Politics, Ethics and the Millennium Development Goals: The Case of Reproductive Health," Brooks World Poverty Institute Working Paper No. 104 (Manchester: University of Manchester, 2009).
62 Sakiko Fukuda-Parr, "Millennium Development Goal 8: Indicators for International Human Rights Obligations," *Human Rights Quarterly* 28, no. 4 (2006): 966–997.

63 See Chapter 4 for a detailed examination of PRSPs.
64 This figure was later revised up to 1.7 billion. See Table 4.1.
65 World Bank, *World Development Report 2000/2001: Attacking Poverty* (Washington, DC: World Bank, 2001), 3.
66 While some World Bank staff was actively using the MDGs for programming, influential macro-economists thought them a waste of space and focused almost exclusively on economic liberalization. An interview with IMF staff summarized their position: "You are encouraged to mention them in the introduction of any report and then ignore them" (Paul Francis, July 2006).
67 Ferial Haffajee, "Monterrey Meet – 'Washington Consensus in a Sombrero,'" *Third World Economics*, No. 277 (March 16–31, 2002), available from http:// www.twnside.org.sg/title/twe277f.htm
68 See Chapter 4.
69 Shaohua Chen and Martin Ravallion, "The Developing World is Poorer than We Thought, but No Less Successful in the Fight against Poverty," World Bank Policy Research Working Paper No. 4703 (Washington, DC: World Bank, 2008).
70 FAO, *The State of Food Insecurity in the World* (Rome: FAO, 2009).
71 For up-to-date figures on poverty measures related to the MDGs monitor the annual UN *MDG Reports* and the linked website. For up-to-date consumption poverty estimates monitor the World Bank poverty measurement website.
72 See Chen and Ravallion, "The Developing World Is Poorer," tables 9 and 10.
73 Paul Collier, *The Bottom Billion: Why the Poorest Countries Are Failing and What Can Be Done About It* (Oxford: Oxford University Press, 2007).
74 Christopher D. Elvidge *et al.*, "A global poverty map derived from satellite data," *Computers and Geoscience* 35, no.8 (2009): 1652–1660.
75 Stephen Devereux, "Why Does Famine Persist in Africa?" *Food Security* 1, no. 1 (2009): 25–35.

2 Understanding and explaining global poverty

"When I give food to the poor, they call me a saint. When I ask why the poor have no food, they call me a Communist."

(Hélder Câmara, Former Archbishop of Olinda and Recife, Brazil)

". . . economists are an arrogant bunch, with very little to be arrogant about."[1]

(Dani Rodrik, 2007)

Ideas matter, they can change the attitudes and behaviors of individuals, transform the social norms of entire societies and shape the practices of institutions. In this chapter the many ideas that have fed into the understanding of global poverty, and helped or hindered its progress on the international agenda, are examined. The concept of global poverty has not evolved in a vacuum or in some form of global academic seminar room. It is a product that is intimately related to structures of power and overt and covert processes of political contestation. Those controlling substantial material capabilities (countries, banks, corporations, social classes and political and economic leaders) and influencing powerful institutions are much more likely to shape the evolution of ideas than those without such power. They may do this directly, by pushing for public acceptance of ideas and interpretations of ideas that serve their interests, or indirectly, by resourcing and promoting individuals, think-tanks, media and universities that are aligned to the ideas and forms of analysis that they favor. The best ideas are not always the ones that dominate theory and practice: at times, as Paul Krugman has observed, "bad ideas flourish because they are in the interests of powerful people."[2] An extraordinary range of institutions have contested and contributed to increasing awareness about the idea of global poverty and shaping its conceptual content.

Much of this chapter is about the contest between the World Bank and IMF (both heavily influenced by the material and intellectual power of the United States, OECD countries, corporate capitalism and neo-classical economics in US universities) and UN specialist agencies, especially UNDP, UNICEF and at times other agencies (influenced by a broader set of countries, including developing countries, and a more heterodox set of academic and civil society actors and positions). As was revealed by the disputes over the *World Development Report 2000/2001* that led to the resignation of Ravi Kanbur its Director,[3] civil society pressures may have encouraged the World Bank to broaden the concepts and methods that inform its understanding of poverty, but its predisposition to quantitative analyses focused on growth-mediated poverty reduction remains firm.[4] The UN system incorporates many different positions but, with the lead of the UNDP, it has advanced the idea of human development which appeals to its wider membership and the broader set of intellectual influences that permeate its thinking.[5]

While some poverty theoreticians and measurers view themselves as operating in a domain of pure rationality, divorced from politics and issues of power, such a belief is illusionary. Poverty is not a set of self-evident "facts": it has many potential dimensions and these can be presented in many different ways. As Asuncion St.Clair reminds us, the framing of global poverty is an act of imagination (Box 2.1). The particular concept, or mix of concepts, that an individual or organization adopts has profound implications for the

Box 2.1 The idea of global poverty

"Global poverty is highly contested and politicized. It is an ill-structured and complex social problem able to be defined in different ways, the problem space changing with time and location, and the causal arguments being slippery and difficult to establish. Poverty definitions are not accounts of fact, but rather are 'fact-surrogates' . . . fact-surrogates are partial pictures drawn with the cognitive tools of particular disciplines. In the case of global poverty, the cognitive values of economics such as quantification, simplicity and measurability, just to name the most relevant, are clearly dominant."

Source: Asuncion Lera St.Clair, "Global Poverty: The Co-production of Knowledge and Politics," *Global Social Policy* 6, no. 1 (2006): 58–59.

forms of explanation that it produces and the types of policy or action these highlight to reduce or eradicate poverty.

For example, if poverty is conceptualized as a lack of food then the analysis will be on hunger and under-nutrition and solutions are likely to focus on humanitarian action and improving food supply (ranging from "land to the tiller" reforms to promoting the world's major agribusinesses). If poverty is conceptualized as the lack of prosperity in particular countries or regions then the focus shifts to analyzing why these areas have not experienced economic growth, how industrialization might be initiated (and more recently how "good governance" might be promoted). If poverty is viewed as insufficiency from a multi-dimensional perspective then the analysis and remedial actions (economic growth plus social services plus fairer social relations) become more complex. Finally, if poverty is conceptualized from a social structural perspective then inequality is the main analytical focus and the solutions focus on social and political change (empowerment, land reform or even revolution) rather than direct anti-poverty policies.

The recent framing of the problem of international development as global poverty has had profound impacts on analysis and action. In particular, the concept of global poverty tends to:

1. Indicate that poverty can be uniformly assessed and measured across all parts of the world.
2. Encourage the identification of generic, global policy prescriptions and best practice methodologies (and discourage approaches that argue for policy customization). At the extreme, it can encourage foolish claims that a single global policy (economic liberalization) has reduced the global poverty headcount rather than more useful findings relating to policies and outcomes at national and sub-national levels.
3. Emphasize the role of global institutions – the UN, World Bank, IMF, WTO and others – in analyzing, organizing and acting against poverty (and consequently downplay the role of national and sub-national action).
4. Highlight the role of international causes of, and solutions to, poverty – foreign aid, international trade, international finance, and economic instability. This can lead to a reduction of the focus on domestic causes of, and solutions to, poverty, such as poor governance, public sector reform, predatory behavior of national elites and domestic taxation.[6]
5. Depoliticize thinking and action about development by encouraging the framing of issues as technical, rather than political, challenges.[7]

So a focus on global poverty fosters particular emphases in analysis and action and potentially empowers some actors while weakening the influence of others. This may have clear advantages, such as encouraging all of humanity to see itself as having some responsibility for global poverty reduction. But it may have clear disadvantages, such as exaggerating the contribution that external actors can make to domestic processes of social change.

This chapter has four main sections. The first explores the key questions that have to be addressed when developing a concept for poverty – what are the main parameters of poverty and who should decide this? The second reviews the main concepts that are used to define, measure and analyze contemporary global poverty. The third section examines the ways that these different concepts are used to explain global poverty and identify preferred courses of action for poverty eradication. The fourth section draws together conclusions and warns that the shifts in the conceptualization of poverty that some institutions have publicly flagged have not been matched by comparable shifts in policy and practice.

Understanding poverty – conceptual building blocks

Any attempt to elaborate what global poverty is requires that a series of conceptual issues be addressed either explicitly or implicitly. The most important steps in this process are identified below. Each of these steps incorporates value judgments so that technical and political analyses are woven together in all of the conceptual choices that underpin different notions of global poverty.

Poverty as a narrow or broad concept

Poverty can be framed in narrow or broad terms.[8] Narrow approaches have the advantage of being measurable, so that cross-national and inter-temporal comparisons can be made. Although they often involve complex technical manipulations of data their findings can be made easily comprehensible to policymakers and the general public. Broader approaches have the advantage of more fully exploring the multifaceted nature of poverty and of the processes that create, maintain or reduce poverty. But their findings are likely to lack the clear and simple punch-lines preferred by busy policymakers in today's "sound bite" culture.

At the narrow end of the continuum, following Rowntree's seminal 1901 study of York,[9] comes income poverty – the amount of money needed "to obtain the minimum necessaries for the maintenance of merely physical efficiency."[10] In perhaps the greatest narrowing of the concept of poverty, this approach has produced the "$1-a-day" measure (now $1.25-a-day measure).[11] These one-dimensional conceptualizations contrast with multi-dimensional notions that see poverty as a complex of material and non-material deprivations – having a low income, being illiterate, experiencing poor health, having to drink unclean water, lack of participation in decision-making, experiencing violence, humiliation, lack of respect and powerlessness. While some writers and agencies will argue passionately for a narrow conceptualization so that the major features of global and historical patterns can be identified, others are committed to a broader concept so that the complexity and changing nature of the experience of poverty is fully recognized.[12] Others, as I do in this book, use both narrow and broad conceptualizations in an attempt to weave together a deeper understanding of the dynamic nature of poverty.

Means or ends

There are heated debates about whether poverty should be understood as a lack of means (i.e. income) to achieve a minimally acceptable quality of life or as the actual shortfalls from minimum standards that someone experiences in their quality of life. The concepts of human development and capabilities[13] have convinced many that to be analytically rigorous the focus should be on ends. This leads to a broadening of the concept. It also permits the recognition that the ability of individuals to convert income into capabilities varies (for example, a disabled person may need more income or resources than an able-bodied person to achieve the same minimum standard of living). This adds to the analytical power of the human development conceptualization.

Absolute or relative poverty

In most developing countries poverty is defined in absolute terms and official poverty lines are set at the income or consumption level below which it is estimated a person is unable to access their minimum needs for survival and reproduction. In most countries this is assumed to be around 2,300 calories per day for an adult. This line is often identified as the "extreme poverty" line and another line, 20 to 30 percent higher, may be defined as the "poverty" line as other items (clothing, shelter and fuel) are also judged to be essential.

Such a notion of absolute poverty facilitates measurement and focuses attention on a paramount human need. Without sufficient food people cannot function effectively, their health declines and they cannot reproduce. Prolonged dietary inadequacy is permanently detrimental to physical development (and cognitive development in children) and eventually results in death. The apparent precision of this approach can disguise some of its shortcomings. First, there are big differences in the minimum amount of nutrition that people need according to their age and so "adult equivalent scales" are needed. Second, the costs per person of acquiring food and other essential items reduce with the size of the household so further adjustments have to be made (buying in bulk is cheaper than buying in small amounts). Finally, there are large differences in the minimum calorific needs of individuals depending on their health status and employment. People with malaria or worms (most often poorer people) need additional calories to deal with their ill health. Manual workers may need several thousand more calories a day to maintain their output than an office worker. Thus, the impression that poverty lines are set with scientific precision and are somehow less arbitrary than other approaches needs to be treated with caution.

Critics of income poverty lines also argue that such devices treat people as if they are cattle or livestock – being reared, but not part of a society. From this perspective comes the argument that as human beings are social actors, poverty needs to be defined in relation to other people in a society at the same time. Such arguments have won out in OECD countries where official poverty lines are virtually always defined in relative, not absolute, terms. So in the European countries, for example, the poverty line is usually set at 60 percent of a country's median income.[14] Thus, as a country's prosperity increases so does its official poverty line. This has important policy implications. If poverty is to be reduced then, from a relative poverty perspective, a country's growing income must continuously be monitored to ensure that it is being "shared" across the population.

Interestingly, the idea of a relative poverty line has not been used for assessing global poverty. This may be due to technical difficulties – although the assumptions required to estimate what proportion of each country's population has an income/expenditure below 60 percent of median global income would probably be no more heroic than the assumptions made in estimating $1-a-day poverty headcounts. But, it also has a political dimension. Relative poverty has proved an acceptable concept for both the rich and the poor in European countries, reflecting the degree to which such countries see themselves as based upon common citizenship. The equivalent global concept, global citizenship, has weaker roots and the world's rich (people and countries) seem unlikely to sign up to a global relative poverty goal. For better-off countries and people, saving the poor in other countries from absolute poverty is OK . . . but, promising to continuously share the world's growing wealth with the poor is a step too far.

Objective and subjective poverty

Objective definitions and measures of poverty are specified by researchers who collect and analyze data and decide who is poor and non-poor according to these definitions. Such definitions and measures have the advantages of being rigorously specified and permit comparisons to be made over time and space. However, critics point out that such definitions involve explicit or implicit value judgments and so the claim to "objectivity" needs to be scrutinized.

By contrast, subjective definitions and measures (or assessments) of poverty are made by people about their own status and of others in their community or society. They are subjective as the respondents, not the external analyst, determine what poverty is and what the acceptable "minimum levels" of goods, services, well-being or other factors should be. In terms of knowledge creation this has the great advantage of letting those most knowledgeable about the experience of poverty (i.e. people who live in poor communities) determine "what" poverty is. It can also be argued to be ethically more justifiable than objective approaches, as it recognizes the right of poor people and poor communities to create social knowledge: in development-speak, it empowers them. But it also has disadvantages as people living in different areas set different criteria and, over time, people may change their definitions/perceptions. This makes comparisons difficult or infeasible.

Measuring poverty or understanding impoverishment?

There are considerable tensions between those who pursue conceptualizations of poverty that facilitate measurement (usually narrow, means-based, absolute and objective) and those who believe that such simplifications are fundamentally flawed as they avoid the structural aspects of poverty that are essential to understanding how poverty is produced and reproduced.[15] These are part of a broader intellectual fracture between positivists and post-positivists but also reflect ideological differences. Positivists argue that the procedures of natural science can be applied to the social world; that facts can be separated from values; and that observation permits the collection of facts. Positivists place a priority on measuring poverty as accurately as possible. Post-positivists and realists dismiss the ideas of theory-neutral observation and value-free social science. They argue that poverty is relational and that all poverty analysts must understand that their work is not independent of the social world.[16] The measurement camp is usually occupied by neo-classical economists and econometricians. Governments, the World Bank and IMF, policymakers and center/right of center political parties gravitate towards this camp. In the structuralist camp are heterodox economists, sociologists, anthropologists and political economists. Their analyses are most often used by advocacy Non-Governmental Organizations (NGOs), social movements, trade unionists, environmentalists and sometimes left of center political parties.

One of the clearest and most trenchant criticisms of "reductionist" approaches comes from Andries du Toit on the "poverty measurement blues." He argues that:

> ... the difficulties arise out of the domination of development studies and poverty research by ... the 'econometric imaginary': an approach that frames questions of social understanding as questions of measurement ... [They] are undermined by their reliance on a mystificatory theoretical meta-narrative that tries to imbue poverty judgments with a spurious objectivity, and ... they direct attention away from *structural* aspects of persistent poverty.[17]

By focusing on what is readily measurable at individual and household levels these dominant approaches are accused of neglecting the analysis of culture, identity, agency and social structure that are central to the processes that create wealth and poverty. From this perspective the task of critical social scientists is not to integrate quantitative and qualitative analyses of poverty[18] or pursue cross-disciplinarity,[19] but to create "... powerful and convincing counter-hegemonic accounts [of poverty]."[20] Those committed to poverty measurement approaches are either baffled by these criticisms or amazed that other disciplines get away with "such waffle."

Units of analysis

Finally, any approach to understanding poverty has to determine the unit (or units) of analysis it will focus on. These range from poor individuals, poor households, collectivities of poor people (poor women, social classes, ethnic groups, etc.) to poor countries. One reason why the idea of global poverty has made great progress recently is because of its focus on measuring extreme poverty at the individual level. This depends on the measure, however, and while data on an item such as literacy may relate to an individual, the most commonly used data on individuals, per capita income or consumption, is based on heroic assumptions that gender, age and other inequalities are absent within a household.[21] While comparative analyses of social class and poverty have reduced in recent times with the marginalization of Marxist and neo-Marxist studies of development, gender-based studies have proliferated. These have led to claims that poverty is feminized and that "70 percent of [global] poverty is experienced by women."[22] The notion of the feminization of poverty has fitted comfortably into neo-classical economic and World Bank analyses in a way that class-based accounts do not and cannot.

Analyses of poor countries are also common. Orthodox economists use these to explore differences in economic growth rates: poor people are viewed as living in poor countries that have low growth rates. Human development economists have broadened this and contrast differences in social conditions between nations: commonly they find complex patterns from different measures. Political scientists and political economists use comparative national analyses to explore the ways in which international relations, economic processes and national governance shape the distribution of deprivation and well-being between countries and regions.

Conceptual building blocks and global poverty

The issues raised by each of these conceptual building blocks have influenced thinking about global poverty. Commonly, as such thinking has developed, each item has been incorporated but at times heated debates break out when one side of a debate perceives that its analytical frame is being marginalized (as when those promoting participatory appraisals believe that decisions are taken purely on the basis of objective quantitative analyses).

So global poverty has evolved both narrowly ($1-a-day poverty) and broadly (human development); has focused on means ($1-a-day poverty) and ends (most of the MDGs); has pursued objective (Living Standards Measurement Study surveys) and subjective (participatory appraisals and "Voices of the Poor") methodologies; and, has used a variety of different units for its analyses. The one issue that has not been incorporated relates to choices about whether to view global poverty in absolute or relative terms. The contemporary notion of global poverty has favored an absolute approach – the possibility of having a relative global poverty line (such as 60 percent of global median income) has foundered.

Conceptualizing global poverty

Moving from these generic questions about the framing of poverty, three particular concepts can be seen as having shaped thinking about global poverty in recent times:

- measuring income/consumption poverty more precisely;
- developing multi-dimensional concepts and measures of poverty; and,
- adopting participatory methods for knowledge creation so that poor communities and poor people have a say about "what" poverty is.

Interestingly, each of these advances has intellectual roots in South Asian scholarship and/or social action but their elaboration has largely occurred in Western institutions.

Income and consumption poverty

Most of the small number of analysts working directly on poverty in the 1970s was micro-economists experimenting with Rowntree's ideas of minimum subsistence needs at the household level. In particular, Indian researchers[23] applied and advanced these ideas and, partly as a result of their work, the ideas of national poverty lines and the identification of the poor through a "biological" approach became widely accepted. The Foster, Greer, Thorbecke (FGT) measures of poverty incidence, depth and severity moved thinking beyond simple headcounts as these made it possible to assess how deeply a population is experiencing income poverty and the relative distribution of different levels of poverty among the poor.[24] With the support of the World Bank many developing countries began to mount nationally representative Living Standards Measurement Study surveys so that quantitative poverty analyses became increasingly common.

While most poverty analysis focused on the national level, and often agonized about the imperfections of this task, bold researchers at the World Bank experimented with ways of generating a global income poverty measure and in the late 1980s invented the $1-a-day global poverty line. As a result, the first attempt to count the global poor (more accurately the first approximation) came in the *World Development Report 1990*. This Report identified 1,116 million extremely poor people in the world.[25]

Multi-dimensional poverty and human development

Critics of income poverty measurement approaches, and also some of the leading poverty measurers themselves, believed that poverty was more than a mere lack of income or food intake. Back in the mid-1970s the International Labour Organization (ILO) had promoted the Basic Needs Approach identifying a multi-dimensional set of human needs – basic education and health services, clean water, clothing and other needs. While this listing had intuitive appeal and was well supported, it lacked a clear theoretical basis. It was Amartya Sen's work,[26] initially on entitlements and subsequently on capabilities and freedoms, which laid the foundations for envisioning poverty as individual human development deprivations.

For Sen, the poor are those whose basic capabilities are so constrained that they cannot achieve a minimum set of the functionings they value (Box 2.2). Functionings are the things that people manage to do or to be (for example, living a long and healthy life, being a respected member of a community, raising a family, achieving satisfaction in sports or cultural activities). From this perspective people experience poverty when they are deprived in terms of a basic capability, such as being able to avoid hunger, achieve literacy, appear in public without shame or take part in social activities.

Box 2.2 Sen's framework for conceptualizing human development

The conceptual foundations of the capability approach can be found in Sen's critiques of traditional welfare economics, which focuses on resource (income, commodity command, asset) and utility (happiness, desire-fulfillment) based concepts of well-being. Sen rejects these frameworks in favor of a more direct approach for measuring human well-being and development, which concerns itself with the full range of human function(ing)s and capabilities people have reason to value. Sen's framework makes the following distinctions:

Functionings. "The concept of 'functionings' . . . reflects the various things a person may value doing or being. The valued functionings may vary from elementary ones, such as being adequately nourished and being free from avoidable disease, to very complex activities or personal states, such as being able to take part in the life of the community and having self-respect."

Capability or freedom. "A person's 'capability' refers to the alternative combinations of functionings that are feasible for her to achieve. Capability is thus a kind of freedom: the substantive freedom to achieve alternative functioning combinations (or, less formally put, the freedom to achieve various life-styles)."

Development. The expansion of freedom is the primary end and principal means of development. Development involves the expansion of human capabilities and the enrichment of human lives.

Sources: Adapted from David Clark, "Capability Approach," in *The Elgar Companion to Development Studies*, ed. David Clark (Cheltenham: Edward Elgar, 2006), 32–44; and Amartya Kumar Sen, *Development as Freedom* (New York: Knopf, 1999), 3, 75.

While much of Sen's work is purely theoretical, he was persuaded by Mahbub ul Haq at UNDP to help work out how complex ideas of human development could be simplified into an operational measure.[27] Out of this came the Human Development Index (HDI), which combined three crude indicators of capabilities – life expectancy, educational attainment and average income – so that progress in human development could be assessed (Box 2.3). The UNDP's *Human Development Reports* (first published in 1990) rank countries according to their HDI in contrast to the World Bank's *World Development Reports* which ranked countries in terms of their average GNP per capita. The HDI measure, like GNP per capita, has been sharply criticized, but it has led to "social" issues – especially health and education – gaining a much higher profile in poverty discourse.

In the 1997 *Human Development Report* the UNDP developed a second measure – the human poverty index (HPI) – which assessed basic human deprivations (Box 2.3). This was an important step on the way to a multi-dimensional measure of poverty, but the HPI has not been institutionalized to the same degree as the HDI, nor has it been included in any of the goals or targets of the MDGs. The quest to establish a widely accepted micro-level measure of human development deprivation continues.[28]

Box 2.3 Measuring human development and human poverty

Human Development Index. The Human Development Index (HDI) measures the average achievement in a country in three basic dimensions of human development – longevity, knowledge and a decent standard of living. A composite index, the HDI thus contains three variables: life expectancy, educational achievement (adult literacy and combined primary, secondary and tertiary enrolment) and real GDP per capita (in PPP$).

Human Poverty Index. The Human Poverty Index measures deprivation in basic human development in the same dimensions as the HDI. The variables used are the percentage of people expected to die before age 40, the percentage of adults who are illiterate, and overall economic provisioning in terms of the percentage of people without access to health services and safe water and the percentage of underweight children under five.

Source: UNDP, *Human Development Report 1997: Human Development to Eradicate Poverty* (Oxford: Oxford University Press, 1997).

Participatory approaches to poverty assessment

The third major conceptual innovation influencing thinking about global poverty has been the development of participatory methods for poverty assessment. These methods were originally developed by Indian NGOs and involve mounting a series of exercises with people from poor communities so that they can collaboratively collect data about living conditions and livelihoods and analyze this data using their own mental constructs.[29] Such methods offer, at least, two specific advantages over orthodox data collection approaches. First, they may permit better quality data to be collected as people can use their own mental constructs, can share knowledge and experience and debate what has happened and why. Participants are not forced into answering closed questions based on the researchers' analytical framework as in orthodox approaches. Second, it can be argued that they empower people in poor communities as they reinforce their right to be involved in the construction of knowledge. More generally, it can be seen as contributing to processes of local democracy as people deliberate on their experiences and future courses of action.

For global poverty this advance has been applied in two concrete ways. First, researchers at the World Bank have used such methods to provide global overviews of what the experience of poverty is like for poor people and how they explain and cope with deprivation. This has been done by reports such as *Voices of the Poor*[30] although it must be noted that the methods by which 60,000 voices are turned into a coherent account remain to be explained.[31] Second, participatory approaches to poverty assessment have become a formal component of the global infrastructure to plan poverty reduction. The Poverty Reduction Strategies (PRSs) that most developing countries have to prepare to access foreign aid require that Participatory Poverty Assessments (PPAs) be conducted alongside conventional statistical analyses of "objective" data. It is argued that combinations of orthodox, quantitative analysis and participatory, subjective assessment produce deeper understandings of the nature and causes of poverty so that more effective poverty reduction policies can be designed. There are debates, however, about whether such differing approaches can be integrated and/or whether PPAs are a mere "add-on" to "objective" analyses to keep NGOs and civil society groups happy.

The causes of global poverty

If World Bank presidents dream, one could imagine former President Jim Wolfensohn dreaming of a short, bullet-point list of the causes of global poverty. Alongside each item would be an associated policy solution. From what we know of the World Bank in the late 1990s it had a desperate need for such a list, to rehabilitate its image and policies after the disappointments of structural adjustment. Moreover, Wolfensohn had the ambition and ego to think "big."[32] However, despite the conceptual and measurement advances of the 1990s, such a grand, theoretical simplification has not been possible.[33] Global poverty has proved not to be a well-structured problem, which can be understood through intellectual cogitation and then remedied, but an ill structured mess. The level of our understanding of the causes of global poverty requires that we appreciate that there is no clear "solution." Rather, global poverty reduction, like its antecedent rural development, is about trying ". . . to change the functioning of a complex, dynamic system in order to make progress in attaining multiple objectives."[34]

While the complexity of, and limited state of knowledge about, global poverty reduction has been evident to many, for the dominant group of policy advisors – economists – this has not necessarily been the case. After more than a decade of increasingly sophisticated econometric analysis, examining a growing number of datasets whose quality was improving, a recent study by a panel of Europe's leading poverty econometricians found that "country heterogeneity" was the main pattern that emerged across poverty variables. The belief that there would be some clear, underlying pattern of relationships in all countries – economic growth leads to improvements in social development leads to strengthened governance leads to more growth – had proved illusory. Paradoxically, the difficulties of developing a single clear explanation of "why" global poverty occurs has helped the consensus about the need for an organized assault on global poverty to emerge. The fact that by the late 1990s there was no single dominating account about what to do helped facilitate the Millennium agreements. The consensus on global poverty reduction that developed at that time concentrated on global goals and global calls to action but left open decisions about exactly what to do.

Historical accounts of poverty in the colonies commonly identified two main causes: geography and race. "Native" people were poor because of the tropical environments in which they lived, as heat sapped their energy and made them lazy, or because of negative characteristics caused by the genetics of non-European races. While the geography explanation has remained part of academic debate[35] the racial explanation is not part of the contemporary literature, but remains powerful at a popular level in some regions (for example, Russia and many of the states from the former Soviet Union).

In recent times, the most common way of examining theories of why mass poverty occurs is through the sequence of ideas that have dominated the history of international development. This charts the rise and fall of grand theories in terms of three main eras.[36] The first, modernization theory of the 1950s and 1960s, posited that the lack of development in Third World countries (and associated mass poverty) was the result of economic backwardness and traditional social structures. Once these countries "caught up" with the industrialized world – technologically, institutionally, socially – mass affluence would eradicate poverty everywhere. Typical of this era was Walt Rostow's "take-off" theory which was highly influential at this time. Developing countries would go through five predictable stages over a generation until they achieved mass consumption.[37]

The modernization account was attractive. However, by the late 1960s, when there was mounting evidence that the "non-Communist manifesto" of modernization was not delivering on its promises,[38] this analysis was powerfully challenged by neo-Marxists and dependency theorists.[39] They explained that the immiserization of developing countries was caused by active processes of underdevelopment.[40] The Third World had been integrated into the world economic system in a way that permitted its exploitation through "unequal development." The poor were kept poor so that the elites and bourgeoisie of wealthy countries could have high material living standards. This analysis demanded radical and confrontational actions – peasant revolution, autarky and strategies of autonomous development. These arguments played out well in much of academia but most of the countries that pursued autarkic development strategies (Sri Lanka in the early 1970s, Nicaragua, Mozambique, Tanzania in the 1970s and 1980s) did not fare well.[41]

By the late 1970s a quite different set of radical ideas were on the ascendant. These neo-liberal ideas became dominant, intellectually and in policy, in the 1980s. They posited that countries, and their people, were poor because of public policies that distorted prices and incentive systems and public institutions that were wasteful and rent-seeking. Once economies were liberalized and opened up to international trade then competition would promote efficiency and a country could pursue its comparative advantages. Economic growth would ensue, fueled by foreign direct investment. The trickle-down from growth, through increased demand and job creation, would reduce poverty and fuel prosperity. A particularly powerful and well-organized epistemic community[42] developed around these neo-liberal ideas, gaining key positions in US universities, the US government, the World Bank and IMF and in the finance ministries and central banks of many developing countries. The Washington Consensus[43] (held by the World Bank, IMF and US Treasury) on the necessity for policies of "structural adjustment" in developing countries was championed by this epistemic community.

These policies were pursued with varying degrees of enthusiasm by countries in Africa, Asia and Latin America. The results were generally weak (and/or gains took many years to occur) and were often negative for poor people (especially with the introduction of user fees for health and education).[44] However, it was the full-blooded adoption of these policies in Russia after the end of the Cold War that revealed their weakness.[45] The short, sharp shock expected after a massive shift to the market turned into a chronic, catastrophic collapse – in GDP, life expectancy and institutions. Where economic growth and poverty reduction did occur in the 1990s was in China and India, but in both of these countries it came through a gradual opening up to the market while retaining heterodox economic policies in which the state played a major role. As the new millennium neared the sweeping policy narratives of the second half of the twentieth century appeared to have faltered and more pluralist frameworks, such as the Post Washington Consensus[46] and agreement on the MDGs, began to fill the global policy space. These frameworks recognized major roles for the market, the state and civil society and encouraged the pursuit of a range of goals including the strengthening of institutions – growth was not enough. There was an increased recognition of the complexity of poverty and the breadth and variety of policies that might be needed to reduce it in different countries and for different groups. Despite attempts by the US Treasury Department to ensure that the World Bank's flagship Millennium publication (*World Development Report 2000–2001*) highlighted economic growth and market-led policies, the report produced a framework based on three integrated strategies – opportunity (market-based growth), empowerment (social and political reform) and security (a social safety net to protect people from vulnerability).[47] Thinking since that time has become increasingly nuanced and, in particular, social policy in developing countries has moved beyond health and education and now includes social protection policies, such as cash transfers for the poor and non-contributory old age pensions.[48]

Why poverty occurs

It is no surprise, given all the debates about "what" poverty is, that there are also many competing theories about "why" poverty occurs in an affluent world. Charting all of these would require an encyclopedia. Here the ambition is more modest. The major positions in the debate are identified and illustrated through an examination of recent key books on poverty. To aid analysis and ensure that a full range of explanations are examined three major ideological positions are illustrated through the literature:[49]

1. Global poverty is caused (or mainly caused) by a lack of economic growth because markets are constrained by state action and/or poor governance.
2. Global poverty is caused by contemporary capitalism, globalization and socio-economic inequality.
3. Global poverty is caused by a lack of growth in poor countries (because of lack of access to finance and technology) and a lack of compassion

(charity, morality, fairness) in rich countries. Both the market and the state, in rich and poor countries, are jointly responsible.

This review is broken into two sections. The first examines relatively polemical works that present simple, stylized accounts of poverty and identify a single major cause. These are the sorts of account that many readers may have come across in the media. The second section moves beyond these polemics to examine works that see poverty as having multiple causes, as being contextual and contingent and, as a consequence, requiring relatively complex prescriptions for its eradication.

Polemics of global poverty

In this section we examine the arguments put forward by Surjit Bhalla, Walden Bello and Jeffrey Sachs. Each of these writers has made a passionate case that claims to identify the main reason why hundreds of millions of people stay poor and then prescribes a form of magic bullet that will permit poverty to be eradicated.

At one ideological extreme comes Bhalla with *Imagine There's No Country: Poverty, Inequality and Growth in the Era of Globalization.*[50] For him poverty is caused by a lack of economic growth. His position is clear: indeed, the more criticism it has attracted the sharper and simpler it seems to have become. Analytically he determines that the ordering of key issues ". . . is growth first, poverty second and inequality a distant third. Many (including Marx) have it in exactly the reverse order."[51] His empirical analyses of the linkages between these three variables leads him to conclude that growth explains progress in poverty reduction and ". . . that we have just witnessed the best 20 years [1980–2000] in world history – and doubly certainly the best 20 years in the history of poor people."[52] This leads to a very firm conclusion – ". . . can economic growth alone be sufficient for poverty reduction? Yes . . . the conclusions differ from the conventional wisdom that 'attacking poverty requires actions beyond the economic domain.' Such actions are not needed. Growth is sufficient, period."[53] Critics within economics argue that Bhalla's dataset and methodology are flawed and lead him to exaggerate the reduction in poverty over 1980 to 2000.[54] It can also be pointed out that the associations of globalization with growth and growth with poverty reduction are basically correlations – the evidence of a direct causal linkage would need additional analysis. Nevertheless, his polemic has been persuasive and is widely cited by proponents of liberalization.

At the other extreme comes Walden Bello with *Dark Victory: The United States, Structural Adjustment, and Global Poverty* and, more recently,

Deglobalization.[55] Bello, like Bhalla, is passionate about his arguments but they derive from a quite different analytical framework. Bello eschews orthodox economics and the examination of large cross-country datasets. His approach is from a Marxist political economic position and is based on sociological, case study analyses of unequal economic and social relations and case studies. He uses these to argue that the world is becoming more unequal and that a variety of problems[56] (poverty, unemployment, economic crisis, hunger, injustice and land degradation) are actually caused by the spread and deepening of capitalism, i.e. caused by globalization, which he characterizes as "[A] sweeping strategy of global economic rollback unleashed by Northern political and corporate elites to consolidate corporate hegemony in the home economy and shore up the North's domination of the international economy."[57] Actors in the US political system, the IMF and World Bank, and multinational corporations (MNCs) are seen as spearheading these processes. Globalization may create wealth but this is through David Harvey's "accumulation by dispossession."[58] While it makes some very wealthy it imposes poverty on the mass of humanity – wealth does not trickle down as Bhalla argues.

Bello's diagnosis and prescription are radical. Contemporary capitalism does not merely need re-regulating or reforming, as others critics of globalization argue.[59] It needs replacing – "Whether one calls the alternative socialism, social democracy, democratic capitalism, or people-centered development is less important than its essence: the subordination of the market, of the institutions of production and distribution to the community."[60] While Bello's arguments have been highly influential in civil society movements, such as the World Social Forum, neo-classical economists have cast them aside as "journalism" that lacks analytical rigor.

The third polemic is equally passionate but takes the middle ground. Jeffrey Sachs believes that market-based, economic growth is needed for poverty reduction but it is not enough. Concerted public action (locally, nationally and internationally) is needed to eradicate multi-dimensional poverty in the short term and to connect poor people to the market-based opportunities that will permit them to avoid poverty and to steadily accumulate the assets to improve their economic and social position in the longer term. Poor countries and poor people lack the finance and technology to eradicate poverty. This can be provided by rich countries once they have the "political will" to commit to caring for distant strangers.[61] In *The End of Poverty: How We Can Make it Happen in Our Lifetime* he calls for a massive increase in foreign aid and other financial transfers to poorer countries.[62] This infusion of finance will transform the social and economic conditions of the poor and allow the MDGs to be achieved by 2015. A "big push" model of development lies behind this proposition – a one-off massive infusion of capital will improve social conditions and kick-start economic growth in parts of the world that have been economic laggards. Sachs's work has been highly influential: he has been/is a special adviser to Kofi Annan and Ban-ki Moon and led the UN's Millennium Project.

However, his work has also been heavily criticized. From the right,[63] critics such as Bill Easterly have pointed out the naivety of believing that foreign aid would be used effectively if it was rapidly scaled up: many countries appear to already be at or past their aid absorption capacity. Sachs assumes that selfless individuals and organizations will be available to use aid effectively and provide poor people with the goods and services they need. From the left, the criticisms are that he lacks an understanding of social and political relations. The United States, and most other rich countries, are highly unlikely to increase their aid budgets to the levels for which Sachs calls. Aid is often captured by local elites and foreign companies and contractors. His assumption that unreformed capitalism will take care of poor people once they have had an aid-financed "hand up" fails to understand the way in which globalization actively creates poverty.[64]

Each of these writers has attracted media and public attention with their simple diagnoses of why global poverty occurs and how it might be attacked. For Bhalla it is a lack of economic growth and the problem can be overcome by economic liberalization and globalization. For Bello the cause is globalization (and associated neo-liberal economic policies) and a socialist alternative to capitalism is the answer. Sachs sees the problem as a lack of finance and technology – a massive one-off transfer of finance to poorer countries will create a form of caring capitalism that can eradicate poverty. While each of these positions has generated substantial support, usually from like-minded spirits (respectively, free-marketeers or anti-globalizers or fans of foreign aid) each has been heavily criticized for the fundamental conceptual and empirical oversimplifications in their accounts.

The task of coming up with more nuanced and sophisticated analyses – theorizing multiple causal factors that interact in different ways, recognizing the importance of context and timing, and understanding how institutions evolve and processes of governance change – has been taken up by other writers whose work is examined in the next section.

Global poverty: complex issues need complex analyses

If global poverty is recognized as a complex problem, involving economic, political and social factors whose interaction varies at different times in different places, then more nuanced analysis is required. There are many different positions that attempt these more complex approaches but most are characterized by a number of common features:

- Multiple causal factors are identified.
- Globalization is viewed neither as hero or villain – its impacts depend on country-specific factors and the ways in which individual countries select policies to manage the opportunities and problems presented by globalization.
- Historical factors are seen as very important, especially processes of state formation, the composition of the domestic polity, levels of conflict, the structure of the economy and the forms of international linkage.
- All see governance and/or institutions as a key factor for explaining the present situation and assessing future prospects.

The approaches vary with the discipline, interests and personal values of the analyst. Economists tend to focus on economic growth, often through cross-country comparisons, and on measurable aspects of governance and institutions. Political scientists and political economists focus more on international relations and the structural dynamics of the domestic polity. Anthropologists and sociologists have commonly taken a post-developmental stance, usefully pointing out the extreme complexity of understanding poverty (and that all analysts are part of the issue under examination rather than objective outsiders) but often slipping into the error of treating the IMF and World Bank as monoliths responsible for most problems.[65] The main lines of analysis are illustrated by five writers. Four of these (Easterly, Craig and Porter, and Collier) can be very roughly "mapped" over the polemicists discussed in the previous section. The fifth, Rodrik, focuses on the development of an analytical method that permits the different reasons why different countries stay poor to be identified at the country level.

At the growth end of the spectrum comes Bill Easterly with *The Elusive Quest for Growth* and *The White Man's Burden.*[66] While aid is a major focus for his work it looks more broadly at growth and the prospects for poverty reduction,[67] incorporating a broader analysis of why poor people stay poor. His perspective is historical with poor countries (and/or countries with significant numbers of poor people) seen as highly varied. While he recognizes the relevance of processes and outcomes from many centuries ago, Easterly's main focus is on the colonial and post-colonial eras. He argues that the neo-Imperialist policies of the colonial period damaged both the growth and governance prospects of most countries that are poor today. More recently, super-power competition during the Cold War led the first world (the United States and its allies) to actively sponsor "bad government" through its foreign aid programs and military interventions. The end of the Cold War has done little to improve aid impacts and he sees the UN, IMF and World Bank as encouraging over-ambitious plans for growth and poverty reduction and continuing to support bad governments. Within his conceptualization of "bad government" are corruption and nepotism (leaders and other elites using state resources and power to amass wealth and influence for themselves and their cronies) and excessive government (dysfunctional regulation and red tape, state-owned enterprises and excessive resource allocation to the public sector). While individual rich countries and bilateral aid agencies add to these problems it is the multilateral agencies that are particularly responsible according to Easterly.

While there is much in this analysis that many across the spectrum agree with, behind Easterly's detailed arguments lies an overarching neo-liberal framework that is weakly conceptualized. Individuals and agencies engaged in public policy and planning ("planners") exaggerate their understanding of, and mis-diagnose, problems. This reduces the opportunities for "searchers" (private and social entrepreneurs) to achieve piecemeal advances in creating wealth and producing jobs, goods and services for the poor. What is needed, according to Easterly, are home-grown and largely market-based strategies that will create wealth and gradually (although exactly how is not explained) raise the likelihood of improvements in national governance. While Easterly's argument avoids the crude market fundamentalism of Bhalla it leans toward that analysis: private action, commercial and philanthropic, should be the basis of any strategy and state action should be limited to building on what works.[68] In his account he plays down the role of state planning in successful experiences (South Korea, Hong Kong, Singapore, Malaysia, Taiwan and now China) and bundles very different sources of failure as being caused by "planners" (from central planning in communist countries to World Bank/IMF structural adjustment policies). Easterly's political analysis concentrates on the failure of global governance to address world poverty. While he is critical of some US policies and activities, there is no real consideration of the overarching influence of the United States on ideas and practices for tackling, or not bothering to tackle, global poverty.

Craig and Porter provide an analysis that contrasts sharply with Easterly's.[69] Their perspective is political and political-economic and they focus on the recent conversion of "development" into "poverty reduction." This means that their argument is framed in ways that bring it closer to Bello – but this is no simple condemnation of globalization or US hegemony or MNC duplicity. It presents a detailed analysis of late twentieth- and early twenty-first-century capitalism from a long-term historical viewpoint. The causes of poverty (understood as a lack of economic and social development) lie in many areas but these are traced back to the overarching dominance of liberalism (Box 2.4) in framing thinking and action about the forms of governance and nature of institutions and policies that guide human progress. Over the last 400 years liberalism has been "lurching in Polanyi-style 'double movements' between security-embedding and market-disembedding approaches."[70]

This is traced through early British colonialism (the East India Company), Victorian colonialism, imperial development plans (*pax Britannica* and the Lugard Plan) and the "security-embedded Development" of the Cold War. During the 1970s and 1980s conservative neo-liberalism maintains and creates poverty in many parts of the world and sets the stage for the contemporary period in which poverty reduction and good governance become the cornerstones of an inclusive neo-liberalism (Box 2.4). Their judgment is that neo-liberal institutionalism has over-reached itself and has not been able to discipline its own processes or those of the governments with which it engages. It struggles with the territorial modes of government that remain so strongly embedded in poorer countries. Contemporary development, with its focus on governance and poverty reduction, is primarily a top-down response led by the BWIs and the G7. As a result, compensatory mechanisms, subordinating markets to domestic social issues, are not arising and the "double movement," that would permit economic and social progress, is stalled.

Box 2.4 **Definitions of liberalism**

Liberalism: A political ideology and form of governance that has hybridized over time, but generally emphasizes the benefits of markets, the rule of universal law, the need for individual human and especially property rights. In its approach to poverty, it eschews major redistribution, and emphasizes moral discipline and (again) markets.

"Inclusive" neo-liberalism and "positive liberalism:" While retaining core conservative neoliberal macroeconomic and pro-market policy settings, "inclusive" neo-liberalism adds "positive liberal" approaches emphasizing "empowerment" to enable participation (and ensure "inclusion") of countries and people in global and local markets. These include: institution building and an enabling state ensuring global market integration; building human capital via services (health, education); empowering and protecting the rights of the vulnerable through participatory voice and legal access; engendering moral obligations to community and work.

Source: David Craig and Douglas R. Porter, *Development beyond Neoliberalism?: The Poverty Reduction Paradigm* (London: Routledge, 2005), 11–12.

Through this very different framework, Craig and Porter reach conclusions that are both very similar and very dissimilar to Easterly. They agree that the universal doctrine of the present day – MDGs, PRSs, increased aid, good governance – is unsuitable and argue for more territorially based (locally and nationally) strategies and agendas. But, where Easterly sees this as requiring "more" liberalism (a reduction in the role of the state and more market-based strategies to create space for local entrepreneurs), Craig and Porter see it in terms of promoting countervailing social and political responses. They conceptualize this as "smart re-politicization" permitting heterodox policy approaches to economic growth and poverty reduction as proposed by Dani Rodrik, Robert Wade and Ha-Joon Chang. These involve state guidance of industrial policy and of the linkages between human development policies, employment creation, productivity and growth. This is not a precise prescription of "what" the strategy should be – but it is not intended to be. Rather, they seek to move away from the idea of identifying a sweeping "technical and consensual solution"[71] to accepting that such choices need to be addressed politically at the national and sub-national levels. Efforts to dress liberalism up as the source for universal best practice poverty reduction policies need to be stopped. Plans need to be country-specific and external actors must work not only with national and sub-national governments but with political parties (assisting with manifestos), voter education, NGOs and professional associations. This smart re-politicization also has an international dimension – reforming the BWIs and World Trade Organization (WTO) so that they are more internationally accountable. Like Easterly, Craig and Porter seek to create space for neglected actors in the development process – but, where Easterly sees these as "searchers" (commercial and social entrepreneurs) Craig and Porter seek to strengthen the role of domestic political activists and the influence of political activism more widely.

Somewhere between the arguments of Easterly and Craig and Porter comes Paul Collier's recent work. Although like Easterly he is an economist with World Bank experience and a predilection towards market-based policies, his analysis has broadened in recent years and he sees his work as positioned between the pro-state and pro-aid case of Sachs and the anti-aid and anti-state argument of Easterly.[72] He has broadened his analysis from a total reliance on vast cross-country comparisons, many of which have been disparaged by serious econometricians, to include more detailed economic and political examinations of case studies. In addition, he now recognizes the significance of history and particularly processes of state formation.

Collier, like most economists, sees the lack of growth in poor countries as the proximate cause of poverty.[73] He explains this in terms of four "traps" that keep poor people in poor countries poor:[74]

- The conflict trap – many poor countries have experienced decades of violent conflict. This makes economic growth unlikely or impossible, leads to stagnant or declining social conditions and makes it highly likely that, even if peace breaks out in a country it has a high probability of falling back into conflict in the future.
- The natural resources trap – poor countries with mineral and hydrocarbon resources commonly experience a "resource curse." Their leaders and elites compete for "rents" from these resources so that public investment, agriculture and industry are neglected and the probability of civil war increases.
- The landlocked with bad neighbors trap – landlocked countries are comparatively disadvantaged in economic terms (as the costs of their imports and exports are higher than coastal countries) and they are highly dependent on their neighbors' policies and political stability.
- The bad governance in a small country trap[75] – bad governance, and associated bad policies, can destroy the economy and institutions of a country "with alarming speed." This is particularly the case for countries that have few economic opportunities, for example landlocked countries.

Various combinations of these traps keep poor countries poor and the nature of this combination means that each country will require a customized approach. Policies need to be set in both geographical and historical context. Geographically, much depends on the size, topography and location of a country. Historically, the recent rise of China and India may mean that the strategies for catching up that have worked in the past (establishing ready-made garments manufacturing and later moving on to electronics assembly; out-sourcing of services) may no longer be possible.

Collier argues that neither the market, in the form of globalization, nor the state, in the form of aid-financed national plans, will come to the rescue of countries in these traps. Moreover, simplistic prescriptions of economic liberalization or massive foreign aid programs will not be a panacea for the 70 or so nations covered in his analysis. The main changes needed to reduce poverty are not seen as being in the international sphere but at the local, national and regional level. The best outsiders can do is try to support gradual, progressive change within countries and "do no harm." Depending on the context an evolving set of instruments are emerging for foreign countries to assist the bottom billion. These include targeting aid on infrastructure in landlocked countries, providing well-designed technical assistance to tackle bad governance, mounting conflict prevention initiatives (including military intervention), strengthening international laws and charters, reducing international corruption (such as bribes by MNCs), fairer trade policies (but not "fair trade") and better aid coordination. This is not simply a technical exercise – foreign governments need to identify and support progressive political reformers within poor countries and re-shape public opinion in their own countries.

The work of Dani Rodrik in *One Economics, Many Recipes*[76] does not map over the polemics reviewed earlier in this chapter. Rodrik believes that analysis should focus on the national level as cross-national analyses, and their universal prescriptions, are theoretically and methodologically flawed. Poverty can be caused by too little globalization in some contexts and by too much (or the wrong forms of) globalization in others. The pathway out of poverty is not simply a total reliance on the market, nor a rejection of the market, nor some identifiable universally optimal accommodation between market forces and state intervention – it depends! Countries are poor, and as a result large proportions of their populations are poor, for different sets of reasons depending on their geography, their history and the particular institutional endowments they have. The role of poverty analysis is not to identify the global average cause for a lack of growth, and a surfeit of poverty, in developing countries, but to develop a diagnostic approach that permits the specific obstacles (and opportunities) facing each country to be identified, prioritized and acted upon.

Rodrik is a neo-classical economist and believes that "economic growth *is* the most powerful instrument for reducing poverty."[77] But, by making the analysis of context paramount in his framework, he is able to focus on understanding why specific countries have not experienced growth. This entails detailed empirical analyses that permit national geographies and institutions to be understood. While his approach follows the neo-classical orthodoxy, and views private sector activity as the basis for growth, Rodrik also ". . . believe[s] in the ability of governments to do good and change their societies for the better". But this does not mean that an optimal role can be identified – that depends on the context and what governments can do is partly constrained by structural factors, but these change over time. Serendipity and imperfect knowledge also shape policy choices and outcomes. As governments have a limited capacity to pursue policies then the diagnostic exercise also needs to prioritize and sequence policies and explore selectivity and targeting. This produces country-specific industrial policies reflecting a collaboration between the private and public sectors. This process is based on three main steps: (i) the analysis of growth diagnostics (ii) policy design, and (iii) the on-going institutionalization of the diagnostic and policy design activities – so that growth is not merely kicked off but can become sustainable.

While Rodrik's analysis,[78] like most neo-classical economists, frames poverty reduction as sustained economic growth at the national level he does not present growth as a panacea for poverty reduction. This more nuanced form of economic analysis is of great significance, moving economists away from their "flat Earth" analytical frameworks of the last decade which assume that countries are identical except for a few key parameters. Indeed, the approach could be extended into "poverty diagnostics." If this is developed it would permit the diagnosis to move beyond a focus on industrial policy to other macro-economic areas (such as taxation and redistribution) and social policy (education, health and social protection). Rodrik's approach makes it difficult to relate to the polemics with which we started this section – as its focus on context means that it rejects the idea of global poverty as a uniform problem with a standard solution. That is its strength as it allows for contextualized explanations of poverty and customized country responses to the challenges and opportunities they face. Its weakness is that for policymakers seeking "clear answers" it may appear too eclectic.

Conclusion

This chapter has shown that while ending global poverty might appear to be a clear and agreed goal for national and international actors, the understanding of "why" so many people are poor and "what should be done" remains a highly contested issue. There are heated debates about "what" poverty is – a lack of income, a failure to meet basic needs, a set of multi-dimensional capability deprivations or an abrogation of human rights. These are not mere semantics as the way one envisions poverty has profound implications for the types of actions one believes are needed to eradicate or reduce poverty. The political economy of the late twentieth and early twenty-first centuries has permitted the issue of global poverty to become part of the international agenda through the efforts of aid donors, UN agencies and the General Assembly and civil society (particularly in rich countries). But the power of different actors, reflecting their material capabilities, has allowed them to frame the ways in which global poverty is understood and determine the processes (MDGs, Heavily Indebted Poor Countries initiative, PRSPs, access to finance) by which it is to be tackled. While the neo-liberal explanatory frameworks and policies of the 1980s have been weakened, orthodox economic analysis still privileges economic growth over human development and key institutions, such as the IMF and World Bank, are suspicious of heterodox economic strategies that open up more of a role for state action. The policy statements of the BWIs, UN agencies, national governments and many NGOs may make it sound as though there is a consensus on prioritizing global poverty reduction and adopting a multi-dimensional view of poverty. But, there are often gaps between what organizations say and what they do – what Catherine Weaver calls the "hypocrisy trap."[79] Ideas about poverty have shifted over the last decade, but not as much in practice as in public statements – as Weaver argues, this is particularly the case for the BWIs.

While the polemicists discussed in this chapter can identify a single overriding cause for poverty, and prescribe a universal response that will reduce poverty everywhere, more rigorous and less aggressively ideological analysts of global poverty demonstrate the causal complexities. A set of economic, social and political factors, varying from country to country, and often within countries, and over time, have to be understood. These factors interact in complex ways so that prediction, and hence prescription, is not straightforward. To be effective and to contribute to the strengthening of institutions, which is essential for poverty reduction and for growth, strategies need to be determined at the national level and by national governments and civil societies. Policies and actions in support of poverty eradication require both *a priori* technical analysis (thinking through) and on-going social learning (acting out). Interventions are not only about getting the policies right but also about changing social norms, raising the likelihood of institutions becoming more effective and governance improving over time.

This chapter has focused on the concepts and ideas that have battled to raise global poverty onto the international agenda and shape its content. But ideas are only part of the story – they are promoted and obstructed by institutions and in turn they re-shape those institutions. These are the focus of the next chapter.

Notes

1   Dani Rodrik, *One Economics, Many Recipes: Globalization, Institutions, and Economic Growth* (Princeton, NJ; Woodstock: Princeton University Press, 2007), 5.
2   Paul Krugman, "Cycles of conventional wisdom on economic development," *International Affairs* 71, No. 4 (1996): 717–732.
3   Robert H. Wade, "US Hegemony and the World Bank: The Fight over People and Ideas," *Review of International Political Economy* 9, no. 2 (2002): 215–243.
4   As is discussed later, the Bank's Research Department has been keen to prove a direct causal link between economic liberalization, growth and poverty reduction. A 2006 evaluation, chaired by Angus Deaton, found that some of this work had ". . . such deep flaws that, at present, the results cannot be regarded as remotely reliable." See Angus Deaton, Abhikit Vinayak Banerjee, Nora Lustig and Ken Rogoff, *An Evaluation of World Bank Research, 1998–2005* (Washington, DC: World Bank, 2006).
5   However, some believe that the UNDP's influence has waned since the mid-2000s due to the retirements of key staff.
6   Nancy Birdsall, Dani Rodrik and Arvind Subramanian, "How to Help Poor Countries," *Foreign Affairs* 84, no. 4 (2005): 136–152.
7   See Sam Hickey, "The Return of Politics in Development Studies (I): Getting Lost Within the Poverty Agenda?" *Progress in Development Studies* 8, no. 4 (2008): 349–358.

8 Ruth Lister, *Poverty* (Cambridge and Malden, Mass.: Polity, 2004).
9 B. Seebohm Rowntree, *Poverty: A Study of Town Life* (London: Macmillan, 1901).
10 Rowntree, *Poverty*, quoted in Ravi Kanbur and Lyn Squire, "The Evolution of Thinking About Poverty: Exploring the Interactions," in *Frontiers of Development Economics: The Future in Perspective*, ed. Gerald M. Meier and Joseph E. Stiglitz (Oxford: Oxford University Press and World Bank, 2001), 186.
11 See Chapter 4 for a detailed discussion.
12 The "Sarkozy Report," produced by the Commission on the Measurement of Economic Performance and Social Progress, provides a detailed critique of narrow measures of development (especially GDP) and explores multi-dimensional measures and approaches that incorporate assessments of the sustainability of progress – see Joseph Stiglitz, Amartya Sen and Jean-Paul Fitoussi, *Report by the Commission on the Measurement of Economic Performance and Social Progress* (2009) at http://www.stiglitz-sen-fitoussi.fr
13 Amartya Kumar Sen, "Development as Capability Expansion," in *Human Development and the International Development Strategy for the 1990s*, ed. Keith Griffin and John B. Knight (Basingstoke: Macmillan, 1990); Amartya Kumar Sen, "Capability and Well-Being," in *The Quality of Life*, ed. Martha Craven Nussbaum and Amartya Sen (Oxford: Clarendon Press, 1993).
14 Lister, *Poverty*.
15 David Hulme and Maia Green, "From Correlates and Characteristics to Causes: Thinking about Poverty from a Chronic Poverty Perspective," *World Development* 33, no. 6 (2005): 867–879.
16 For an introduction to the literature on positivism, anti-positivism and post-positivism see Loïc Wacquant, "Positivism," in *The Blackwell Dictionary of Modern Social Thought*, ed. William Outhwaite, (Oxford: Blackwell, 2006), 507–510.
17 Andries du Toit, "Poverty Measurement Blues: Some Reflections on the Space for Understanding 'Chronic' and 'Structural' Poverty in South Africa," in Tony Addison, David Hulme and Ravi Kanbur, *Poverty Dynamics: Cross-disciplinary Perspectives* (Oxford, Oxford University Press, 2009).
18 Ravi Kanbur, ed., *Q-Squared: Combining Qualitative and Quantitative Methods in Poverty Appraisal* (Delhi: Permanent Black, 2001).
19 David Hulme and John Toye, "The Case for Cross-Disciplinary Social Science Research on Poverty, Inequality and Well-Being," *Journal of Development Studies* 42, no. 7 (2006): 1085–1107.
20 du Toit, "Poverty Measurement Blues," 20.
21 Lawrence Haddad and Ravi Kanbur, "Is There an Intra Household Kuznets Curve? Some Evidence from the Philippines," Policy Research Working Paper Series, No. 466 (Washington, DC: World Bank, 1990).
22 My thanks to Sakiko Fukuda-Parr for pointing out to me that this oft-quoted statistic does not have an authoritative empirical base.
23 See Sreenivasan Subramanian, *Measurement of Inequality and Poverty* (New Delhi: Oxford University Press, 1997) for a collection of classic papers and reviews.
24 James Foster, Joel Greer and Erik Thorbecke, "A Class of Decomposable Poverty Measures," *Econometrica* 52, no. 3 (1984): 761–766.
25 See Table 4.1 (Chapter 4) for a summary of the various estimates of $1-a-day and $1.25-a-day 1980 to 2005.

26 See Amartya Kumar Sen, *Resources, Values and Development* (Oxford: Blackwell, 1984); Sen, "Development as Capability Expansion"; Sen, "Capability and Well-Being"; Sen, *Development as Freedom* (New York: Knopf, 1999).

27 Amartya Kumar Sen, "Human Development Index," in *The Elgar Companion to Development Studies*, ed. David Clark (Cheltenham: Edward Elgar, 2006).

28 See David Hulme and Andy McKay "Identifying and Measuring Chronic Poverty: Beyond Monetary Measures," in *The Many Dimensions of Poverty*, ed. Nanak Kakwani and Jacques Silber (Basingstoke and New York: Palgrave, 2007), 187–214.

29 See Robert Chambers, "The Origins and Practice of Participatory Rural Appraisal," *World Development* 22, no. 7 (1994): 953–969.

30 Deepa Narayan, Raj Patel and Kai Schafft, *Can Anyone Hear Us? Voices of the Poor* (Washington, DC: Oxford University Press and World Bank, 2000).

31 Students have suggested to me that this may be ". . . one of the greatest robberies of all times" with the World Bank holding copyright over the testimonials of 60,000 poor people.

32 Sebastian Mallaby, *The World's Banker: Story of Failed States, Financial Crises, and the Wealth and Poverty of Nations* (New York: Penguin, 2004).

33 The MDGs are such a list but they were produced by a political process and are not a theoretically reasoned position on poverty or poverty reduction.

34 Bruce F. Johnston and William C. Clark, *Redesigning Rural Development: A Strategic Perspective* (Baltimore: Johns Hopkins University Press, 1982), 26. Johnston and Clark were referring to "rural development" around the world, but over the years rural development has morphed into poverty reduction.

35 For a discussion of "geography" see Jeffrey D. Sachs, "Tropical Underdevelopment," NBER Working Paper 8119 (Washington, DC, National Bureau of Economic Research, 2001). Recently, Daron Acemoglu, Simon Johnson and James A. Robinson ("Reversal of Fortune: Geography and Institutions in the Making of the Modern World Income Distribution," *Quarterly Journal of Economics* 117, no. 4, (2002): 1231–1294) have argued that "good institutions and not geography explains the poverty of nations."

36 For a detailed discussion of these three eras, and of earlier colonial accounts of why native populations were poor, see Alastair Greig, David Hulme and Mark Turner, *Challenging Global Inequality: Development Theory and Practice in the 21st Century* (Basingstoke: Palgrave Macmillan, 2007).

37 Walter W. Rostow, *The Stages of Economic Growth: A Non-Communist Manifesto.* (Cambridge: Cambridge University Press, 1960).

38 Some supportive evidence was emerging from South Korea, Hong Kong and Singapore but, during the 1960s, this was too limited to claim an "economic miracle" and/or identify "tiger" economics.

39 Neo-Marxists and dependency theorists applied Karl Marx's concepts to international development but in a way that differed from Marx's analysis.

40 A classic study is Andre Gunder Frank, *Capitalism and Underdevelopment in Latin America: Historical Studies of Chile and Brazil* (New York and London: Monthly Review Press, 1969). Also see the chapters in Robert I. Rhodes, ed., *Imperialism and Underdevelopment* (New York: Monthly Review Press, 1970).

41 Cuba is the exception as despite low growth rates and anti-capitalist strategies its social indicators improved greatly.

42 An epistemic community is a network of knowledge-based experts with a strongly held common analytical position. See Peter M. Haas, "Epistemic

Communities and International Policy Coordination: Introduction," *International Organization* 46, no. 1 (1992): 1–35.
43 See Table 5.1 (Chapter 5) for the ten main policy priorities of the Washington Consensus.
44 Though Paul Mosley (pers. comm.), a critic of structural adjustment in the 1980s and 1990s, now points out that in the longer term structural adjustment has underpinned growth and poverty reduction in countries such as Ghana, Tanzania and Uganda.
45 See Joseph Stiglitz, *Globalization and Its Discontents* (London: Penguin, 2002), chapter 5.
46 See Table 5.1 (Chapter 5) for a listing of the policies of the Washington Consensus and "Augmented" Washington Consensus.
47 See Wade, "US Hegemony."
48 See Armando Barrientos and David Hulme, eds., *Social Protection for the Poor and Poorest: Concepts, Policies and Politics* (London: Palgrave, 2008).
49 Jean-Philippe Thérien, "Beyond the North-South Divide: The Two Tales of World Poverty," *Third World Quarterly* 20, no. 4 (1999): 723–742 argues that there are two main "tales of world poverty" and contrasts the BWI paradigm and the UN paradigm. As his study relates to institutional positions rather than ideas more generally, his work is discussed in the next chapter.
50 Surjit S. Bhalla, *Imagine There's No Country: Poverty, Inequality, and Growth in the Era of Globalization* (Washington, DC: Institute for International Economics, 2002).
51 Bhalla, *Imagine There's No Country*, 3.
52 Bhalla, 202.
53 Bhalla, 206.
54 Martin Ravallion, "Measuring Aggregate Welfare in Developing Countries," *World Bank Staff Working Paper 2665* (Washington, DC: World Bank, 2001).
55 Walden Bello, Shea Cunningham and Bill Rau, *Dark Victory: US Structural Adjustment and Global Poverty* (London: Pluto Press, 1994); and Walden Bello, *Deglobalization: Ideas for a New World Economy* (London and New York: Zed Books, 2002).
56 Like many critics of globalization Bello is concerned about a variety of problems and does not focus exclusively on poverty. The overarching concern of Bello, as with many left wing writers, is with inequality, and a notion of growing relative poverty seems to be inferred by his analysis.
57 Bello, Cunningham and Rau, *Dark Victory*, 2–3.
58 David Harvey, *A Brief History of Neoliberalism* (Oxford: Oxford University Press, 2005).
59 Joseph E. Stiglitz, *Globalization and Its Discontents*; Ha-Joon Chang, *Bad Samaritans: Rich Nations, Poor Policies and the Threat to the Developing World* (London: Random House Business, 2007).
60 Bello, Cunningham and Rau, *Dark Victory*, 113.
61 Sachs has moved a long way from his disastrous prescription of neo-liberal "shock therapy" for the Soviet Union in the early 1990s.
62 Jeffrey D. Sachs, *The End of Poverty: Economic Possibilities for Our Time* (New York: Penguin Press, 2005).
63 Easterly's ideological position is difficult to classify but much of his work in the mid-2000s was picked up by right wing critics of aid and, willingly or unwillingly, it is identified with this perspective.

64 Robin Broad and John Cavanagh, "The Hijacking of the Development Debate: How Friedman and Sachs Got It Wrong," *World Policy Journal* 23, no. 2 (2006): 21–30.

65 Reflecting my own prejudices I have not included any detailed comment on post-developmentalists, such as Escobar (1996). While their work provides many interesting insights, I believe that their failure to say "what" poverty is or "who" is poor limits their contribution to understanding poverty.

66 William Russell Easterly, *The Elusive Quest for Growth: Economists' Adventures and Misadventures in the Tropics* (Cambridge, MA and London: MIT Press, 2002); William Russell Easterly, *The White Man's Burden: Why the West's Efforts to Aid the Rest Have Done So Much Ill and So Little Good* (Oxford: Oxford University Press, 2006).

67 Easterly would see the notion of poverty eradication as utopian and likely to lead to mis-diagnoses and dysfunctional policy prescriptions.

68 This applies to both domestic and international policy and, his assumption is, that very little public action can be empirically shown to "work."

69 David Craig and Douglas R. Porter, *Development beyond Neoliberalism?: The Poverty Reduction Paradigm* (London: Routledge, 2005).

70 Craig and Porter, *Development beyond Neoliberalism?*, 11.

71 Craig and Porter, 270.

72 Paul Collier, *The Bottom Billion: Why the Poorest Countries are Failing and What Can be Done* (Oxford: Oxford University Press, 2007). See also Paul Collier and Stefan Dercon, "The Complementarities of Poverty Reduction, Equity and Growth: A Perspective on the World Development Report 2006," *Economic Development and Cultural Change* 55, no. 1 (2006): 223–236.

73 Collier and Dercon, "The Complementarities of Poverty Reduction," 11.

74 Importantly, Collier's work has little to say about poor people in India and China – at least half of the world's dollar-a-day poor. He appears to assume that because India and China have economic growth then eventually poverty will become a residual issue in both countries.

75 Collier is unclear about why this is a particular problem for small countries. He seems to go for this label to avoid the Bangladesh case – if bad governance is so bad why has Bangladesh experienced economic growth and poverty reduction?

76 Rodrik, *One Economics*.

77 Rodrik, 2.

78 Also see the work of Ricardo Hausmann, Bailey Klinger and Rodrigo Wagner, "Doing Growth Diagnostics in Practice: A 'Mindbook,'" CID Working Paper No. 177 (Cambridge, Mass.: Harvard University Press, 2008).

79 Catherine Weaver, *Hypocrisy Trap: The World Bank and the Poverty of Reform* (Princeton: Princeton University Press, 2009).

3   The institutional landscape for attacking global poverty

"Never has the need for international organizations like the IMF, the World Bank and the World Trade Organization been greater, and seldom has confidence in them been lower."

(Joseph Stiglitz, 2006)[1]

"A recurring theme of the evaluation concerned the disconnect in external perceptions between the IMF's rhetoric on aid and poverty reduction and what it actually did at country level . . . [with] . . . a staff professional culture strongly focused on macroeconomic stability . . . the IMF gravitated back to business as usual."

(Independent Evaluation of the IMF, 2007)[2]

The institutional landscape for tackling global poverty is a vast terrain which lacks clear boundaries and involves a web of multilateral, national, sub-national and local institutions spread across the public sector, private business and civil society. It is also a dynamic landscape comprised of institutions reflecting the power structures and principles of different era. While several of the key institutions date back to the founding of the UN and Bretton Woods Institutions (BWIs) in the 1940s there are many new institutions based on twenty-first-century international power relations, such as the G20, and complex public-private partnerships, such as the Global Fund for AIDS, Tuberculosis and Malaria. There are many ambiguities about the roles of different institutions and about their overlapping mandates. While the assumption underpinning the UN institutions is of unquestioned state sovereignty, with wise men negotiating compromises between well-articulated national interests, contemporary practices of deliberation, decision-making and practical action on global poverty have increasingly been influenced by the growing number, and increasing influence, of non-state actors. These different institutions have differing interests and visions of "what should be done" and coalesce into a variety of formal and informal associations and networks.

From the outset it must be understood that the institutions, associations and networks examined here are not elements of a rationally designed international institutional architecture. Their roles, responsibilities and authorities are often unclear and they overlap, sometimes in ill defined ways. While some are mandated to eradicate poverty around the world, others have taken poverty reduction on as an additional goal to a pre-existing mission. Policies, plans and actions occur on both a coordinated and uncoordinated basis and involve different sets of players in multiple arenas. As for other global issues – such as food supply, climate change and financial sector regulation – there is no overarching or agreed institutional framework of authority and, as a result, no-one is "in charge" of global poverty eradication.

The values that underpin international efforts to tackle global poverty, and the policies and actions that are pursued, are constrained – some would say are undermined – by the day-to-day realities of power politics in international relations. While the most powerful nations can agree that the contemporary architecture, the UN and the BWIs, is inadequate, agreeing changes has proved difficult. The most important institutions were designed to meet the needs and serve the interests of the power structure of the mid-twentieth century. Reforming them to recognize the configuration of economic and military power in the early twenty-first century remains work in progress. The acronyms of many new organizations litter this chapter – the G20 (a recognition that no longer are there a mere handful of industrial powers), GAVI (the Global Alliance for Vaccination and Immunisation – a recognition of the significance of the commercial and non-profit sectors) and others. While both the old and the new institutions and associations are commonly identified as having specific policies and interests, it is important to recognize how porous their boundaries and positions are. For example, radical critics of the World Bank present it as a monolithic organization with all its departments and staff determinedly pursuing a clear mission and set of policies to neo-liberalize the world. In reality the Bank is more complex, with departments set against each other and staff networking with "like-minded" people in other institutions – sometimes to challenge or oppose Bank policies and actions. Forms of influence that are not focused on specific institutions – such as the epistemic community of "Chicago economists" spread throughout the BWIs and ministries of finance and universities around the world (see later) – have been and can be very powerful.

The following section looks at the multilateral institutions that lead the attack on global poverty. The third section explores the roles that national governments, and sub-national governments, are playing. The fourth section explores the role of the increasingly important non-state players – social movements, NGOs, civil society organizations (CSOs) and the business sector. The following section discusses the emergence of the cross-sectoral institutions that have recently been established to pursue MDG goals. In the conclusion a central paradox of global poverty reduction efforts is highlighted – that it is rich world institutions (national governments, social movements, NGOs and coalitions) that have pushed this issue onto the international agenda more than institutions based in those countries where extreme poverty is most common. The conclusion also examines whether the contemporary institutional landscape is "chaotic" and a cause for concern, or reflects the "multi-multilateralism" that Fukuyama sees as the best way forward for international relations.[3]

Multilateral institutions

At the heart of debates and plans for global poverty reduction lie multilateral institutions. While components of the UN system have been central to the emergence of the idea of global poverty and policies for global poverty reduction, other players, such as the OECD, also have played influential roles.

The UN General Assembly

With its 192 member states, and its "one country one vote" constitution, the UN General Assembly has unprecedented global representation and legitimacy. While right wing critics of the UN caricature it as a nascent world government seeking to wrestle sovereignty away from nation-states, in practice the UN is as much engaged with normative change as with policy making and implementation for the issue of global poverty. General Assembly meetings, and the UN conferences and summits approved by the General Assembly, have sought to raise awareness about the extent of extreme poverty around the world and to encourage UN member states, individually and collectively, to devote more resources and policy attention to the eradication of poverty at home and abroad. The UN cannot order rich countries to increase foreign aid or make their trade policies fairer to poor countries. Nor can it tell poor countries to improve public management or allocate more resources to basic social services. It can, however, encourage member states to move in these directions unilaterally, through domestic policy changes influenced by UN debates and declarations, and multilaterally, by signing up to binding agreements about future action.

Until the 1990s the UN's effectiveness in persuading member states to recognize and tackle poverty, as a global moral issue, achieved relatively little political traction. While the world's rich nations mounted bilateral aid programs and provided finance for the UN and World Bank, and poor countries produced national strategies and five-year plans, their public statements at the General Assembly were rarely matched by equivalent actions. In most

industrialized countries the resources committed to international development, and the policies pursued, were strongly influenced by geo-political
maneuvering around the Cold War and domestic interest groups (such as
farmers, agribusiness, export industries and engineering contractors).[4] In
poor countries, policies commonly served to meet the needs of the elites
holding power and their networks of patronage. At other times they were
ineffective and sometimes deeply flawed (as with Tanzania's *Ujamaa* program).[5] Successive UN Secretaries-General found their agenda overwhelmed
by urgent emergency and security issues so that long-term international
development received relatively scant attention.

The environment within which the UN operated changed dramatically
around 1990 with the end of the Cold War and the growing realization that
in most countries the BWIs' structural adjustment policies were not yet
stimulating growth nor assisting poor people. The UN General Assembly
approved a series of international conferences and summits which influenced world leaders, national political parties and the general public in many
countries. From a global poverty perspective the highpoint of these events
came in March 1995 when 117 national leaders met at the World Summit
for Social Development in Copenhagen and declared global poverty eradication a priority. These declarations, and others, were built on in 2000 when
189 nations (and 149 national leaders) affirmed their commitment to a set
of poverty reduction goals in the Millennium Declaration of the General
Assembly.

These goals were crafted into the UN Millennium Development Goals
(MDGs) which have become the centerpiece of efforts for global poverty
reduction.[6] Subsequently, the UN's Finance for Development (FFD) summit
in 2002 produced the Monterrey Consensus, with rich countries committing themselves to increased funding to achieve the MDGs and developing
countries promising improved governance. However, the influence of the
UN's "millennium moment" soon faded and, despite the continuing and
resounding rhetoric of UN member states, the "Millennium plus 5" (2005)
General Assembly and the 2008 General Assembly high level event on the
MDGs merely kept global poverty on the agenda: they did not advance
its position. For the majority of the UN's member states the "noughties"
(2000–2009) have meant "business as usual" at the General Assembly –
making grand statements about the eradication of poverty but not matching
this with actions.

The UN organ specifically tasked with promoting economic and social
development across the world – the Economic and Social Council (ECOSOC),
an elected body of 54 member states – has been unable to create the momentum to drive the poverty reduction agenda forward. Similarly, the G77 (an
informal grouping of the UN's "developing" countries that now has 130

member states, some of which are now upper middle income countries), has played a relatively limited role in placing global poverty reduction on the General Assembly's agenda and its proposals have lacked support.[7] As its member states hold almost all of the world's $1-a-day poor it might be expected to energetically promote the idea of global poverty reduction. In practice it has taken a relatively reactive role at the General Assembly and at UN conferences and summits. Part of the explanation for this is that by seeking unanimity from its large and diverse membership it can rarely set an agenda, as one or more of its members will object. Its main engagements with the debates about global poverty have been to force the removal of reproductive health from the Millennium Declaration and MDGs in 2000[8] and argue that goals for rich countries (Goal 8) be included in the MDGs. The energies that lay behind the General Assembly's turn of the millennium focus on global poverty came from civil society, social movements, the Secretary-General, UN specialized agencies and a handful of rich countries, rather than the UN's G77 member states. Paradoxically, placing global poverty eradication on the UN agenda has been more the focus of richer states than of poorer states.

The UN Secretariat

This is the body that supports the work of the General Assembly. It is headed by the UN's Secretary-General, who is the public face of the UN, and it employs some 40,000 international public servants. While theoretically the Secretariat merely advises the Assembly, in practice it has the opportunity to set the UN agenda and to make UN positions more coherent. The personal commitment of Secretary-General Kofi Annan (1997–2007) to eradicating extreme poverty helped to ensure that this topic became a major item on UN agendas and was influential in making poverty eradication a central component of the Millennium Declaration. Senior advisors at the Secretariat, such as John Ruggie and Michael Doyle, and personal advisors to Annan such as Jeffrey Sachs, were able to shape the content of UN declarations and proposed actions.[9] The appointment of Jeffrey Sachs, an influential economist from Columbia University, as personal advisor on poverty to Kofi Annan in 2002 was an important decision. Many insiders saw it as signaling that the secretariat and UNDP lacked the intellectual muscle in the field of economics to chart a way forward for the MDGs. They report that Sachs was given "carte blanche" to do some "big thinking" about MDG implementation. He did this by establishing the Millennium Project, which harnessed a large number of intellectual heavyweights to prepare a plan.[10]

UN funds, programs and specialized agencies

A bewildering array of official multilateral agencies is engaged in promoting, analyzing, planning, implementing and monitoring global poverty reduction. They fall into three main groups: the UN agencies that report directly to the General Assembly; the IMF and World Bank that are part of the UN System but have their own boards; and the WTO.

The UN funds, programs and agencies are the greatest in number and include the UNDP, FAO, WHO, ILO, UNESCO, UNIFEM, UNAIDS, UNEP, UNICEF, UNFPA and many others[11] (for full names see the "List of abbreviations"). As components of the UN system all of these organizations have agreed to contribute to achieving the MDGs and all have identified some role in global poverty reduction. These roles vary with agency mandates: so UNICEF specializes in child health, UNFPA in reproductive health, UNIFEM on gender equality and so on. However, the significance and effectiveness of agency contributions to global poverty reduction vary greatly and are often linked to the quality of their leaders.[12] For example, in the 1990s UNICEF was widely acclaimed for its achievements in reducing child mortality and morbidity, and spearheading the Convention on the Rights of the Child. By contrast, the FAO has been criticized for not predicting the food price rise of 2007 and 2008 which pushed tens of millions into poverty and hunger. While there is evidence that some UN agencies have been "ahead of the curve"[13] in placing ideas about global poverty on the international agenda, the overall contributions of UN agencies to the effective planning and implementation of poverty reduction policies is generally seen as being mixed. Many who work in these organizations find them "bureaucratic" and coordination between agencies remains weak despite Annan's efforts to create "one UN."

For global poverty, it is the UNDP that has the most important overarching role within the agencies reporting to the General Assembly. It has offices in most developing and transitional countries (or regions), so that it has an opportunity to influence national policies. UNDP headquarters in New York has also played an important ideational role in promoting the idea of poverty as multi-dimensional deprivation that needs to be tackled through both economic and social policies. Throughout the 1990s the UNDP promoted the concept of, and policies for, human development through the *Human Development Report*, by computing the HDI for all UN member states and other work. This helped to both frame the MDGs and create a supportive environment for them.[14] The UNDP's then Administrator, Mark Malloch Brown, was one of the principal "message entrepreneurs" engaged in the decanting of the Millennium Declaration into the MDGs.[15] However, the leading role envisaged for the UNDP in 2002 and 2003, when the Millennium Project and Millennium Campaign were set up, has not been realized.[16]

Although the UNDP provides support to national "poverty units" it is the World Bank and IMF that have played the main role in shaping national Poverty Reduction Strategies (PRSs).[17]

While the BWIs are part of the wider UN system they differ greatly from the UN agencies that are accountable to the General Assembly. First, the BWIs are accountable to member state shareholders whose votes are weighted according to their share of capital. So rich countries hold a majority on their Boards and, as a result of being the leading shareholder, US influence on the IMF and World Bank is very strong.[18] Both institutions have their headquarters in Washington, DC and so close ties with US government agencies, particularly the Treasury Department, are maintained. The second main difference between the BWIs and UN agencies is that the former have substantial funds to allocate to countries as loans, and sometimes grants. (In 2008 the Bank made loans totaling US$24.7 billion while the IMF disbursed US$25.7 billion in the financial year 2008–2009, though it should be noted that this was particularly high due to the financial crisis). This gives them substantial policy leverage with borrowing countries and they can require that recipient countries agree to significant conditions to access loans or grants.[19] As a result, they can dictate policy conditions to needy countries in a way that UN agencies cannot.[20]

While there are considerable differences in these organizations' roles – the IMF focuses on short- to medium-term economic stability while the World Bank's[21] mandate is to promote long-term development – both see economic growth as a priority. Since the mid-1990s the Bank has shifted towards a more direct attack on poverty reduction and the vision it declares in its atrium is of "a world free from poverty." Arguably, the World Bank is the most influential organization in terms of setting the agenda on global poverty. This is partly because of its lending but also because of its capacity to shape thinking. It has the largest concentration of development economists anywhere in the world and its ". . . analytical machine has more intellectual juice in it"[22] than other multilaterals and development agencies. By contrast, the IMF's commitment to direct poverty reduction remains shallow. One of their senior economists for Africa advised me in 2006 that ". . . the MDGs are European social policy. The IMF doesn't do European social policy."[23]

While the public pronouncements of the UN agencies and the BWIs have converged in recent years (they are all pursuing the MDGs and poverty reduction is their prime goal) their ideological and policy orientations have been and remain very different. Jean-Philippe Thérien[24] argues that two competing "tales of world poverty" can be identified: a "Bretton Woods paradigm" advanced by the IMF and World Bank (and also the WTO) and a "UN paradigm" advanced by ECOSOC, UNDP, ILO, UNICEF and other UN agencies. The Bretton Woods paradigm favors globalization and sees the roots of poverty as laying in the policy choices of national governments. The UN paradigm views globalization as ". . . a multiplier of inequalities . . . and emphasizes the lack of international cooperation" as the major cause of poverty. "These differences in perspective ultimately result in highly disparate political projects: the Bretton Woods paradigm favors a complete market liberalization, while the UN paradigm insists on the need to subordinate the functioning of the world economy to objectives of social equity and sustainability." In effect, the BWIs are presented as "bastions of liberal capitalism" while the UN is seen as having a social democratic political orientation. While this contrast oversimplifies many of the nuances of these institutions' ideological and policy stances – the UN agencies are too fragmented to speak with one voice and there are sometimes major disagreements between the Bank and Fund[25] – it does provide a good basis for understanding many of the overt and covert battles of the last 20 years about the content and policy focus of international declarations and policy choices about global poverty. Indeed, the MDGs can be seen as a form of compromise between these "two paradigms."[26]

While the original division of labor envisaged that the UN agencies would work on ideas and policies while the Bank and Fund would work on financial transfers, the Bank has gained the leading position in terms of conducting research on development, and more recently poverty, and shaping policies. It has been able to do this by devoting resources to research and recruiting leading development economists (the Bank pays significantly higher salaries than the UN). However, in recent years the credibility of its research findings have been questioned by the Deaton Review and by other detailed studies of the biased way in which parts of the Bank have manipulated data to argue that economic liberalization always produced growth and that such growth reduced poverty.[27]

The WTO, by contrast, is not a "development" organization, but it has been tasked with helping to tackle global poverty through the declaration of its Doha round of trade negotiations as a "development round" – that is, a round that is meant to benefit developing countries and reduce poverty. Also, it is not formally part of the UN system. Its origins lie with the more informal General Agreement on Tariffs and Trade (GATT). The WTO differs markedly from the World Bank and IMF in its operation. Unlike the Fund and Bank, the WTO has no autonomous leverage over its member states and no mandate to forge agreements between members, though the Secretariat has been accused of doing so at the margins. The WTO operates instead as a forum in which states negotiate trade deals, which it then monitors and provides a system through which members can bring enforcement actions and resolve disputes. Being a "member-driven" organization rather than one in which the Secretariat makes decisions, inevitably the process by which trade agreements are made is highly political. Each member has influence broadly in proportion to the size of their economic muscle, with the result that poor countries have traditionally been excluded from the negotiation process. This led to the trade rounds negotiated under the GATT being imbalanced, with the commercial interests of the powerful industrialized states being privileged while those of developing countries were marginalized. This culminated in the highly imbalanced Uruguay Round of trade negotiations of 1986–1994, which created the WTO. Partly as a result of the imbalance of the Uruguay Round, which was estimated by UNDP to make sub-Saharan Africa US$1.2 billion a year worse off,[28] the first WTO round was termed a "development round." Though the Doha Development Agenda is yet to be concluded, it is generally considered to be highly unlikely to provide a pro-poor agreement.

Associations of states

Apart from meeting at the UN, states also meet in a variety of formal and informal associations. For rich countries the key formal grouping is the Organisation for Economic Co-operation and Development (OECD) with its secretariat in Paris and a membership of the 30 richest countries (in 1990 it had only 24 members). The OECD's interests in international development and global poverty are articulated through its Development Assistance Committee (DAC) which runs regular meetings of the administrative heads of bilateral development agencies and annual meetings of ministers of international development or development cooperation. The DAC has played a leading role in making the case, and mobilizing public support, for foreign aid and global poverty reduction in the rich world. The content and "results-based management" format of the MDGs were heavily influenced by DAC.[29] Subsequently it led on the Paris 21 initiative (to improve statistical capacity in developing countries with a particular focus on poverty monitoring) and the Paris Declaration for improved donor coordination. While the DAC pursues a moral mission, its actions also serve the needs of its membership – making the case for foreign aid. An unfortunate consequence of the DAC's involvement in leadership of the global poverty eradication agenda has been the exaggeration of the role of foreign aid in achieving the MDGs.

The roles and interests of regional associations in global poverty differ. The African Union (AU), with its 53 African member states, has been seen as having special significance because of the potential role it could play in improving governance and policies across the continent – and thus reducing poverty and violent conflict. Its New Economic Partnership for African Development (NEPAD), established in 2001, was intended to spearhead AU efforts to improve governance by introducing a peer review process. This would put pressure on African leaders and governments to perform better but it would not be seen as the rich world or non-Africans telling Africans "what to do." Unfortunately, this mechanism is credited with little success. Indeed, in 2007 President Abdoulaye Wade of Senegal claimed: "Expenses adding up to hundreds of millions of dollars have been spent on trips, on hotels. But not a single classroom has been built, not a single health center completed. NEPAD has not done what it was set up for."[30]

Box 3.1 The New Economic Partnership for African Development (NEPAD)

NEPAD arose from the Organization of African Unity (OAU) tasking five heads of state (Algeria, Egypt, Nigeria, Senegal and South Africa) to prepare a strategic framework document. This document was formally adopted by the OAU in July 2001. NEPAD's primary objectives are:

i.   To eradicate poverty;

ii. To place African countries, both individually and collectively, on a path of sustainable growth and development;

iii. To halt the marginalization of Africa in the globalization process and enhance its full and beneficial integration into the global economy; and

iv. To accelerate the empowerment of women.

It identifies five key priority action areas:

i.   Operationalizing the African Peer Review Mechanism. This is a voluntary OAU program in which participating members review each other's policies to ensure that they conform to agreed political, economic and governance standards, promoting human rights and democracy;

ii. Supporting regional infrastructure programs covering Transport, Energy, ICT, Water and Sanitation;

iii. Facilitating implementation of the food security and agricultural development program;

iv. Preparing coordinated African positions on trade, aid and debt issues; and

v.   Monitoring and intervening as appropriate to ensure that the health and education MDGs are met.

(Box continued on next page)

When launched NEPAD did not receive a very positive response from civil society, partly as a result of their exclusion from its negotiation process which they saw as being driven by African elites and corporate interests. Over 40 African organizations signed an "African Civil Society Declaration on NEPAD" in July 2002 criticizing it point-for-point, in particular for being too similar to the Washington Consensus policies of the BWIs, that civil society generally saw as having led to great hardship for Africa's people, particularly the poor.

While the Peer Review Mechanism has been initiated and reports have been produced these are not viewed as having impacted on prospects for poverty eradication and/or improved governance in Africa. Progressive African leaders, major donors and independent analysts appear to see NEPAD as increasingly irrelevant.

Sources: http://www.nepad.org; "African Civil Society Declaration on NEPAD," July 8, 2002, available from http://www.fntg.org/news/index.php?articleid =399&op=read; and author.

The EU has made some progress. While it struggles to find a common external position at the UN, OECD and other institutions, it has managed to reach an internal agreement about focusing on the MDGs, increasing aid and inducting its new member states into international development. One of the conditions imposed on new EU member states is that they must develop an aid budget that will reach 0.33 percent of GNI by 2015. Internally, the EU has established a regional norm for global poverty reduction that has promoted the idea of extreme poverty anywhere in the world being morally unacceptable for citizens of European countries.[31] However, progress with the institutionalization of this norm within EU member states varies dramatically.[32] Other regional associations are either ineffective, for example South Asian Association for Regional Cooperation (SAARC) which is widely seen within its region as purely a talking shop, or have not identified poverty reduction as a major focus, as with ASEAN.

The Organization of the Islamic Conference has an Islamic Development Bank (IDB) to ". . . foster the economic development and social progress of Member States and Muslim Communities individually as well as collectively in accordance with the principles of the Shariah." In 2006 the IDB was entrusted with the following objectives: (i) reducing poverty; (ii) eliminating illiteracy; (iii) eradicating major communicable diseases such as malaria, tuberculosis and AIDS; and, (iv) building the human and productive capacities particularly in the least developed members of the Organization. Little information is available about the activities and performance of the IDB in pursuit of these objectives, and regional specialists advise that, at best, the wealthy Arab and Middle Eastern states see aid purely as charity.

Among the informal associations of states, the most significant is the G7/8 – the annual meetings of the national leaders of Canada, France, Germany, Italy, Japan, United Kingdom and United States, and since 1998, Russia. Hodges characterizes it as ". . . a forum, rather than an institution . . . a closed international club of capitalist governments trying to raise consciousness, set an agenda, create networks, prod other institutions to do things."[33] While the G7/8 has focused most of its attention on the pressing interests of its members – trade policy, conflict and security, energy policy, financial stability – in recent times it has taken an interest in poorer countries. In 1988, and later in 1998 and 1999, it re-shaped debt relief; in 2001 and 2002 it looked at African development; and, in 2005 at Gleneagles, it included Africa, debt cancellation and increasing foreign aid on its agenda. While "global poverty" has never explicitly been on the G7/8 agenda, its focus on increasing aid, canceling debt and assisting Africa was aimed at global poverty reduction.

In 2008, in response to the deepening effects of the global financial crisis on the real economy, the G8 realized that in the "Asian Century" a larger forum was essential. Any agreement made without China and India was likely to be ineffective, and forums that excluded Latin America, Africa, Asia and the Islamic world stoked resentment and were increasingly seen as illegitimate. Furthermore, much of the finance for the bank bailout and stimulus packages implemented by Western countries (particularly the United States and United Kingdom) was borrowed from surplus countries such as China and Saudi Arabia, increasing their influence over global financial matters. These factors led to a shift in forum from the G8 to the more inclusive G20. While the G20's 2009 meeting, chaired by Gordon Brown in London, focused on stabilizing the global financial system and stimulating the global economy, Brown worked hard to ensure that his deep personal commitment to tackling global poverty reduction influenced the meeting. This involved mobilizing support in the United Kingdom and from other national leaders and succeeded in producing a G20 commitment to provide US$50 billion for social protection in low income countries. It was also agreed that the G20 would effectively take over as the forum for the discussion of global financial matters. Though the G8 continues to meet its focus is likely to shift away from economic issues, though what its new focus will be is not yet clear.[34]

National and sub-national governments

While the contemporary focus on global poverty leads to a highlighting of the roles of international institutions and associations of states the practical action for poverty reduction occurs largely at the national and sub-national level.

National governments

National governments are still recognized as being the most important institution for reducing poverty. International agencies can supply finance, forgive debt, provide policy advice and improve the trade regime that countries operate in, but it is national governments (in countries with large numbers of poor people) that create the conditions for economic growth and oversee the delivery of basic services that can free people from poverty. As a result, the main instruments for the achievement of global goals are national PRSs[35] and related documents. Similarly, and despite the vast increase in non-state activity to tackle poverty, it is the national governments of rich countries that largely determine the volume of international finance allocated for poverty reduction in the poorest countries and that have most influence over the policies of international institutions.

With more than 65 national governments independently engaged in implementing PRSs or related plans, it is difficult to generalize about what developing country governments are doing and how committed and effective they have been. It is clear that commitment and achievement vary greatly. One can point to specific examples were there is evidence that national governments are committed to poverty reduction and, in collaboration with their development partners (UN agencies, World Bank, IMF and bilateral donors), have developed strong plans that are well implemented and are effective. My personal experience suggests that the governments of Brazil,[36] Ghana, Mozambique, Rwanda, Tanzania and Vietnam would be widely seen as falling into this category. Towards the other extreme are national governments that appear to be either unconcerned about tackling poverty or give it a low priority – as with Angola, Kenya, Sudan, Yemen and several Central Asian countries. This group of weakly committed national governments may be the most common. A study by the Chronic Poverty Research Centre[37] of the implementation of 13 PRSs concluded that implementation was relatively weak, indicating that the commitment of national governments to poverty reduction is shallower than would appear from an appraisal of the documents they produce. At the very extreme are national governments that systematically keep their populations poor and hungry and/or actively create poverty. These include Myanmar under the military junta, North Korea under Kim Jong Il and Zimbabwe under Mugabe.

For the national governments of rich countries a similar pattern of mixed levels of commitment and action can be identified. The Commitment to Development Index (CDI) provides a partial means of objectively assessing how seriously rich countries are taking their promises to eradicate global poverty (Figure 3.1). It assesses governments' performance with regard to how pro-development their policies on aid, trade, investment, migration, environment, security and technological are. At the "strong commitment" end come the governments of the like-minded group of donors (the Netherlands, Sweden, Norway and Denmark) with high levels of foreign aid, a major focus on poverty reduction and policies that support development in poorer countries. Over the last 10 years the United Kingdom has sought to join this group with an increased aid budget, improved aid effectiveness and more pro-poor policies on trade and migration. Indeed, in terms of political commitment to poverty reduction the United Kingdom has aspired to become the leader of the world's rich countries. The UN General Assembly's 2008 high level event to try and engineer a re-commitment to the MDGs was driven forward by Gordon Brown, who pressed other heads of government to attend through personal telephone calls. A special team in the Cabinet Office and Department for International Development (DFID) masterminded the event.

In the middle, with relatively low CDI scores, are a group of economically important countries – France, Germany and, most significant of all, the world's only superpower of the late twentieth and early twenty-first centuries – the United States. These countries have matched their low CDI scores politically by avoiding playing leading roles in events and debates on global poverty. Indeed, under President Bush the United States appeared highly ambivalent to the idea of global poverty reduction. A study published by the US National Bureau for Economic Research estimates that the implicit weight that the US assigns to the welfare of foreigners is 1/2000th of the weight it assigns to US citizens. This suggests ". . . that US policy is consistent with social preferences that place essentially no value on the welfare of the citizens of the poorest countries, or that implicitly assumes that essentially all transfers are wasted."[38]

At the bottom end of rich country government commitment to development come Greece, Italy, Japan and South Korea, with small aid budgets (as a percentage of GNI), aid programs that are politically and commercially targeted and other policies that are not supportive of economic and social development in poor countries. These countries are prepared to sign up to agreements about global poverty reduction but only pretend to take on the responsibilities that this entails. The UN has no authority to sanction such behavior and the electorates of these countries do not or cannot hold their leaders accountable for promises made to help the distant needy.

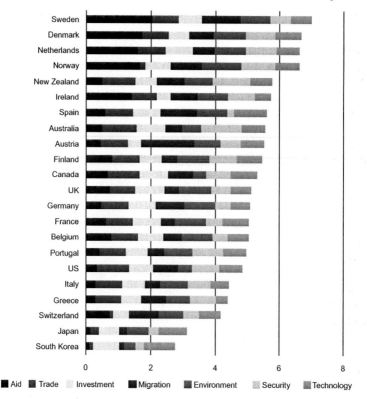

Figure 3.1 The commitment to development index 2009

Source: http://www.cgdev.org/section/initiatives/_active/cdi/

Sub-national governments

Sub-national governments – local governments, district councils, *panchayats* and municipal authorities – are the "Cinderellas" of development efforts. The vast literature on global poverty barely mentions them but they are at the coalface of poverty reduction. When they function well, basic health and education services are available, potable water can be accessed and local infrastructure – feeder roads, culverts, bridges, markets – facilitates productivity and income growth. When they do not work well, which is common in many poor countries and especially in rural areas, then economic and social progress are unlikely and poverty persists. Indeed, the proliferation and growth of service delivery NGOs in many developing countries is in part a response to the failure of national governments to allocate sufficient resources to local governments and/or reform and re-structure them so that they deliver basic services to poor communities.

National governments from Afghanistan to Zambia have declared that they are pursuing strategies of decentralization to strengthen local governments, improve service delivery and, sometimes, to promote local democracy. Commonly such claims are much greater than the actual practice.[39] In practice, national leaders, political parties and the central bureaucracy are often unwilling to delegate authority and resources to lower levels of government as that reduces their control over money, materials and jobs. When decentralization is genuinely pursued, as in the southern states of India, there is evidence that local services can rapidly be improved and the vulnerability of poor people reduced.

While the idea of global poverty eradication and the MDGs have been seen usually as devices for mobilizing international action, they have inspired some sub-national governments to focus their policies on poverty reduction and even to see if they can achieve the MDG targets at the local level. The best example of this comes from Brazil where MDG achievement is monitored at the local level for all 5,564 municipalities.[40] This has encouraged some mayors to set up "MDG plans" and adds to pressures for improved municipal authority performance in basic service delivery. This example is unusual,[41] however: while we know that sub-national governments are very important for poverty reduction we know next to nothing about the ways in which the declared international focus on global poverty reduction has helped or hindered, or made no difference, to sub-national government performance.

Non-state institutions

Since the end of the Cold War non-state actors have become increasingly influential in international affairs and this has particular significance for global poverty. Civil society groups (NGOs, social movements, faith groups) played a major role in taking the idea of attacking poverty to publics around the world. They have been granted formal recognition at the UN, and for PRSs "civil society participation" is a BWI requirement. More recently, some for-profit businesses have started to relate their "triple bottom lines" (economic, environmental and social) to the MDGs. There are so many actors in this group that here only a small selection of the most significant can be covered.

Social movements

Social movements (an umbrella term that covers forms of collective action aimed at social re-organization), particularly the women's movement and the environmental movement, were heavily involved in shaping the agenda and outcomes of the UN conferences and summits of the 1990s. Directly these movements ensured that gender equality and sustainable development became components of the MDGs. Indirectly they provide support for other poverty reduction goals. Martha Chen took stock of the women's movement contribution to these events.[42] She found that it had not only promoted gender equality and women's rights and empowerment but had more broadly advanced the case for human rights, social justice and reduced inequality.

The key question to pose about social movements is why a distinct movement did not develop around the issue of global poverty.[43] Well-mobilized campaigns have developed around elements of global poverty reduction – especially around debt cancellation and fair trade – but an anti-poverty movement has not emerged. The closest institution to this is the Global Call to Action Against Poverty (GCAP), with its 115 national federations. Despite the success of its "whiteband" initiative in 2005 GCAP has a relatively low international profile and parts of its membership, as in Malawi, take a lead from national level UNDP offices rather than pursuing an autonomous mission within civil society.[44]

One can only speculate about this absence but several potential reasons can be identified. The first is that the issue of poverty is just too broad for effective mobilization – it's about increasing incomes, accessing schools and health services, gender equality, family planning and much more – just too many things around which to create the short, sharp messages needed to mobilize substantial numbers of people for extended periods of time. A particular problem for poverty eradication activists is the difficulty of precisely identifying who are "the enemy" that has to be opposed. The women's movement could identify male chauvinists and the patriarchy, and the environmental movement could point fingers at loggers, mining companies, airports, nuclear power stations and others, but who exactly would be the enemy for an anti-poverty movement? While anti-capitalists could identify banks, multinational corporations, the IMF, World Bank and G8 as the enemy (of the poor, of the environment, of social justice, of animal rights and most other problems), many committed to poverty eradication did not see things that simply. International trade was unfair and needed major reforms – but, closing down trade was not going to make things better for the poor. The WTO and G8 needed changing, but rioting and violence were not legitimate means for creating a better society.

A second possible reason for the failure of an anti-poverty social movement to emerge is that it is difficult to create an identity around poverty or poverty eradication.[45] Feminists and environmentalists created identities for themselves, indeed labels for themselves, but no equivalent has evolved for poverty eradication – people do not identify themselves as poverty reductionists or anti-povertyists. Poor people themselves do not like to be seen as "the poor" and they face the problem that the main identities they recognize, or into which they have been and are socialized – religious, cultural, and ethnic – often keep them apart and/or make them mutually suspicious of or antagonistic to each other.[46]

A third reason could be that the very nature of the concept of poverty makes it difficult to promote the social solidarity that a social movement requires. In the women's movement, poor, middle class and elite women (and later some men) could agree that women were not being treated fairly and find common ways of articulating why this happened and what they thought should be done. People from different countries and different social classes can agree that the environment is under attack (deforestation, pollution, biodiversity loss) and support each other's actions to mitigate this state of affairs. But, the idea of poverty suggests that there are poor and non-poor people – can the non-poor stand shoulder to shoulder with the poor; what are the causes of poverty (is it too much globalization or too little . . . too much government or too little government or ineffective government . . . not being connected to the market or being exploited by the market . . . and many more questions)?

Finally, there is the issue of leadership. The women's movement emerged in the rich world, and was often led by articulate and well-educated women. Over time it diffused to the developing world and a new cadre of leaders developed – again, with the majority of the initial leadership well educated and coming from middle class or elite backgrounds. Similarly, the environmental movement has a cross-class membership but has often drawn its founding leaders from the educated, the middle class and elite. In contrast, the poor by their very condition do not have a middle class or elite within their number. When middle class and elite people seek to assist the poor, the common outcome seems to be the establishment of public benefit NGOs, with boards drawn from the great and the good and with professional, middle class staff providing services to poor people. One major exception – and if one is optimistic perhaps the start of the world's first anti-poverty social movement – is Shack/Slum Dwellers International (SDI). This has mobilized poor urban people in 23 countries and now operates an international federation promoting the interests of the urban poor, led by the urban poor (Box 3.2).

The closest that global poverty reduction has come to achieving the status of a social movement has been when coalitions of NGOs and faith groups have committed to collaborative campaigns, particularly the Jubilee 2000 campaign for debt forgiveness. This coalition of faith groups and NGOs impacted heavily on the 1998 and 1999 G8 Summits and very effectively mobilized public support across the rich world for increased debt reduction for poor countries.[47] Its successor, the Make Poverty History campaign of

Box 3.2 Could poor people form a social movement? The example of Shack/Slum Dwellers International (SDI)

SDI was founded in 1996 and now has affiliates in Latin America, Asia and Africa. It is a transnational network of slum-dweller organizations that work together as federations promoting the interests of the urban poor. A majority of members are women, although men are also involved. A key start-up activity for SDI federations is the operation of savings and credit schemes among slum-dwellers. These are a common need and bring diverse groups of people living in a slum together. Subsequently, other important activities are identified and pursued. Achieving greater security of tenure over land often becomes a major goal and activity. SDI federations also engage in improving water and sanitation services, drawing down resources and technical advice from municipal authorities and running training programs for members.

Source: http://www.sdinet.co.za

2005, raised the public profile of the MDGs, helped push the G8 meeting at Gleneagles into re-affirming earlier commitments to increasing aid and forgiving debt and even made plastic wrist bands a fashion item.[48]

Non-governmental organizations and civil society organizations

The rise of development NGOs (non-profit and non-government agencies usually registered as charities) in the last 25 years has been one of the biggest institutional changes in the field of international development. NGO numbers and involvement in development were well on the rise before global poverty was on the international agenda[49] but they have prospered with public concern about poverty, the increases in foreign aid of the late 1990s, the decision by some donors to disburse aid through NGOs as much as possible, and donor dissatisfaction with the inefficiency and ineffectiveness of many national and sub-national governments in many developing countries. This growth in numbers has been both in the rich and poor countries. Not only have NGOs become more numerous but some have become colossal. For example, BRAC, founded in Bangladesh in 1972 as a relief organization, now employs more than 115,000 staff in that country, reaches 110 million people, has a budget in excess of US$550 million per annum and runs 65,000 primary schools. Its overseas arm, BRAC International operates in three other South Asian countries and five African countries. While NGOs are delivering basic services in most developing countries they are particularly important in poorly governed countries where state service delivery is weak or ineffective. In such circumstances multinational NGOs like CARE have become large scale, non-profit contractors for aid donors.

In the last few years the biggest change in the non-profit sector has been the arrival of a new generation of "philanthrocapitalists." This new generation differs from their predecessors in a number of ways: they have truly global ambitions; they plan to spend their wealth during their own lifetimes; they strive to use business methods to select "investments," monitor performance and ensure efficiency; and their vast wealth is often matched by a celebrity status. While Bill Gates (Box 3.3) is the most highly publicized philanthrocapitalist, this phenomenon is established in India, China, Africa and Latin America.

Box 3.3 Philanthrocapitalism and global poverty: will the Gates Foundation make a big difference?

The Bill and Melinda Gates Foundation was set up in 1994 (originally as the William H. Gates Foundation). It organizes its work around three themes: Global Development, Global Health, and the United States, where it works to increase the opportunities of marginalized groups. It works through providing grants to other organizations, rather than through direct implementation. The foundation has assets (in 2009) of US$29.7 billion, and has to date made grants of US$19.8 billion, including a US$750 million grant to GAVI, US$306 million in agricultural development grants and several large grants to support research into diseases affecting the poor. These are substantial additional funds for the fight against global poverty and Bill Gates's celebrity status means he can raise public awareness on this issue.

The turn (or return) to philanthrocapitalism is not without critics, however. Mike Edwards, for instance, argues that philanthrocapitalism

(Box continued on next page)

is detracting from civil society organizations, with possibly negative results for tackling poverty. Philanthrocapitalists are generally either very quiet about, or outright hostile towards, any idea of reforming the global economic system (presumably because it is precisely that system that has allowed them to amass the wealth to become a philanthrocapitalist). And yet, it is precisely through broad social movements forcing change on governments that the major advances in social justice have been achieved. Also, the basing of philanthrocapitalism in business and market thinking can be detrimental to civil society, placing great emphasis on technical solutions and rapid scaling-up, rather than the evolution of effective public service delivery agencies.

In the same way as sub-national governments are the unsung heroes of public action to reduce poverty, so small scale, local level, civil society institutions are often the unsung heroes of civic action. Local organizations[50] (mosque and temple committees, funeral societies, slum associations, savings and loans societies) and non-organizational institutions (neighbors, relatives, friends) are usually the first to assist poor people at times of crisis and when they are trying to improve their lives. There are many case studies of these institutions but their scale and overall significance to the goal of poverty eradication is not known. Their significance is certainly greater than the minimal mention they receive in most analyses of global poverty.

Faiths

While faith-based organizations and individuals with religious beliefs figured in much of the non-state action to promote an attack on global poverty – particularly in Jubilee 2000 – systematic action by the major faiths was rare. The main documented case is the role of the Roman Catholic Church in opposing the reproductive health goal in the Millennium Declaration and MDGs.[51] (Though it should also be noted that the "liberation theology" promoted by Catholic priests in the 1960s and 1970s was a rallying call for the poor in Latin America.) More recently Christian churches in North America, Europe and Africa have come together in the Micah Challenge and have argued that church members should promote MDG achievement directly, through personal giving, and indirectly, by lobbying for state action. The Challenge has a strong religious element and argues that the Bible is "the poverty and justice Bible" and provides prayer guides that weave a commitment to poverty reduction into the daily practice of Christianity. Interestingly, for a faith that has poverty alleviation as part of its doctrine, there is barely a mention in the available literature of Islamic positions or actions on the idea of global poverty eradication or any of the key instruments for poverty reduction – the MDGs, PRSs, finance for development, personal giving, etc. Whether this reflects a lack of interest in the issue, an orientation to individual charitable acts (based on the idea of *zakat*) or a feeling that the idea of global poverty eradication and its mechanisms are a Western agenda is unclear.

The private sector

The main role ascribed to the "for profit" sector in global poverty eradication is indirect – creating the growth that will provide more and better paid jobs for poor people so that their increased incomes take them above the poverty line. However, an increasing number of businesses are attempting to reduce poverty directly through their corporate social responsibility and fair trade[52] programs. The UN's "Global Compact" of 2000 is a systematic attempt to encourage corporations and private businesses to improve their social performance. It contains ten principles for corporate behavior covering core values in human rights, labor standards, the environment and anti-corruption. Since it was launched in 2000, more than 6,700 participants have signed up to these principals, including over 5,200 businesses. A report undertaken for the Compact found that "the Global Compact has had noticeable, incremental impact on companies, the UN, governments and other civil society actors."[53] Critics, however, point out that only 40 percent of the surveyed companies reported that the Compact had been a significant factor in leading them to change their corporate policies and that the Compact is only a voluntary code, with no capacity for enforcing companies adherence to its principals. As Surya Deva argues, "The language of these principles is so general that insincere corporations can easily circumvent or comply with them without doing anything to promote human rights or labor standards."[54] The Global Compact may just be a low costs means of advancing the private sector's public relations.

The World Economic Forum's (WEF) annual meetings at Davos gives a select group of the business world's elite an opportunity to meet with political, civil society and academic leaders and capture the attention of the global media. Judging whether the WEF is a "convener or a player," a "cabal of wealthy elites" or a multi-stakeholder forum for global problem solving, is an important question but beyond the scope of this book.[55] It is clear, however, that the increasing political and media attention given to global poverty in the new millennium – the Millennium Declaration, the MDGs, the Monterrey Consensus, the placing of the MDGs on the G8, EU and General

Assembly agenda in 2005 – meant that the WEF had to put poverty on its agenda. According to Geoffrey Pigman, "Davos 2005 lived up to its promise to advance global debate on new solutions to ending poverty," with Jacques Chirac proposing a global tax on aviation fuel to fund development, Bono pressing for total debt forgiveness, and Gordon Brown calling for a new International Finance Facility.[56] The 2,250 delegates at Davos also selected "poverty" to head their list of global priorities. The popular media were able to raise awareness of the poor's problems, with photographs of Sharon Stone passing her hat around to raise money to fight malaria in Tanzania while the broadsheets pointed out that the debates at Davos did not see "charity" as the solution to global poverty.

The WEF certainly achieves more media coverage about global poverty (see Figure 3.2), and encourages business and political leaders to make public statements about how it should be tackled, than its anti-capitalist alternative the World Social Forum (WSF). While the WSF can demonstrate greater transparency and inclusivity (100,000 delegates from 119 countries in 2005) it has not managed to achieve much of a global profile beyond already committed civil society activists. Perhaps, however, the act of engaging with the criticisms of the WSF and its support base may have helped shift the agenda of the WEF towards allocating more attention to poverty, inequality and environmental change.

Epistemic communities

Epistemic communities are ". . . network[s] of professionals with recognized expertise and competence in a particular domain and an authoritative claim to policy relevant knowledge within that domain."[57] At the risk of

Figure 3.2 The WEF's dream team for rallying support to end poverty

oversimplification two major epistemic communities can be seen as competing to shape recent thinking and action about global poverty.[58] During the 1970s orthodox liberal economists, many leaning towards neo-liberalism, formed an epistemic community that dominated thinking about international development. These "Chicago School" economists provided the intellectual underpinning for the "Washington Consensus" that promoted structural adjustment. They held the leading technical positions at the World Bank[59] and IMF and were deeply networked across ministries of finance around the world, academia and the economics profession. Although the validity of their theoretical and empirical arguments – deregulate, privatize, roll back the state – was contested by interventionist liberal economists[60] it was not until the mid- to late 1990s that their control of the development agenda weakened. But they were not vanquished, and leading interventionist liberal economists, such as Kanbur and Stiglitz,[61] faced tough times when they challenged orthodox liberal economic policy prescriptions. The allies of the interventionists, the proponents of human development at the UNDP and many other UN agencies, lacked the intellectual muscle to support the likes of Kanbur and Stiglitz within the academic discipline of economics in the United States. While the World Bank now appears to be influenced by both "Chicago"-inclined and "saltwater"-inclined (Harvard, MIT, Berkeley) epistemic communities the IMF remains firmly orthodox.[62] Interventionist economists have found it hard to establish a highly focused epistemic community as the range of positions they cover is wide and their arguments are not as attractive to, and do not muster support from, the corporate world.

New institutional forms

Two new forms of institution have become associated with the attack on global poverty in recent years – complex public-private partnerships and celebrity (while individual celebrities cannot be regarded as institutions the phenomena of celebrity can be treated as a form of institution).

Public-private partnerships

Public-private partnerships are interesting structures as their governing bodies include representatives from the public agencies (UN agencies and the World Bank) that they are designed to bypass. The best-known of these organizations are the Global Fund for HIV/AIDS, Tuberculosis and Malaria (Global Fund) and the Global Alliance for Vaccination and Immunisation (GAVI). GAVI illustrates the strengths and weaknesses of such alliances. It is a partnership involving UNICEF, WHO, the World Bank and the Gates Foundation. Its governing board includes representatives from its main partners, five developing countries, the vaccine industry (developing country), the vaccine industry (industrialized country), NGOs and nine independent specialists. Its supporters point to the US$3.7 billion that it has mobilized and argue that it has immunized millions of additional children. Its critics, however, argue that its vertical delivery approach may be good for vaccination but weakens the prospects for poorer countries to develop effective primary health-care systems that can meet the health needs of the poor across the range of problems they face.[63] Furthermore, there is evidence that the pharmaceutical companies working within the GAVI partnership have not reduced the prices of vaccines – in some cases indeed prices have risen – but have benefited greatly from the expanding markets resulting from increased immunizations funded by GAVI. Prices are still being set by supply and demand considerations and the patent system. To date there is little evidence of corporate philanthropy or changed behaviors on the part of the vaccine industry involved in GAVI.[64]

Celebrity

With a popular media obsessed with celebrity, it is perhaps no surprise that a small number of celebrities have gained considerable influence over the ways in which the problem of global poverty is framed and tackled. As for most other global social or environmental issues – saving the rainforest, climate change, landmines – no major initiative to tackle global poverty is complete without celebrity involvements. As globalization has distanced citizens from their states and the media adopts a frenetic and trivializing stance to most issues, a celebrity face helps raise the profile, and somehow enhance the legitimacy, of national and international (UN, G8, WEF) events. The conveners of such events certainly welcome the increased media coverage and the celebrities appear to enjoy meeting political and business leaders, although their motives do not go unchallenged.[65]

While many celebrities serve purely as ambassadors or compères at events, two celebrities have developed personal platforms around ending global poverty – the U2 singer Bono and the former pop star (and now successful businessman) Bob Geldof. Like other celebrities they can raise public awareness and raise money. But, they have moved beyond this and can attempt to influence the decisions of world leaders and multilateral organizations. They practice what Andrew Cooper terms "celebrity diplomacy" and at times are treated as virtual heads of state.[66] Cooper contrasts the role of Bono, the "master manipulator" (who has graduated from influencing Blair/the United Kingdom to Bush/the United States and subsequently to the WEF and G8) to that of Geldof, "the quintessential anti-diplomat" who regularly confronted leaders and agencies until his 2005 accommodation with Blair, Brown and the

G8. It may seem strange, but the public legitimacy of world leaders engaged in reforming the governance of global poverty is enhanced by the presence of aging rock stars. President Bush's decision to attend the Monterrey Finance for Development meeting and massively increase US foreign aid in 2002 was closely linked to securing a photo opportunity with Bono.[67]

Conclusion

The institutional landscape for global poverty eradication is extremely complex. Tens of thousands of organizations operating at different levels – global, regional, national, sub-national and local – are engaged in shaping, planning and implementing policies and actions towards this goal. Non-organizational institutions – faiths, epistemic communities, celebrity, neighborhoods, and networks of kith and kin – are also involved. Institutions designed to solve the problems of the mid-twentieth century work alongside late twentieth-century social movements and twenty-first-century public-private partnerships and philanthrocapitalists. While there are vast numbers of official partnerships and networks linking agencies, there are also vast unofficial linkages (between individuals, groups and agencies) sharing information and ideas and coordinating activity in ways that are often not publicly visible.

Clearly the project of global poverty eradication needs to involve many organizations, associations and other actors but why are their roles, responsibilities and relationships so weakly coordinated? There are several reasons for this but two have particular significance.

First, as observed in 2008 and 2009 with the global financial crisis, getting world leaders to re-design global institutional architectures, even when this is an urgent and top priority for their countries, has proved very difficult. Open debates highlight the different positions and no nation or alliance of nations has the moral or material capacity to attain a position of hegemony and impose an agreement. Second, for the fading powers of the twentieth century (US, Japan, France, Germany and others) and the emerging powers of the twenty-first century (China, India, Brazil and others) global poverty eradication is a relatively low priority compared to other issues – national and regional security, international trade policy, economic and financial stability, access to natural resources, energy security and mitigating climate change. Global poverty eradication might have been declared the priority at the UN's Millennium Summit when creating an impression of global unity was at a premium and powerful nations and multilateral institutions sought to bolster their international legitimacy. But, since the Monterrey Consensus of 2002, the issue has slid down the agenda of the most powerful institutions and world leaders. Tony Blair and Gordon Brown, for a mix of moral, political party and national interests, may have managed to temporarily elevate the status of global poverty at the G8 in 2005 and the UN General Assembly in 2008. Other rich country leaders do not appear to feel such personal moral responsibility, or experience significant pressure from a domestic political constituency, to match the UK position. Any hope that with the arrival of President Obama the United States might take on a leadership role for global poverty eradication has been dashed. The rise of the Tea Party now makes any concern for the "distant needy" a political liability in the United States and, like his predecessors Clinton and Bush, Obama will probably not show any significant interest in global poverty (or Africa's poor) until he is leaving office.

The second point concerns a deep paradox in the institutional framework for global poverty eradication. The framing of global poverty eradication and its placement on the international agenda has primarily been based on the initiative and energy of leaders, governments and civil society actors in rich countries – the women's movement in the United States, Jubilee 2000 in Europe, Make Poverty History, ONE, the DAC in Paris, G7/8, the Like-Minded Group of northern European countries, the United Kingdom, the Utstein Group, Bono and Geldof. By contrast, the governments, leaders and civil societies of developing countries where the vast majority of the extreme poor live have taken on only a secondary role.

Several factors explain this paradox. First, and most obviously, governments, civil society groups and activists in the "global North" have more resources and better access to multilateral institutions (the UN, World Bank, IMF, DAC, G7/8, etc.) and the international media (CNN, BBC, the *Financial Times*, *The New York Times*, *The Economist*, *Vogue*) than "Southern" actors. As a result, "Northern voices" are louder and more effectively disseminated across the world than "Southern voices." Second, the incentives operating on those leaders of developing countries who are genuinely committed to tackling extreme poverty are to achieve the best deals possible for the poor in their own countries through bilateral agreements with rich countries and bilateral negotiations with the IMF and World Bank. Pursuing cross-national interests through regional associations (such as the AU or SAARC) and the G77, or at the Boards of the IMF and World Bank, might be desirable but appears infeasible. It might be argued that China or India now has the power to lead such collective action – but, as evidenced in negotiations about trade and climate change, they are focused on Chinese development and Indian development, not global poverty reduction. For those developing country leaders who are morally committed a focus on reducing national poverty levels is as far as they can take the poverty agenda.

The materials in this chapter would appear to confirm that global governance is at best haphazard but perhaps in crisis, and that global poverty is a low priority within the processes of global governance. But the picture is not entirely negative. There is evidence of *ad hoc* advances in the system – the formation of the G20 (it is much more representative than the G8),[68] the evolution of a global poverty reduction norm in the EU (only partially institutionalized but that is a start), the capacity of the Utstein Group to promote global poverty eradication (the Group may not operate now but it shows that opportunities can be seized), the adoption of a social agenda by the WEF (it could be co-option but it opens up political space for pro-poor activists and groups to make their case to political and business leaders) and the ability of NGO and faith groups to re-shape public opinion. All of these can be viewed as strengthening the prospects for changes in the institutional landscape that might make tackling global poverty more probable – raising public awareness, developing pro-poor political constituencies, mobilizing resources, modifying international norms, opening up political space for developing country leaders and civil societies. From this perspective progress has been slow, faltering and unsatisfactory, but it has been made. Perhaps, as Francis Fukuyama would argue, the governance of global poverty is shifting from a sclerotic multilateralism to a more energized, but very messy, "multi-multilateralism" (what Fukuyama defines as "a world populated by a large number of overlapping and sometimes competitive international institutions").[69] This is much less than optimal – as authority and responsibility remain diffuse and activity is often uncoordinated – but, within the international political economy of the twenty-first century, this may be "as good as it gets."

While the institutional issues surrounding global poverty have proved hard to address there has been more progress with the "nuts and bolts" operational issues – counting the global poor, agreeing global goals, designing planning mechanisms and mobilizing additional finance. These topics are the focus of the next chapter.

Notes

1 Joseph Stiglitz, *Making Globalization Work*, (London: Allen Lane, 2006).
2 Independent Evaluation of the IMF, *An Evaluation of the IMF and Aid to Sub-Saharan Africa* (Washington, DC: IMF, 2007), available at http://www.imf.org/external/np/ieo/2007/ssa/eng/index.htm
3 Francis Fukuyama, *After the Neocons: America at the Crossroads* (London: Profile, 2006).
4 See Carol Lancaster, *Foreign Aid: Diplomacy, Development, Domestic Politics* (Chicago, Ill.: University of Chicago Press, 2007).
5 The exceptions to this were in East Asia – South Korea, Taiwan, Hong Kong and Singapore.
6 See Chapter 4 and Sakiko Fukuda-Parr and David Hulme, "International Norm Dynamics and 'the End of Poverty': Understanding the Millennium Development

Goals (MDGs)," BWPI Working Paper No. 96 (Manchester: BWPI, University of Manchester, 2009); and David Hulme, "Global Poverty Reduction and the Millennium Development Goals: A Short History of the World's Biggest Promise," Brooks World Poverty Institute Working Paper 100 (Manchester: University of Manchester, 2009) for detailed accounts of the evolution of the MDGs.

7 For example, in preparatory meetings for the 1995 Copenhagen Summit the G77 proposed the establishment of an International Fund for Social Development. This was not included on the agenda but was referred to ECOSOC. It was never heard of again. See Michael G. Schechter, *United Nations Global Conferences* (London: Routledge, 2005), 141.

8 See David Hulme, "Politics, Ethics and the Millennium Development Goals: The Case of Reproductive Health," Brooks World Poverty Institute Working Paper No. 104 (Manchester: University of Manchester, 2009).

9 See Chapter 4.

10 See Chapter 4.

11 For a full listing and details visit http://www.un.org

12 The roles played by UNICEF, UNFPA and UNDP in the forging of the MDGs are discussed in detail in Hulme, "Global Poverty Reduction."

13 Louis Emmerij, Richard Jolly and Thomas George Weiss, *Ahead of the Curve?: UN Ideas and Global Challenges* (Bloomington, Ind.: Indiana University Press, 2001).

14 See Craig N. Murphy, *The United Nations Development Programme: A Better Way?* (Cambridge: Cambridge University Press, 2006). Murphy's history of the UNDP more broadly identifies the role of UNDP in encouraging member states to focus on global issues other than violent conflict.

15 Fukuda-Parr and Hulme, "International Norm Dynamics."

16 See Chapter 4 for a discussion of the Millennium Project and Millennium Campaign.

17 Poorer parts of Eastern Europe and Central Asia may be the exception as there the UNDP has played a bigger role.

18 In addition, Martin Ravallion (interview, July 2006) points out that the major intellectual linkages of the BWIs are with economists in the United States who have pursued rational choice analyses and generally support market-based solutions to economic and social problems. As a result, "US thinking" dominates global thinking.

19 In addition, most other banks and donors will only make loans, and/or provide grants, to countries that have IMF approval. In effect the IMF serves as the credit rating agency for poorer countries.

20 This was particularly the case in the 1980s and 1990s during the era of structural adjustment when access to Bank and Fund loans entailed countries agreeing to scores of policy reforms centred on privatization and economic liberalization. With the recent entry of China into providing finance for developing countries the IMF's pivotal position has weakened.

21 The World Bank Group is comprised of five organizations – the IBRD, IFC, IDA, ICISD and MIGA. Technically these are overseen by a Board of Governors but in practice power resides with the Board of Executive Directors.

22 Sebastian Mallaby, *The World's Banker: A Story of Failed States, Financial Crises, and the Wealth and Poverty of Nations* (New York: Penguin, 2004), 3.

23 This official prefers not to be named because, officially, the IMF is committed to MDG achievement.

24 Jean-Philippe Thérien, "Beyond the North-South Divide: The Two Tales of World Poverty," *Third World Quarterly* 20, no. 4 (1999): 725.

25 Usually these are kept from the public view but when Joe Stiglitz was the Bank's Chief Economist they became daily news items. See Joseph E. Stiglitz, *Globalization and Its Discontents* (London: Penguin, 2002) for his account of World Bank and IMF disagreements.

26 See Chapter 4.

27 For an excellent example see the detailed study on Ethiopia that shows that the Bank's selective use of data allowed them to make false generalizations about policy impacts. Stephen Devereux and Kay Sharp, "Trends in Poverty and Destitution in Wollo, Ethiopia," *Journal of Development Studies* 42, no. 4 (2006): 592–610.

28 UNDP, *Human Development Report 1997: Human Development to Eradicate Poverty* (Oxford: Oxford University Press, 1997), 82.

29 See Chapter 4 and Hulme, "The Making of the Millennium Development Goals."

30 See "Senegal's Wade slams Africa Development Body," Reuters, June 13, 2007, available from http://www.alertnet.org/thenews/newsdesk/L13876054.htm

31 Fukuda-Parr and Hulme, "International Norm Dynamics."

32 On a lecture tour in Estonia in late 2009 I experienced strong arguments that in poorer EU countries "charity begins at home" and foreign aid cannot be afforded. In many of the new EU member states, particularly those formerly under Soviet control, racist attitudes towards Africans and Asians are very strong.

33 Michael Hodges, "The G8 and the New Political Economy," in *The G8's Role in the New Millennium*, ed. Michael Hodges, John J. Kirton, and Joseph P. Daniels (Aldershot: Ashgate, 1999), 69, quoted in Hugo Dobson, "Global Governance and the Group of Seven/Eight," in *Global Governance and Japan: The Institutional Architecture*, ed. Glenn D. Hook and Hugo Dobson (London: Routledge, 2007), xiv.

34 See Patrick Wintour, "The New G20 – How Will it Work?" *The Guardian*, September 25, 2009; Brookings Institute, *The G-20 London Summit 2009: Recommendations for Global Policy Coordination* (Washington, DC: Brookings Institute, 2009).

35 See Chapter 4 for a detailed discussion.

36 Brazil does not have a PRS but the Lula government is seen as creating a set of social and economic policies that has reduced poverty.

37 Chronic Poverty Research Centre, *The Chronic Poverty Report 2008–2009* (Manchester: CPRC, University of Manchester, 2008), available from http://www.chronicpoverty.org

38 Wojciech Kopczuk, Joel Slemrod and Shlomo Yitzhaki, "The Limitations of Decentralized World Redistribution: An Optimal Taxation Approach," *European Economic Review* 49, no. 4 (2005): 1051–1079.

39 For a review of the decentralization experience in developing countries see Mark Turner and David Hulme, *Governance, Administration and Development* (London: Palgrave, 1997).

40 Visit http://www.portalodm.org.br for full details.

41 Another example comes from Spain where the Spanish Federation of Municipalities and Provinces has decided to promote the MDGs to raise public

awareness and question national government commitment to its international declarations.

42 Martha Chen, "Engendering World Conferences: The International Women's Movement and the UN," *Third World Quarterly* 16, no. 3 (1995): 477–494.

43 Implicitly, this was recognized by the UN in 2002 when it set up the Millennium Campaign to raise public awareness about extreme poverty and the MDGs. In effect, this was an acknowledgment that the advance of global poverty eradication on the international agenda in the 1990s was the result of the energies of tens of thousands of organizations and millions of people – but not of a self-sustaining social movement.

44 Clive Gabay, *A Study of GCAP Malawi*, Milton Keynes, mimeo at the Open University (2009).

45 Research by the Joseph Rowntree Foundation found that poverty was not a good label for mobilizing public action in the UK.

46 This has been particularly evident in Kenya in the last few years. Kenya's population is seething with resentment over its poverty and lack of opportunities. But the elites that have impoverished the country manage to mobilize the poor along ethnic lines so that the confrontations and violence are over which ethnic elite will exploit the economy and not about how to replace these poverty creating elites.

47 Ann Pettifor, "The Jubilee 2000 Campaign: A Brief Overview," in *Sovereign Debt at the Crossroads: Challenges and Proposals for Resolving the Third World Debt Crisis*, ed. Chris Jochnick and Fraser A. Preston, (New York: Oxford University Press, 2006), 297–318.

48 It must be noted however that the Make Poverty History campaign coordinated closely with the UK government. It was criticized by more radical NGOs for being co-opted by the United Kingdom's Labour Party.

49 See Michael Edwards and David Hulme, eds., *Making a Difference: NGOs in the Post-Cold War World* (London: Earthscan, 1992).

50 See Milton J. Esman and Norman T. Uphoff, *Local Organizations: Intermediaries in Rural Development* (Ithaca, NY: Cornell University Press, 1984) for the seminal study on this topic.

51 See Hulme, "Politics, Ethics and the Millennium Development Goals."

52 Both Cadbury's and Mars have publicly committed to using only fair trade chocolate in their products. These products have a retail value of more than US$8 billion per annum. Jenny Wiggins, "Mars Goes Sweet on Ethically Sourced Cocoa," *Financial Times*, April 9, 2009.

53 McKinsey and Company, "Assessing the Global Compact's Impact" (London, 2004).

54 Surya Deva, "Global Compact: A Critique of the UN's 'Public-Private' Partnership for Promoting Corporate Citizenship," *Syracuse Journal of International Law and Commerce* 34, no. 1 (2006): 129.

55 For detailed studies see Geoffrey Allen Pigman, *The World Economic Forum: A Multi-Stakeholder Approach to Global Governance* (London: Routledge, 2007) and Kirsten Lundberg, "Convener or Player? The World Economic Forum and Davos," Kennedy School of Government Case Programme C15–04–1741.0 (Cambridge, Mass.: Harvard University Press, 2004).

56 Pigman, *The World Economic Forum*.

57 Peter M. Haas, "Epistemic Communities and International Policy Coordination: Introduction," *International Organization* 46, no. 1 (1992): 1–35.

58 For analytical purposes it is useful to treat the economists discussed here as being in one community or the other. An alternative would be to recognize a continuum with Bhalla at the neo-liberal extreme of orthodox liberal economics and perhaps Chang at the reformist liberal extreme.

59 The arrival of Anne Kruger at the Bank's Research Department was followed by a period of the appointment of only neo-liberal economists.

60 An early example was Giovanni Andrea Cornia, Richard Jolly and Frances Stewart, *Adjustment with a Human Face* (Oxford: Clarendon Press, 1987). From 1990 onwards the UNDP's *Human Development Reports* were an annual challenge to orthodox liberal economists.

61 Ravi Kanbur resigned as editor of the *World Development Report 2000/2001* rather than agree to shift the argument towards a more market-led development strategy. Joe Stiglitz resigned as Chief Economist of the World Bank because of the tensions arising from his criticisms of the IMF's insistence on orthodox liberal policies as a solution to all problems. See Robert H. Wade, "US Hegemony and the World Bank: The Fight over People and Ideas," *Review of International Political Economy* 9, no. 2 (2002): 215–243.

62 Bessma Momani, "IMF Rhetoric on Reducing Poverty and Inequality," in *Global Governance, Poverty and Inequality*, ed. Jennifer Clapp and Rorden Wilkinson (London: Routledge, 2010).

63 See http://www.healthmetricsandevaluation.org/resources/pubs.html

64 Benedicte Bull and Desmond McNeill, *Development Issues in Global Governance: Public-Private Partnerships and Market Multilateralism* (London: Routledge, 2007), 84–85.

65 For example, see Timothy L O'Brien, "Can Angelina Jolie Really Save the World?" *The New York Times*, January 30, 2005.

66 Andrew Cooper, "Celebrity Diplomacy and the G8: Bono and Bob as Legitimate International Actors," CIGI Working Paper No. 29 (Waterloo: CIGI, 2007).

67 See Mallaby, *The World's Banker.*

68 The G20 may not be globally representative but it is a great advance on the G8 as it covers two-thirds of the world's population rather than the 13 percent living in the G8 countries.

69 Fukuyama, *After the Neocons.*

4 "Doing" global poverty eradication

All change or no change?

"They [the MDGs] envelop you in a cloud of soft words and good intentions and moral comfort; they are gentle, there is nothing conflictual in them; they are kind, they offer only good things to the deprived . . . No wonder it is the juggernaut of all bandwagons."

(Ashwani Saith, 2006)[1]

"Measuring poverty at the local level is straightforward; at the national level it is hard but manageable; and at the level of the world as a whole it is extremely difficult, so much so that some people argue that it is not worth the effort.

(Angus Deaton)[2]

Introduction: global poverty and the policy cycle

The re-framing of international development as global poverty eradication at the end of the twentieth century was associated with many changes in systems and procedures. Depending on your perspective this can be seen as transformational or alternatively as a cynical attempt to disguise "business as usual." This chapter examines the practice of global poverty eradication – how activities towards this grand goal are programmed, planned, financed and delivered – and analyzes whether the changes that have occurred are merely superficial.

Identifying the main components is a challenge as this goal is pursued by almost 200 sovereign states supported by scores of multilateral organizations and associations and tens of thousands of public, civil society and private organizations engaged in advocacy and with national and sub-national plans and projects to tackle poverty. While many ideas have influenced policy selection and a vast array of institutions have been and are engaged in planning and implementing global poverty eradication, it is material capabilities, especially "finance for development" that is most often seen as the critical resource. Critical in its own right, and critical in terms of indicating whether key institutions – rich and poor governments, multilateral agencies – have moved beyond rhetoric and into action. Promoting global poverty eradication entails changing national and international economic policies and strengthening social policies. This has potentially adverse impacts on the capacity of powerful countries, corporations, economic classes and wealthy individuals to retain their control over finance and other resources.

One way of approaching such an analysis is to treat global poverty eradication as a global public policy and identify its key components through the lens of a rational-linear policy cycle:[3] what are the goals; how are policies and programs selected; how are they financed; what mechanisms are used for implementation and, how do monitoring and accountability processes operate? While such a clear policy process has never occurred for the problem of global poverty, many of the international civil servants, and some politicians, engaged in the activity have attempted to make global efforts more comprehensible by envisaging their work as part of a public policy cycle. From this analysis (Figure 4.1) the main elements of the day-to-day tackling of global poverty become evident: the $1-a-day poverty measure; the MDGs; the Millennium Project and Millennium Campaign; national PRSs; the Finance for Development initiative; processes for implementation; and monitoring and accountability processes (the UN and World Bank Monitoring Reports, special sessions of the UN General Assembly and national accountability processes).

In the following sections each of these main elements is examined. The conclusion considers whether these processes and mechanisms demonstrate

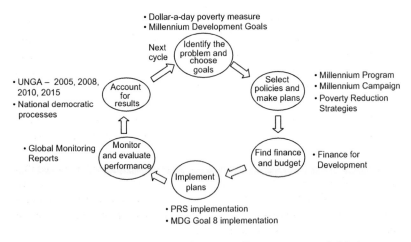

Figure 4.1 The public policy cycle and corresponding components of global poverty eradication efforts

that global poverty eradication is being seriously pursued or whether they give an impression of "all change" when in truth very little has changed.

The $1-a-day poverty measure[4]

Rational approaches to public policy demand that social issues be specified as precisely as possible and that "target groups" be clearly identified. Early attempts to mobilize efforts to tackle world poverty, such as Myrdal and Galbraith,[5] were relatively vague and saw the global poor as the sum of all poor people in low income countries. This seemed logical but, as different countries used different types of measure and had different poverty lines, it was a rather vague target group.

A technical breakthrough at the World Bank in the late 1980s – the invention of the $1-a-day poverty line – brought the specificity that policymakers like to see. It permitted the number of extremely poor people, in absolute terms, to be estimated by using a common measure for all countries. At one level the $1-a-day measure is a scientific activity around which there remain many technical debates. At another level it is a highly political activity with deep political ramifications, as it profoundly expanded the imaginations of politicians and policymakers. An old adage says, "What counts is what can be counted" and in the measurement conscious, results-based management public policy context of the 1990s the $1-a-day measure made "global poverty" legible for policymakers. If the global poor could be counted then it would be possible to estimate budgets and assess the effectiveness of different policies by monitoring how many of the poor were "escaping" poverty. It might even be possible to set quantitative targets to reduce poverty.

The breakthrough at the World Bank followed the standard three steps of poverty measurement.[6] First, the selection of a welfare indicator: in this case, the average per capita consumption of a household in US dollars, adjusted for purchasing power parity (PPP). The PPP adjustment is to ensure that the value of a dollar in any specific country would have the same purchasing power, i.e. would buy the same basket of goods and services (see Box 4.1). The second step is to set a poverty line: to identify the number of dollars below which a human being's most basic needs – food, clothing, fuel – cannot be met.[7] This requires sophisticated analysis but, as Martin Ravallion who led the World Bank team cautions, ". . . there is no escaping the fact that there is a degree of arbitrariness about any poverty line."[8] This is because determining exactly what a person's "minimum needs" are is a value judgment: it is a qualitatively different scientific activity from determining the temperature at which a substance melts.

For the *World Development Report (WDR) 1990* that Ravallion was working on, several different poverty lines were assessed. (The selection of the

Box 4.1 Purchasing Power Parity

Purchasing Power Parity (PPP) is defined as the number of units of a country's currency required to purchase the same amount of goods and services in the domestic market as one US dollar would buy in the United States. That is, PPPs convert one currency into another through equalizing their purchasing power. In general, non-traded goods and services (such as haircuts) are much cheaper in poor countries because wages are lower. One US dollar will therefore buy more in a developing country than in an industrialized country. Using market exchange rates rather than PPPs will usually underestimate the size of developing countries' economies and their citizens' real consumption.

There are, however, potential problems. PPPs are calculated by comparing the prices of a basket of goods and services weighted in proportion to their shares in international consumption expenditure. This has implications for their reliability, in that the consumption patterns of individual countries differ greatly. In particular, the consumption of the poor is unlikely to resemble international consumption patterns, being concentrated instead on basic necessities. Because of this, PPPs can overstate the value of poor people's income, arguably making the method inappropriate for comparing the purchasing power of those in poverty.

line has great significance as the lower the line, the smaller the number of people counted as poor, and thus the smaller the "problem" appears to be.) These were derived from analyzing the national poverty lines for seven poor countries.[9] The lowest poverty line that the team considered was US$275 (adjusted to 1985 PPP$) and the upper line was US$370. The third step was to select a way of aggregating the data. The *WDR 1990* chose two methods: the headcount index (the number of people below the poverty line in absolute terms and as a percentage of the population) and the poverty gap (the aggregate consumption shortfall of those below the poverty line as a percentage of the total consumption of the population). In the academic and policy literature, and in the media, the poverty gap measure is rarely examined despite its potentially significant analytical utility.

The background papers and the *WDR 1990* warned about the accuracy of the estimates – because of the low quality of poverty data, conceptual challenges and data problems with the PPP adjustments, and the arbitrariness of selecting any particular poverty line. However, once the findings fed into policy debates and the media they were headlined as the number of people "living on less than $1-a-day" (as US$370 divided by 365 days was around a dollar a day). Concerns over assumptions and dodgy data that would have greatly increased or decreased the headcount figures fueled professional discussions of these estimates for several years. However, these technical debates did not impact much on policy: for policymakers it was clear that in the late 1980s 1,116,000,000 people lived in extreme poverty and 33 percent of the population of developing countries was extremely poor. The global poor had been "discovered." People were used to photographs of hungry African children and overworked Bangladeshi women but now there was a headcount figure the pressure for something to be done increased.

Over time the data has improved in quality, the methods for manipulating data have become more sophisticated and, as living standards in China, India and other countries have improved, the poverty line has been adjusted up.[10] The 1985 PPP$1-a-day (actually $1.01-a-day) became 1993 PPP$1.08 for *WDR 2000/2001* and, in 2008, became $1.25-a-day.[11] This has led to revisions of estimates of the global poor and, in 2008, to the World Bank arguing that earlier figures underestimated the headcount in 1990 by 542 million, i.e. that there were more than half a billion additional extremely poor people in 1990 than had originally been estimated (Table 4.1). While this means that the number of extremely poor people is much greater than had originally been thought, the rate of poverty decline remains unchanged – so the 1990s and early 2000s are still seen as a period of unprecedented reduction in extreme poverty.

There are many different views as to whether the $1-a-day measure has been an analytical advance. These range from the highly technical, critiquing the methods and data, to the more ideological, as some believe the figures have been manipulated to exaggerate the benefits of economic liberalization and globalization.[12] Three specific perspectives on global poverty measures must be noted.

Public awareness and the media

The $1-a-day measures have made it easier for politicians and advocacy groups to raise public awareness and gain media coverage about extreme poverty. Having a big number for media headlines helps get attention – it probably makes no difference to media coverage whether the figure is 1.2 billion or 1.7 billion, just as long as it is a big number. In addition, the idea of $1-a-day poverty (or $1.25-a-day as it became in 2008) gives non-poor people, especially in richer countries, a feeling of "what" extreme poverty is

Table 4.1 Counting the poor: $1-a-day poverty estimates (1980–2005), in millions (as percentage of population)

Source	Measure	1980	1981	1984	1985	1987	1990	1993	1996	1998	1999	2001	2002	2005
WDR 1980	Indian poverty line	780* (36)												
WDR 1990	$370 p/a at 1985 PPP				1,116 (33)									
WDR 2000	$1.08-a-day at 1993 PPP					1,183 (28)	1,276 (29)	1,304 (28)	1,190 (25)	1,199 (24)				
Ravallion and Chen (2004)	$1.08-a-day at 1993 PPP		1,482 (40.4)	1,277 (32.8)		1,171 (28.4)	1,219 (27.9)	1,208 (26.3)	1,097 (22.8)		1,096 (21.8)	1,089 (21.1)		
World Bank 2008	$1.25-a-day at 2005 PPP		1,900 (52)	1,813 (47)		1,723 (42)	1,818 (42)	1,799 (39)	1,658 (34)		1,698 (34)		1,601 (34)	1,374 (25)

Sources: WDR 1980, WDR 1990, WDR 2000, Chen and Ravallion, "How Have the World's Poorest Fared Since the Early 1980s?" in *World Bank Research Observer* 19, no. 2 (2004): 141–169 and World Bank (website 2008).

* Excluding China

as they know what a dollar can buy. The sentiment, "Gee, how could anyone live on a $1-a-day, it wouldn't even buy you a cup of coffee," helps mobilize concern and sympathy for the poor even though the implied comparison is inaccurate as the $1 refers to what could be bought in poorer countries and not in New York or London.

Global targets

While the MDGs (see next section) set targets to tackle multi-dimensional poverty it is no accident that Goal 1/Target 1 is "halving the proportion of people living on less than a dollar a day." This shorthand version of the MDGs generates headlines and sound bites and provides an easy means for political leaders to summarize what the MDGs are about. Who could object to such a simple and humane target?

Economic liberalization, globalization and poverty reduction

Most controversial of all is the way in which some analysts on globalization began to associate the drop in $1-a-day poverty rates reported in *WDR 2000–1* with globalization. The linking of the $1-a-day estimates (with their data problems and debatable assumptions) to the complex policy changes of the 1980s and 1990s led to some seeing the invention of the $1-a-day poverty as a conspiracy to keep the Washington Consensus alive. India and China had partly opened their economies though in a much managed form, but where the "medicine" of the Washington Consensus had been most directly applied, the former Soviet Union and Africa, poverty had often deepened.

Despite the controversies around the $1-a-day measure the idea captured the attention of politicians and publics in the rich world in a way that no other attempt to present extreme poverty had done before. The $1-a-day measure made global poverty apparently real and tangible and so it became the common currency for framing debates about global poverty.

The Millennium Development Goals

The MDGs are the centerpiece of efforts for global poverty eradication. They have been endorsed by all of the UN's member states, usually by the head of state or government, and are identified as the goals of virtually all multilateral and bilateral aid agencies. Although there are many civil society critics, most of the large international NGOs now frame their activities in relation to the MDGs and the private sector in the industrialized countries increasingly talks about its role in MDG achievement.[13] One might expect that actors and agencies in developing countries would be the leading proponents of the

MDGs but this is not the case. Rich country leaders (and aid agencies) usually place greater emphasis on the MDGs than poor country leaders. NGOs in the developing world tend to highlight rights-based approaches to tackling poverty over the basic needs approach underpinning the MDGs.[14]

Although there is a widely held belief that the MDGs were proclaimed at the Millennium Summit in 2000, their evolution was much more complicated and contested than that.[15] Most of the goals within the MDGs were part of the declarations of the UN conferences and summits of the 1990s. They were drawn together at the "World Social Summit" at Copenhagen in March 1995, which converted the idea of international development into global poverty eradication. Subsequently, a set of International Development Goals (IDGs) produced by the OECD's DAC in May 1996 in the report *Shaping the 21st Century* took forward the idea of compiling a global list of goals. The Millennium Declaration drew on the conferences, summits and IDGs and also: (i) highlighted goals for rich countries in support of tackling global poverty; and (ii) removed the goal of "reproductive health for all" in response to lobbying by the Holy See and a handful of conservative Islamic states.[16] The "final" MDG listing emerged a year after the Millennium Summit in Kofi Annan's "Road Map."[17] This list was produced by the major formal multilaterals (IMF, OECD, UN, World Bank) with sufficient political guidance to ensure a "deal" that developed and developing countries could approve. After the 2005 UN General Assembly the MDGs' 18 targets and 48 indicators were extended to 21 targets and 60 indicators with the addition of targets for "decent work" and "reproductive health."

For a listing that came out of an intensely contested ideological and political process the MDGs are surprisingly coherent (see Table 1.3 for a summary and Appendix 1 for a full listing). They cover four main areas: a goal for improving the material conditions of the poor – income/consumption and nutrition (Goal 1); five goals promoting social development – education, gender equality, reduced child and maternal mortality and improved health (Goals 2 to 6); a goal to ensure the environmental sustainability of development (Goal 7); and a goal and six targets promising a global partnership for poverty eradication (Goal 8).

The MDGs represented a compromise between the BWI paradigm of neo-liberalism and UN paradigm of human development.[18] Their formatting can be summarized as "human development meets results-based management."[19] Amartya Sen's writing on capabilities helped shape the content of the MDGs in arguing for a multi-dimensional conceptualization of poverty reduction. By contrast, the format of the MDGs – a nested set of goals and targets with multiple quantitative, time-bound, objectively verifiable indicators – comes straight out of business school textbooks on results-based management. This strange marriage of left of center economics and moral philosophy with right of center prescriptions from management studies reflects the diverse interests of the many different actors who influenced the target-setting processes. Three important observations need to be made about the MDGs. First, they focus on what is to be achieved and say relatively little about how this will happen. Well before their finalization it was clear that opening debates about "what to do" would make agreement impossible. The international community of states could reach a compromise on goals but not on strategies for goal achievement. Second, the focus on quantitative goal, target and indicator achievement by poorer countries (Goals 1 to 6) reflected rich country distrust of the leaders, governments and elites of developing countries and the power of rich countries over the MDG agenda. While the MDGs were a global vision, the individual UN member states, and their various associations, were keen to ensure that they did not commit themselves to global poverty eradication more than other states and associations. Third, the content of the MDGs, the version of human development that they incorporate, is a relatively materialist "basic needs" conceptualization and not the broader vision of universal human rights or global social justice for which many of the norm entrepreneurs and civil society organizations engaged in the goal setting processes had argued.

Opinions (Box 4.2) about whether the MDGs are an historic social advance (Sachs), an opportunity that needs to be carefully managed (Vandemoortele), a misplaced utopian ideal (Easterly) or a cynical attempt to maintain the status quo while claiming things had changed (Antrobus) vary with the perspective

---

Box 4.2 Opinions about the MDGs

"The end of extreme poverty is at hand – within our generation . . . [t]here already exist a bold set of commitments that is halfway to that target: the Millennium Development Goals . . . are bold but achievable . . . [t]hey represent a crucial midstation on the path to ending extreme poverty by the year 2025."

(J. D. Sachs and J. W. McArthur, "The Millennium Project: a plan for meeting the Millennium Development Goals," *The Lancet* 365, no. 9456 (2005): 347–353)

"The misinterpretation of the MDGs . . . has tangible consequences. Nothing is more disempowering than to be called a poor

(Box continued on next page)

performer when one is doing a perfectly respectable job. The real enemies of the global anti-poverty agenda are pessimism, scepticism and cynicism . . . global targets such as the MDGs have their place but they also need to be kept in place."

(Jan Vandemoortele, "The MDGs: 'M' for Misunderstood?"
WIDER Angle (2007): 6–7)

"The setting of utopian goals means aid workers will focus efforts on infeasible tasks, instead of the feasible tasks that will do some good."

(William Russell Easterly, *The White Man's Burden: Why the West's Efforts to Aid the Rest Have Done So Much Ill and So Little Good* (Oxford: Oxford University Press, 2006))

"I do not believe in the MDGs. I think of them as a Major Distracting Gimmick . . ."

(Peggy Antrobus, "Presentation to the Working Group on the MDGs and Gender Equality," Paper presented at the UNDP Caribbean Regional Millennium Development Goals Conference, Barbados, July 7–9, 2003)

that is taken and the role the MDGs are assumed to play in international relations. While some view the MDGs as a concrete tool for planning, budgeting and monitoring global poverty eradication, others see them in more fluid terms – raising awareness, motivating support and shaping public norms over the long term. Supporters argue that the MDGs are the first global agreement to tackle extreme poverty, are re-shaping social norms and public opinion in the rich world, have gained unprecedented media attention for the poor, have reversed the downturn in aid flows of the 1990s and have improved donor coordination. Critics argue that the MDGs are too ambitious (or too un-ambitious), neglect human rights, see poverty from a residualist viewpoint, fail to appreciate the importance of economic growth, are unfair to Africa and exaggerate the role of foreign aid in poverty reduction.[20]

One way of judging such arguments is to examine the empirical record. This is complex as there are several criteria that could be used and demonstrating MDG causality is difficult. For me the "jury is still out" on this verdict. There is both positive and negative evidence.[21] The pragmatic case is clearer: the MDGs were "as good as it gets" for such efforts within the political economy of the early twenty-first century. They may be only partially honored by rich and poor countries but they have raised the hurdle and are, and can be, used to focus public attention and strengthen commitment to policies and actions to tackle poverty. One major policy change that was seen as essential if the MDGs were to be achieved was an increase in the amount of finance available for poor countries to invest in development.

Finance for development

In 2000 and 2001, looming behind all the negotiations about "what" global poverty reduction goals would look like was the question of "where" the additional resources to achieve them would come from. To avoid risking the Millennium Summit degenerating into a squabble over money, the Millennium Declaration specified that there would be a high level event in 2001 to negotiate "Finance for Development" (FFD). A number of factors delayed this event but eventually it was agreed that it would be held in Monterrey, Mexico, in March 2002.

In preparation, a committee chaired by Mexico's former President Ernesto Zedillo estimated that an extra US$50 billion per annum would be needed to achieve the MDGs. The World Bank came up with roughly similar figures. Their calculation of how much extra finance was needed to boost economic growth in poor countries to rates that would halve $1-a-day poverty by 2015 came out at US$54–62 billion per annum. An alternative estimate of the direct costs of achieving the education, health and environmental goals came out at US$35–76 billion per annum.[22] While the idea of having an aggregate figure appealed to politicians, such as Gordon Brown who latched onto the idea of "doubling aid," and was a device that helped to mobilize public support for increased aid in some countries, other technical analysts pointed out that none of the available methods could ". . . yield robust or accurate cost estimates."[23]

Up until the last minute the prospects of a successful FFD meeting were in doubt. While the EU and several of its members were talking up what could be achieved, the US position was unclear. Indeed the US position was undecided. The Bush administration was almost entirely focused on the "war on terror." Its foreign policy analysts had little knowledge of or interest in development and global poverty and they believed that engagement with the UN led to the United States having to pay the lion's share to finance programs that were not US priorities. If the United States – the world's biggest economy, biggest aid donor, biggest shareholder in the IMF and World Bank and biggest contributor to the UN system – did not show commitment to increasing FFD then the recent consensus on tackling global poverty would falter.

Fortunately for the FFD meeting, US Secretary of State Condoleezza Rice was keen that the United States show its support for the world's poor to help draw in support for the ambitious war on terror that was being planned in Washington, DC. She managed to outmaneuver Finance Secretary Paul O'Neill, who did not want the aid budget increased, by arranging a meeting between Bush and Christian rock star-cum-global poverty eradication celebrity Bono. Bono pressed the President to contribute to the money needed to achieve the MDGs and they prayed together. Immediately afterwards Bush organized an unexpected press briefing and announced he would go to Monterrey and greatly increase US aid.[24]

A few days later he and more than 50 other leaders approved the Monterrey Consensus which included a commitment to substantially increase "ODA and other resources." While the Consensus did not specify time bound targets, several leaders did. Bush committed the United States to ". . . a 50 percent increase in our core development assistance over the next three years." Romano Prodi, President of the European Commission, announced that by 2006 EU aid would reach 0.39 percent of GDP. What was being promised fell far short of the US$50 billion target UK Finance Minister Brown was pushing for but it was much more than many had expected. As a result, Monterrey was declared a success.

The available evidence suggests that the Monterrey Consensus and the Millennium Summit made a difference. Around 2000 the long-term decline in ODA stopped and in the early 2000s ODA began to increase. Between 2000 and 2005, net ODA increased from about US$70 billion to a little over US$107 billion – a rise of 53 percent. Unfortunately this apparent success was not the breakthrough it might appear. The bulk of this "new money" was once-off debt forgiveness grants supplemented by increased humanitarian aid in response to the 2004 Asian tsunami. The debt cancellations were essentially paper transactions as the likelihood of DAC members being repaid by highly indebted poor countries was negligible. In effect, this was writing off unrecoverable loans and not the transfer of real resources. If debt forgiveness is excluded then the underlying increase in DAC ODA 2000–2005 was only 2 percent per annum – well below what was promised at Monterrey. In January 2005 the UN's Millennium Project Report roughly confirmed the earlier studies estimates for the "MDG financing gap." In 2006 an extra US$59 billion in aid would be needed, declining to an extra US$32 billion by 2015.[25]

The failure of the rich countries to significantly increase long-term aid commitments spurred Tony Blair and Gordon Brown to make poverty reduction and assisting Africa the centerpieces of the G8 agenda at Gleneagles in 2005. The leaders attending this meeting responded to the United Kingdom's rallying call and promised to double ODA to the poorest countries from

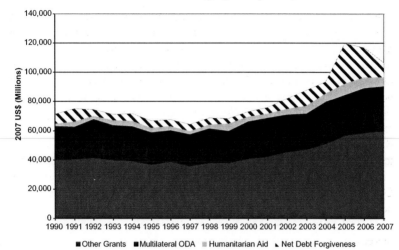

Figure 4.2 Components of DAC donors' net ODA, 1990–2007
Source: DAC website

US$25 billion to US$50 billion by 2010. This was a cleverly packaged commitment. First, it was laudable: this was a lot of money and by focusing the pledge on the poorest countries, where need was greatest, it could draw in public support and direct resources towards Africa. Second, by focusing the increase only on the poorest countries (and not on all recipient countries) it meant that aid could be "doubled" without doubling the size of aid budgets. However, the momentum behind these watered-down promises nearly stalled a few months later. The Millennium Summit plus 5 UN General Assembly meeting (September 2005) was chaotic – with UN Ambassador John Bolton appearing to be withdrawing the United States from efforts at global poverty reduction, Hurricane Katrina throwing the host country (United States) into turmoil and then President Bush committing the United States to the MDGs. The meeting eventually re-affirmed the Monterrey Consensus: rich countries would provide more aid and poor countries would improve their governance and reduce corruption.

But making promises has proved easier than taking action. Since 2005 ODA has fallen away sharply and registered a decrease of 8.5 percent between 2006 and 2007 – before the global fuel, food and financial crises began to exert pressure on public expenditures in rich countries. If debt relief grants are excluded then the picture improves, with an increase in levels of 2 percent: this sounds better but it is far below the levels needed to meet the Monterrey and Gleneagles promises. In particular, the Gleneagles promises are well off track and ODA to Africa would have to increase at more than

17 percent per annum over 2007–2010 to achieve the promised "doubling." It was hoped that the MDGs High Level Event at the UN General Assembly in September 2008 and the Follow-up Conference on Finance for Development (Doha, December 2008) would maintain and perhaps re-mobilize commitment to aid targets. However, with only one G8/OECD national leader turning up to the Doha meeting (Nicolas Sarkozy on behalf of the EU) and the heads of the IMF and World Bank both "too busy" to attend it seems likely that the financial crisis and looming public deficits in rich countries will push ODA promises even further into the future.[26]

The breaking of these promises might be less important if the original FFD meeting's aim of stimulating "innovative" forms of finance had led to new flows – but this was not the case. Gordon Brown's idea of setting up an International Finance Facility, to allow aid donors to front load aid budgets (spend future budgets by borrowing money now that would be repaid from future aid budgets) received little support.[27] Other ideas – the Tobin tax, an international tax on flights, global premium bonds, and a global lottery – were debated but no breakthrough occurred in supplementing existing sources of finance. The new mechanisms, such as GAVI and the Global Fund for HIV/AIDS, have won substantial volumes of aid but most of this comes from conventional sources and is not additional.

The Millennium Project and Millennium Campaign[28]

The Millennium Project and Millennium Campaign are, perhaps, the most rational-linear designed component of efforts to tackle global poverty. Soon after the endorsement of the MDGs in September 2001, Kofi Annan, Mark Malloch Brown (then head of UNDP) and their advisors met to work out how to implement the "Road Map."[29] They identified two activities that required new organizational bases. First, they needed to identify the best practice policies for countries to pursue to achieve the MDGs. This became the Millennium Project. Second, they needed a mechanism to propagate these policies to poor countries and donors and more generally maintain and raise awareness about the MDGs. This led to the Millennium Campaign. It was believed that these two activities would be discrete but complementary. However, once operational the Millennium Project and Millennium Campaign did not develop good relations. The bottom-up and participatory approach of the Campaign clashed with the top-down and expert-led philosophy of the Project, and the Campaign soon re-defined its role (see below).

The Millennium Project, an independent advisory body to the UN Secretary General, was launched in July 2002 and hosted by the UNDP, New York. It was led by Jeffrey Sachs of Colombia University, a highly reputed economist who had the intellectual capacity, personal commitment and ego to take on such a challenge. He approached the MDGs as a rational-linear project. The MDGs specified project targets, his job was to select the best strategies, specify and help mobilize the necessary resources and identify the means for implementation. He structured this exercise around three main tasks. First, identifying the policies and technologies needed to achieve the MDGs. This involved convening ten task forces of world leading scientists and researchers to analyze the main MDG issues: combating AIDS, malaria and TB; raising agricultural productivity; improving water supplies for slum-dwellers; re-orienting science and technology research towards the priorities of the poor and other analytical tasks. These task forces produced 13 detailed reports that were launched, with a synthesis report, *Investing in Development: A Practical Plan to Achieve the Millennium Development Goals*, in January 2005.[30]

The second task was specifying a mechanism to link task force findings into national plans. Sachs envisaged these as "MDG-based poverty reduction strategies" that would supplement or displace the pre-existing PRSPs and PRSs that the IMF and World Bank required before loan or grant approval. These would be ". . . a bold, needs-based, MDG-oriented framework . . ." quite different from the modest, incremental poverty reduction initiatives included in most PRSPs (Figure 4.3). UNDP country teams were expected to help countries shift to this more ambitious format. In practice this depended on the UNDP's political leverage relative to the IMF and World Bank in each country. In some parts of Eastern Europe and Central Asia, the UNDP made inroads, but in Africa, Asia and Latin America national governments continued to take the IMF/Bank approach. The BWIs controlled ODA flows so why antagonize them?

The third task was estimating the resources needed to implement MDG-based PRSs and working out how to mobilize them. This was based on (a) multiplying average unit cost estimates of achieving MDG targets by numbers of poor people and (b) calculating the ODA needed to supplement household and national public expenditure resources. This allowed Sachs to estimate the "ODA gaps" in rich country aid provision by 2015. It also meant that he identified the United States and Japan as the countries likely to be most responsible for the under-funding of the MDGs.

Inevitably, such an ambitious project generated tensions. Individuals within task forces had major differences in their technical judgments. Tensions also arose because of the pressures Sachs put on task forces to identify universal solutions to major problems: he called these "quick wins." These pressures were resented by many experts who felt that Sachs – an orthodox, neo-classical economist – did not fully appreciate the regional, country and social group specificity of the actions needed to achieve MDG targets. Sachs appeared unaware of the United Kingdom's Secretary for

Typical poverty reduction strategy

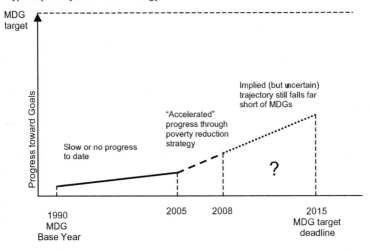

MDG-based poverty reduction strategy

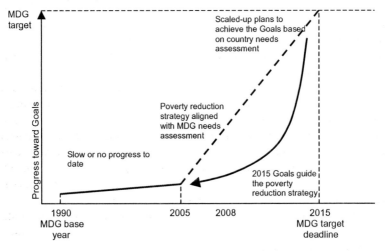

Figure 4.3 An MDG-based poverty reduction strategy

Source: UN Millennium Project, *Investing in Development: A Practical Plan to Achieve the Millennium Development Goals* (London: Earthscan, 2005), 57.

International Development Clare Short's dictum – "take the MDGs seriously but don't take them literally."[31]

However, the main obstacle to the Sachs Plan, and indeed the main reasons why its formal influences[32] were so limited, came from the BWIs and some rich countries. For the Bank and IMF, national plans and medium-term expenditure frameworks had to be based on what was judged to be affordable not what was needed. They controlled PRSs in many countries and believed that Sachs's "MDG-based PRSs" would be disastrous: these would fuel inflation, the aid could not be absorbed effectively and they would lead to a bloated state. For the United States and Japan, the levels of aid Sachs's report indicated they should contribute were regarded as totally unreasonable.

Finally, there was Sachs's personal reputation and image.[33] Many pro-MDGs and pro-aid professionals, especially those who are left of center, distrust Sachs as in the early 1990s he was a leading advocate of free markets. Why had he changed his policy advice by 180 degrees but was still claiming his advice to the former Union of Soviet Socialist Republics had not been bad? Others felt he was "just another middle-aged white man" presenting himself as the savior of Africa and Asia's poor.

Whatever the reasons, the Millennium Project had a grand launch but it rapidly slipped off the radar of global poverty eradication. Sachs himself did, however, win a substantial consolation prize. A philanthropist gave him US$5 million to trial Millennium Project strategies in Kenya and subsequent grants (US$25 million from the Japan International Cooperation Agency and US$50 million from George Soros) now support "cutting-edge, science-based solutions" in 80 African villages – the Millennium Villages. These are managed by a non-profit organization, Millennium Promise, headed by Sachs. Opinions about this experiment vary from the highly positive to accusations of them ". . . damaging the mindset of Africans. It means they expect solutions from the West and not from their own government."[34] A recent review[35] reported substantial gains in living standards in the Millennium Villages but cautioned about the feasibility of the initiative being scaled up.

The Millennium Project's "sister," the Millennium Campaign, could hardly be more different. Within a relatively short time after its inception it became almost a reverse image of the Millennium Project (Table 4.2). The Campaign explicitly takes a bottom-up approach, focuses on working with civil society, adopts a human rights focus in its work, highlights the need for accountability and better governance, eschews a "one-size-fits-all" approach, believes in country-specificity and takes a low profile approach (it wants the credit to go to its partners not itself). Depending on its activities it sometimes promotes the MDGs and at other times keeps clear of them. These two agencies may have been established by the same committee and were based in the same UNDP building, but there the similarities end.

Table 4.2 A comparison of the main characteristics of the Millennium Project and
Millennium Campaign

Characteristics	Millennium Project	Millennium Campaign
Approach	Top-down	Bottom-up
Key actors	Scientists and specialists	Civil society organizations and citizens
Strategy	Detailed plans and implementation	Political mobilization
Focus on aid	More aid, less poverty	Donor and recipient governments should be much more accountable for volume, quality and use of aid
Goal	Deliver basic needs	Promote human rights and empowerment
Role of leader	Lead from the front, high profile	Let partners lead, stay in the background
View on MDGs	Total acceptance	Useful for "newcomers" but experienced people and organizations want locally specific goals

Source: David Hulme

The Millennium Campaign is programmed to run until 2015 with support from the Nordic, Netherlands and UK governments. Around 75 percent of its US$10 million budget (2007) is spent on "national programs" in 25 target countries and the remainder on international programs. Its approaches and objectives in developed and developing countries contrast markedly.

In the rich world it has chosen target countries in terms of two criteria. First, which are the worst-performing countries (in terms of aid volume, aid effectiveness, debt cancellation and trade policy)? Second, what are the possibilities for effective engagement in these countries? On this basis it selected Italy, Spain, Germany and the United States in 2002. A few years later it added Australia and Canada. It has a continued interest in Japan but has found it difficult to find civil society groups with which to partner. In the United States it has worked with the ONE campaign and encouraged faith groups to focus on extreme poverty. In Europe it has supported efforts to re-shape public opinion about international development in Italy and Spain; this helped to strengthen support for the EU committing itself to the 0.7 percent aid target by 2015 at the EU's 2005 Luxembourg Summit.

In the developing world it targets around 20 countries in Africa, South Asia and South-east Asia. It focuses on larger countries in the belief that progressive change in these countries often diffuses to smaller neighbors through regional associations and other links. The main focus is on promoting accountability and transparency, to improve local and national governance, and thus strengthen voice and service delivery for the poor. It works with networks of civil society groups, often encouraging them to use the media (such as FM radio in West Africa) and it encourages local governments to base plans on the needs that poor people identify.

The highest profile international activity of the Millennium Campaign has been the "Stand Up" Campaign asking people to stand up and shout for global poverty eradication each 17 October (World Poverty Day). In its first year, 2006, it mobilized 23 million people. By 2009 this reached 173 million and was especially popular in India. This initiative is explicitly to raise public awareness so the MDGs are the main message. The Millennium Campaign found that the MDGs ". . . are ideal for mobilizing children and youth and newcomers to development and poverty reduction."[36] For other initiatives, and when working with experienced civil society activists and groups, the MDGs are avoided as their one-size-fits-all message is self-evidently inaccurate (and potentially disempowering). As Millennium Campaign Director Shalil Shetty reports, "we need to be discerning about precisely how to use the MDGs in our efforts for social change."[37]

The Millennium Campaign has also been influential in the formation and strategic direction of the Global Call to Action Against Poverty (GCAP), an international network of NGOs, trade union, advocacy agencies and faith groups with chapters in 115 countries. The Campaign has striven to move beyond simplistic "more aid, less poverty" advocacy and promote more sophisticated messages – about the accountability and transparency of public bodies and their commitments to poverty eradication – in the developed and developing worlds. The Millennium Campaign has played an arbitration role between GCAP's Northern and Southern members. Northerners tend to prefer short (one-year) highly focused campaigns – "more aid" or "forgive debt." Southerners see a need for innovative long-term campaigns to improve governance and raise the voice of the poor by promoting accountability.[38] In its recent strategy GCAP has decided to run multi-year campaigns to 2015, and make accountability its top priority issue.

Evaluating the contribution of the Millennium Campaign is difficult. In any activity it is only one of several actors and it explicitly seeks to have a low profile as its philosophy is that credit and media attention should go to front-line organizations. For an agency based in the UN it is exceptional – relating directly to citizens rather than governments. Its financiers, progressive North European governments, clearly think it is worth supporting.

Poverty Reduction Strategies

From a policy cycle perspective (Figure 4.1) PRSs, originally rather foolishly called Poverty Reduction Strategy Papers (PRSPs), might appear to be a component of a logically designed global poverty reduction process: the device by which global goals, the MDGs, are customized into national goals and action plans. This is not the case. The PRSP format was developed to achieve different goals and was led by the World Bank, with acquiescence from the IMF – not the UN or DAC or national governments. The timing of their "invention" over 1999 to 2002 (like the MDGs, Millennium Project, Millennium Campaign and Monterrey Consensus), is no coincidence. The civil society pressures for an assault on global poverty, as the new millennium dawned, spilled over to the Bank and IMF and forced them to develop "new" strategies and lending mechanisms.

During the 1990s the BWIs attracted much criticism, and often hostility, outside of Washington, DC (the Clinton administration seemed satisfied with them). The IMF was widely regarded as having bungled its response to the 1997 Asian financial crisis and there was increasing criticism of the poor results of its Enhanced Structural Adjustment Facility loans. These criticisms were not merely from anti-globalizing radicals, but also came from respected economists including the World Bank's Chief Economist.[39] At the same time, the World Bank was still being criticized by concerted campaigns focused on its Structural Adjustment Programs (from African, European and South Asian NGOs) and its environmental impacts (from the environmental movement in the United States). It was public knowledge that the two organizations could not even coordinate their national level operations through their joint Policy Framework Papers.

At the same time the policy environment was shifting in support of a massive, second round of debt forgiveness for highly indebted poor countries (HIPCs) in what came to be known as HIPC2. Political pressure on the G7 and OECD member states, from the Jubilee 2000 coalition, NGOs, faith groups and celebrities like Bono, was building support for a "broader, deeper, faster, better"[40] debt cancellation initiative. While the creditor countries moved towards accepting this idea they demanded that HIPC2 would have to ensure that debt relief was "spent well." Overseeing such spending and creating the new modalities would be tasks for the IMF and World Bank.

Two very different sources generated the ideas that underpin the PRSP design. The first was Uganda's home-grown Poverty Eradication Action Plan (PEAP) that was approved in summer 1997. This plan arose out of dissatisfaction in Uganda about World Bank proposals for the country to reduce poverty through a trickle down growth strategy allied to increased expenditure on primary education and basic health services.[41] Ugandan ministers and technocrats felt this was "business as usual" and they were supported by bilateral donors and international NGOs, especially Oxfam. This led to Uganda supplementing the Bank's poverty assessment with a participatory poverty assessment – consulting people around the country and drafting a plan directly aimed at national poverty eradication – the PEAP. This raised the profile of poverty and broadened the range of policies the government would use to tackle it. It also served political purposes: demonstrating to donors that HIPC money would reach the poor and that Uganda's "non-party" democracy promoted civil society participation in policy making. World Bank officials based in Kampala observed the PEAP process and reported this back to Washington, DC.[42]

The second source of ideas was the Comprehensive Development Framework (CDF) written by World Bank president James Wolfensohn over his Christmas/New Year holiday in 1998/99.[43] This sought to reposition and re-orient the Bank in response to the sharp criticisms that Wolfensohn had constantly encountered and, by drawing on the "newest" ideas about development, create a new mechanism for the Bank to work with countries. The CDF would be long-term and holistic, would be based on a Bank-country partnership led by the country, would involve civil society consultation and use the latest "participatory" techniques. It would also be results-oriented. Surprisingly, given Wolfensohn's ability to spot messages that would show him and the Bank in a good light, the only major issue the CDF omitted was a focus on poverty!

From these two very different sources – the Ministry of Finance in Kampala and Wolfensohn's holiday home at Jackson Hole, Wyoming – a set of five core principles were derived to build PRSPs (Box 4.3). These ideas matched the mood of the moment and, in record time the IMF and World

---

Box 4.3 Five core principles for PRSPs

- Country-driven: involving broad-based participation by civil society and the private sector in all operational steps
- Results-oriented: focusing on outcomes that would benefit the poor
- Comprehensive: recognizing the multi-dimensional nature of poverty
- Partnership-oriented: involving coordinated participation of development partners (bilateral, multilateral and non-governmental)
- Based on a long-term perspective for poverty reduction.

Source: World Bank website, http://go.worldbank.org/ZLBKFM2V90

Bank agreed in September 1999 that PRSPs would be their new mechanism for handling HIPC2 resources. The PRSP design provided a device by which the BWIs could explain to critics how they had changed – a poverty focus, no longer narrow macro-economics, countries would lead, partnerships and civil society participation would underpin relationships – and HIPC2 money would be focused on the results-oriented poverty reduction that creditor countries, and their publics, demanded.

As the new millennium opened the BWIs were able to signal to their main stakeholders, in Washington, DC, Paris, London and Tokyo, that they were ready for a new way of doing business: indeed, the PRSP seemed a panacea for BWI public relations, suggesting a shift from economic growth to multi-dimensional global poverty reduction. The IMF renamed its Enhanced Structural Adjustment Facility as the Poverty Reduction and Growth Facility (PRGF); the Bank's Structural Adjustment Programs were replaced by Poverty Reduction Support Credits (PRSCs); and, in 2002, it was decided that all ODA disbursed by the Bank and Fund would require a PRSP. This meant that non-HIPC borrowers would now need a PRSP. As virtually all OECD donors require recipients to be BWI-compliant this meant that an approved Interim Poverty Reduction Strategy Paper (IPRSP) or full PRSP became essential to access most foreign aid.

However, despite its apparent coherence and its commitment to a country-led development process, a number of factors militated against the PRSP initiative's achievements. First, despite "stealing" the PRSP idea from Uganda's PEAP (and related ideas in Bolivia, Mozambique and Tanzania), there was little input from developing country governments at the design phase. The PRSP process was designed by the IFIs and their key bilateral partners with some consultation with international NGOs. Second, although PRSPs were to be "country led" and "nationally owned," they would not come into effect until an IMF/Bank Joint Staff Assessment had been conducted and the Executive Boards of both institutions had approved the paper. PRSPs were clearly not the end of BWI conditionality. Third, the technical capacity of many developing countries to prepare PRSPs was limited (not least because the BWIs had been encouraging the closure of "national planning" units for 20 years and promoting a focus on short-term macro-economic management). Many IPRSPs and PRSPs were prepared, sometimes hastily, by foreign consultants. Fourth, PRSPs envisaged the processes of policy selection and prioritization as a technical exercise of evidence presentation and dialogue. In democratic and partly democratic countries, where policy contestation and disagreement was likely to occur, this "depoliticization" distanced PRSPs from the real world of national decision-making. Finally, the culture of the BWIs changed much more slowly than their documented mechanisms. In many cases they remained both arrogant and controlling[44] – as they do to this day. As a World Bank official joked in 2001, ". . . the PRSP is a compulsory process wherein the people with the money tell the people who want the money what they need to do to get the money."[45]

A vast empirical literature contains debates about the progress and achievements of the PRS initiatives. There is widespread agreement that the "first generation" PRSs (2000–2003) did not lead to significant changes in policy content or the policy process around key decisions.[46] Things have become more complicated with "second" and now "third generation" PRSs as some countries have built up capacity and become more assertive. While radical critics see PRSs as a continued sham[47] more detailed examinations show results that vary from country to country. Geske Dijskstra found ". . . the results are disappointing . . . [and PRSs have had] . . . unintended and sometimes harmful consequences" in Bolivia, Honduras and Nicaragua.[48] In Ethiopia, ". . . before the PRSP ink was barely dry, key policy decisions, for resettlement, education, water sector reforms, all differed from the PRSP commitments."[49] In other countries, such as Rwanda, Mozambique and Ghana, more favorable impacts are reported on national capacities to analyze poverty, debate policy options and select an effective customized policy response. The IMF's 2004 PRSP evaluation[50] reported mixed impacts, both beneficial and negative, on policy processes. Significantly it found that: "BWI measures of the quality of policies and institutions suggest that PRS countries generally started out in a better position than non-PRS countries but did not improve at a faster pace . . . Short-term growth outcomes in PRS/PRGF countries do not show much change from earlier periods . . ."[51] This report details many shortcomings of the way the IMF managed PRSs.

Detailed examinations of policy changes show similarly mixed results. Both the IMF and its critics agree that PRSP linkages to macro-economic policy and Medium Term Expenditure Frameworks are weak. The IMF evaluators were concerned about the lack of PRSP "feedback" into broader macro-economic policies and structural areas,[52] but Craig and Porter see this as a deliberate design of the PRSP mechanism. A shift from conservative neo-liberalism to inclusive neo-liberalism may have occurred but domestic policy debates, challenging neo-liberal macro-economic analyses, are actively discouraged by the BWIs.[53] On the positive side, for those favoring human development and social protection policies, there is evidence of a real shift in World Bank lending (also see Chapter 5 and Table 5.2). Bank lending for Human Development increased from 2 percent of portfolio (pre-PRSP) to 13 percent (PRSCs) and Social Protection from 5 percent to 21 percent. Conversely, Bank spending on Finance and Private Sector Development and Economic Management dropped dramatically, reflecting the concerns of economists who are worried that PRSPs and the MDGs are driving down investment in the productive sectors. Very few countries have related PRSPs to growth strategies and/or explored how pro-poor growth will be achieved.[54]

Many observers have commented upon the weak links between PRS policy statements and implementation. A Chronic Poverty Research Centre study of PRS implementation in 13 countries found that even in second generation PRS countries implementation was weak. PRSs commonly made statements about goals and priorities but there was limited evidence of shifts in budgets or attempts to reform delivery systems.[55]

To date, PRSs have worked well for the BWIs. PRSs have helped to improve their image without significantly reducing their influence and control over Medium Term Expenditure Frameworks that set ceilings on public expenditure and macro-economic policy in poorer countries. However, BWI influence over PRSs and development policy is now being challenged in two ways. The first is through the UNDP. Following on from the Millennium Project, a unit within UNDP continues to promote MDG-based National Development Strategies structured around meeting basic needs rather than maximizing the impact of "what is affordable" from an IMF macro-economic analysis (see above). In theory these could facilitate increased social expenditures partly supported by increased aid flows. This is a very weak challenge, however, as the UNDP's international and national leverage is very limited compared to the IMF. The UNDP can offer small amounts of technical assistance: the IMF can open up, or close down, all ODA flows for a country.

The second challenge over who shapes poverty reduction plans is potentially more significant as it comes from developing countries themselves. When PRSPs, and later PRSs, were first launched most recipient countries had little idea about what they were for or how to do them. Indeed, the World Bank had to produce a 1,260 page manual[56] and run scores of training courses on preparing PRSPs. Over time, however, countries have gained experience and strengthened their analytical capacities so that in third generation PRSs there is much greater potential for the "national ownership," originally promised in 1999, to occur. But, is the BWIs' concept of ownership appropriate for sovereign states or does this need to be re-negotiated? Zambia and Malawi re-named and re-structured their PRSs into national development plans in 2006 and 2007. In 2008 a visit to Uganda revealed that it was withdrawing from the PRS format. Uganda had unilaterally decided that the best way for it to advance the interests of its citizens was to shift from a three-year PRS to a five-year National Development Plan pursuing both growth and poverty reduction. Bilateral donors to Uganda (the United Kingdom, the Netherlands and Austria) reported being unsure about how the BWIs would react to this. It seemed unlikely that they would be brazen enough to tell the Government of Uganda that it did not have the right to choose the time frame, format and focus of its national plans. More likely were private negotiations between the BWIs and Government of Uganda that would agree that the National Development Plan will meet BWI needs for official documentation – as long as the IMF retains influence over the main parameters of its macro-economic policies. Similar negotiations around moving away from the PRS format have and are occurring in Ghana, Vietnam, Bangladesh, Tanzania and other countries.

Implementation

Global poverty eradication is an idea – it is an idea that maps well onto international institutions, global goals and international trade and finance. It maps much less well over implementation and practical actions to reduce poverty as most of this occurs at the micro-level in local health posts, village schools, women's micro-finance groups, farmer associations, community water pipes and visits by the field staff of public agencies and NGOs. Indeed, most of the grand goals and plans for global poverty eradication assume that the pre-existing, local level institutional frameworks will deliver the expanded and improved services that have been promised. The processes through which specific policy changes and programs work out on the ground – on making household or community decisions, on motivating and training field workers, on delivering services – were not directly changed by the MDGs, additional finance or PRSs. Rather, higher level changes induced by the idea of global poverty eradication cascade down, or perhaps trickle down, to implementing agencies in the form of increased budgets, improved access to medical supplies, better organized or higher paid staff, better extension advice to small farmers and many other ways.

The effects of this cascade vary from country to country, locality to locality and organization to organization. Their achievement depends on the perspective that is taken. If one adopts a transformational perspective, as promised by the global declarations, and asks "Has what happens on the ground been transformed?" then the assessment will be negative. If one takes a more incremental perspective and asks "Has the pursuit of global poverty eradication improved what happens on the ground?" then the assessment is probably more positive. While there is no authoritative, cross-country data on this topic, an interview with Armando Barrientos,[57] a leading international researcher and consultant on social protection policies and extreme poverty who works on sub-Saharan Africa, Central and South-east Asia and Latin America, illustrates the gradual changes that have and are occurring (Box 4.4). His experience (which matches my own experience in South Asia) indicates that at the national and sub-national level in several African countries

Box 4.4 The effects of the pursuit of global poverty eradication on policy implementation in Africa: an interview with Armando Barrientos

"It is simply not accurate to claim that the moves toward global poverty eradication – the MDGs, PRSs, poverty measurement and monitoring, poverty-focused aid – have not changed what happens in developing countries. In African countries you can see the changes over the last ten years. The Ministry of Finance now has to take an interest in poverty and not just economic growth and stability. As it is usually the most powerful ministry this means that poverty reduction is now on the agenda when policies are being chosen and budgets allocated. Previously poverty was the concern of the Ministries of Social Welfare: these were politically and technically weak and had little or no influence on major decisions.

"There are also more statistics about poverty in most countries – on the geographical distribution of poverty and on the extent to which public expenditure reaches those in poverty, the coverage of programs, how many children are not in school, etc. Their quality is improving and sometimes these provide evidence on the impacts of policies and programs on poverty. These data improve decision-making. There is growing interest and understanding of vulnerability to poverty which is evident in second generation Poverty Reduction Strategies. Nowadays the donors in a country are much more likely to have a poverty focus, because of the MDGs and PRSs and ministerial statements, and they are increasingly harmonizing their activities which makes it easier for governments to plan and implement. The ILO has shifted to 'decent work'; the World Food Programme (WFP) looks at social protection and not just food aid; and, in agencies such as DFID, UNICEF and the World Bank there are more country staff with professional interests in poverty. Some PRSs have opened up political space for civil society voices – look at the Livingstone Process, where African ministers and leaders discuss social protection policies, and civil society demands for social protection programs in Uganda. This knocks down to the local

(Box continued on next page)

level – it creates pressures for field staff to focus services on poor people, to set up simple monitoring systems, to set targets. Nothing has changed as much as was promised in the grand declarations and summits – but, that does not mean that change is not happening."

the mechanisms associated with global poverty eradication have raised the prospects for resources to be allocated for poverty reduction and field staff having to think more about who they serve and how to monitor the poverty impact of their actions. His account challenges those who would dismiss the recent focus on global poverty as a distraction. What is happening is far from optimal but "... that does not mean that change is not happening."

Monitoring global poverty reduction and accountability processes

At the end of the public policy cycle comes monitoring and evaluation – to allow activities to be re-programmed so that goals are achieved and to facilitate accountability for the use of resources and the levels of achievement. This is probably the area where the most publicly visible impact of the idea of global poverty eradication has occurred. The years from 2000 to 2005 saw a phenomenal increase in attention and resourcing for poverty monitoring. The primary focus was on monitoring the progress towards the 48 (later 60) indicators of the MDGs. This fostered technical debates and was also associated with a substantial increase in quality newspaper coverage (and associated TV/radio coverage) of global poverty as MDG success or failure, and being on or off target, provided journalists with a "hook" for introducing stories. The secondary focus was on PRS monitoring to see whether national PRS targets were being achieved. Both these forms of monitoring can serve a variety of purposes but two are of particular importance. These are assessing whether MDG achievement is "on track" and whether processes of public accountability have improved.

The former seeks to maintain the commitment of national governments and international agencies by regularly showing what is being achieved and encouraging adjustments in policy and resourcing. For MDGs that are "on track" or better this usually infers that present actions should be continued. For MDGs that are off track, so it appears the MDG indicator will not be achieved by 2015, then the inference is that policy needs to be improved and that additional resources may be needed. The story emerging from the many reports monitoring the MDGs has proved to be fairly consistent – there has been progress but it has been "mixed" or "uneven" both geographically and in terms of different goals and targets (see Chapter 7). Generally progress has been on track (or close) in East Asia and South Asia but off track in sub-Saharan Africa. In terms of goals then universal primary education has made progress in most areas while reducing maternal mortality has proved very hard to attain in any region.

One important point to note on the monitoring process is that both the UN and the BWIs produce separate annual reports – the *Millennium Development Goals Report* (UN) and the *Global Monitoring Report* (IMF and World Bank). Whether this is good practice, as it creates two opportunities to raise awareness and attract attention, or alternatively whether it shows that these agencies are still competing over the "UN paradigm" and the "BWI paradigm"[58] is a matter of judgment. I see competition as the main reason. While both reports agree on the measurement details the BWI report focuses more on economic growth trends and prospects and their implications for MDG achievement. Generally the UN report focuses more on the human development indicators.

While there is much technical and policy debate among professionals about the findings of these reports this data should be part of much broader political processes of public accountability. If goals and targets are on track then accountability processes should provide positive feedback to those engaged in global poverty reduction. Conversely, if goals are not being achieved then accountability processes should test whether these targets are reasonable and, if they are, should put pressure on governments, multilateral agencies and their leaders to perform better. International accountability processes are always complex and this is particularly the case when a vast number of autonomous agents are involved in producing a large number of public goods – such as global poverty reduction. Assessing the contribution, or lack of contribution, of each agent to the goal, and relating that to goal achievement, may appear virtually impossible. This issue of accountability has played out in many ways over global poverty but three are of particular relevance for this book.

The first concerns whether the MDGs should be monitored purely at the global level or whether a focus on the national level is more appropriate. The UN's Millennium Project, and particularly its Director, Jeffrey Sachs, have argued that the MDGs are "country goals" as (i) in a world of sovereign states their operationalization has to be at the country level, and (ii) they ". . . need to be applied at the country level so governments can be held accountable for signing on to them."[59] Sachs is particularly concerned that high levels of achievement in China and India would mean that global targets are met while progress in some parts of the world is negligible. Implicitly, Sachs does not trust the governments of many, perhaps most, countries. He has publicly railed against the United States and, to a lesser degree, other rich countries for not meeting targets, but he is probably equally suspicious of many poor country governments. But in attempting to demand global accountability is he undermining the sovereignty of poor countries and the right of their citizens to demand national government accountability?

Jan Vandemoortele (now retired from the UN but a member of the MDG design team) and other colleagues in the UN, believe that Sachs and others who wish to monitor the MDGs at country level have "misunderstood" the goals. He argues that they were set for the global level from analyzing historical global trends and were never intended to be applied to countries or regions. Vandemoortele is particularly concerned about reporting that identifies countries as being "poor performers," despite the fact that economic and social conditions in those countries are improving. He believes that this will both disempower national governments and undermine public support for the MDGs as national monitoring generates reports of "MDG failure." For Vandemoortele what is needed at the country level is a country-led process of defining national poverty reduction goals based on the trajectories of MDG indicators for that specific country and developing a plan to meet those targets through a series of intermediate targets (probably every three years). In this way poverty reduction becomes part of the national political agenda and can be directly linked to national budgets and plans. In effect, Vandemoortele sees the MDGs as a device for mobilizing rich country commitment to global poverty eradication, and encouraging the setting of national targets and more effective national plans by poor country governments.

In practice, accountability for poverty reduction is weak at both the global and the national levels. The UN General Assembly can agree global goals for poverty reduction but it lacks the authority to hold member states accountable for their contributions and achievements. Even in the most extreme and clear situation, with Robert Mugabe and the ZANU-PF government actively creating poverty in Zimbabwe for almost a decade, the UN has proved virtually powerless. If the UN can do nothing about a government that by all the objectively verifiable indicators has driven millions of its people into poverty and tens of thousands into easily preventable deaths, what could it do about a leader or government that was moderately "off track"? Vandemoortele's proposal for a genuinely national level accountability process is more feasible, in a world of sovereign states and in terms of relating actions to results, but it assumes that states are operating democratically and that poverty reduction is genuinely a major political concern. Unfortunately, these assumptions appear to be rarely valid.[60] In most low income countries PRSs have not set explicit goals, so accountability is diffuse, and PRSs and/or poverty have not become a central issue on the national political agenda. Instead, poverty targets and plans have tended to be documents to keep international agencies and donors satisfied – not something for citizens to take seriously. In many high income countries the situation has not been much better. National leaders and governments have signed up to agreements to increase aid, reduce debt, make trade fairer and reduce climate change. They have then walked away from these commitments and little or no demands for accountability have been made by their citizens.[61]

Conclusion

Ten years after what appeared to be fundamental changes in how global poverty eradication would be tackled (reducing $1-a-day poverty, the MDGs, PRSPs, FFD and other changes) there is little evidence that the planning, financing and implementation of efforts to assist the poor have transformed. While everything has apparently changed – policies are focused on poverty, national governments now own national strategies, poor countries and their donors work in partnership, assessments of performance against targets feed into iterative plans and accountability processes, commitments to increased aid, fair trade and mitigating climate change have been made – it can be argued that most of these changes have been superficial. The international political economy of policy-as-practice continues to maintain international relations that serve the interests of the most powerful countries, business corporations and the elites and middle classes (in rich and poor countries).

Policy statements about poverty reduction have proliferated but plans remain based on what can be afforded and not what is needed. There is a little more national control over poverty reduction plans but other key policy issues, the Medium Term Expenditure Framework and setting key macro-economic parameters, are overseen by the BWIs and especially the IMF; developing countries now own their national policies, as long as these stay close to orthodox neo-classical economic thinking; civil society can participate more in debates about poverty reduction but party politics and national assemblies make only bare mention of poverty; aid levels have risen but now they are falling back. While everything has changed in the public documents about poverty, what happens on the ground has changed very little. The power relations and economic structures that keep poverty as a low priority issue continue.

At the heart of this "all change – little change" nexus lie accountability processes. These have remained resilient to change. At the UN and BWIs there is global poverty monitoring and country reporting – but, these have little consequence. The way that the IMF and World Bank went about organizing PRSs made it clear that recipient countries would own their plans . . . as long as they met BWI requirements. The EU has committed to increasing aid but while some of its northern members seem likely to stick to this some of its other members are indicating that they will use the recent downturn as an excuse to cut back on aid. The WTO's Doha round has been declared a development round: great progress apart from the fact that eight years on no agreement has been reached. With relatively few exceptions, national governments and leaders in the poor and rich worlds can make promises about poverty reduction targets and actions and know that they will not be held to account by their citizens or put under pressure because of non-compliance with international norms. While the rhetoric of global poverty reduction has been transformed the practice has only slightly shifted in a progressive direction.

Notes

1 Ashwani Saith, "From Universal Values to Millennium Development Goals: Lost in Translation," *Development and Change* 37, no. 6 (2006): 1167.
2 Angus Deaton, "Measuring Poverty," in *Understanding Poverty*, ed. Abhijit Vinayak Banerjee, Roland Bénabou and Dilip Mookherjee (New York: Oxford University Press, 2006), 12.
3 The reader must understand that this is an analytical device. It is not the way that global poverty has been tackled.
4 For discussions of poverty measurement and $1-a-day measure see Deaton, "Measuring Poverty"; and Stefan Dercon, "Poverty Measurement," in *The Elgar Companion to Development Studies*, ed. David Alexander Clark (Cheltenham and Northampton, Mass.: Edward Elgar, 2006).
5 Gunnar Myrdal, *The Challenge of World Poverty: A World Anti-Poverty Program in Outline* (London: Penguin, 1970) and John Kenneth Galbraith, *The Nature of Mass Poverty* (Cambridge, Mass.: Harvard University Press, 1979).
6 See Dercon, "Poverty Measurement."
7 See Chapter 2 to gain a fuller understanding of the challenges surrounding such a definition.
8 Martin Ravallion, "The Debate on Globalization, Poverty, and Inequality: Why Measurement Matters, Volume 1," Policy Research Working Paper No. WPS 3038 (Washington, DC: World Bank, 2003), 10.
9 Bangladesh, Egypt, India, Indonesia, Kenya, Morocco and Tanzania.
10 The *World Development Report 1990* acknowledged that poverty was subjective and that as a country's GNI per capita rose so did thinking about where a poverty line should be set. See World Bank, *World Development Report 1990: Poverty* (Washington, DC: World Bank, 1990), 27.
11 The Asian Development Bank, *Comparing Poverty across Countries: The Role of Purchasing Power Parities* (Manila: Asian Development Bank, 2008) argues for a higher poverty line for Asia – $1.35-a-day.
12 See Sanjay G. Reddy, "Counting the Poor: The Truth about World Poverty Statistics," *Socialist Register* 42 (2006): 169–178; and Thomas Pogge and Sanjay G. Reddy, "Unknown: The Extent, Distribution, and Trend of Global Income Poverty," Institute of Social Analysis Working Paper, University of Columbia (2006).
13 See, for example, the UN Private Sector Forum of 2008 on the Millennium Development Goals and Food Security.

14 See Paul Nelson, "Human Rights, the Millennium Development Goals, and the Future of Development Cooperation," *World Development* 35, no. 12 (2007): 2041–2055.

15 See David Hulme, "Global Poverty Reduction and the Millennium Development Goals: A Short History of the World's Biggest Promise," Brooks World Poverty Institute Working Paper 100 (Manchester: University of Manchester, 2009) and Sakiko Fukuda-Parr and David Hulme, "International Norm Dynamics and 'the End of Poverty': Understanding the Millennium Development Goals (MDGs)," BWPI Working Paper No. 96 (Manchester: BWPI, University of Manchester, 2009).

16 See David Hulme, "Politics, Ethics and the Millennium Development Goals: The Case of Reproductive Health," Brooks World Poverty Institute Working Paper No. 104 (Manchester: University of Manchester, 2009) for a full account.

17 "Road Map towards the Implementation of the United Nations Millennium Declaration," report of the Secretary-General to the UN General Assembly, A/56/326, September 6, 2001.

18 See Jean-Philippe Thérien, "Beyond the North-South Divide: The Two Tales of World Poverty," *Third World Quarterly* 20, no. 4 (1999): 723–742; and Alain Noel, "The New Global Politics of Poverty," *Global Social Policy* 6, no. 3 (2005): 304–333.

19 See David Hulme, "The Making of the Millennium Development Goals: Human Development Meets Results-Based Management in an Imperfect World," BWPI Working Paper No. 16 (Manchester: University of Manchester Press, 2008).

20 William Easterly, "Can the West Save Africa?" *Journal of Economic Literature* 47, no. 2 (2009): 373–447; William Russell Easterly, *The White Man's Burden: Why the West's Efforts to Aid the Rest Have Done So Much Ill and So Little Good* (Oxford: Oxford University Press, 2006); Sakiko Fukuda-Parr, "Millennium Development Goal 8: Indicators for International Human Rights Obligations?" *Human Rights Quarterly* 28, no. 4 (2006): 966–997; and Thomas Pogge, *World Poverty and Human Rights: Cosmopolitan Responsibilities and Reforms* (Cambridge: Polity, 2008).

21 See David Hulme, "Governing Global Poverty? Global Ambivalence and the Millennium Development Goals," in *Global Governance, Poverty and Inequality*, ed. Jennifer Clapp and Rorden Wilkinson (London: Routledge, 2010) for a listing of this evidence and also see Chapter 7.

22 Shantyanan Devarajan, Margaret Miller and Eric V. Swanson, "Goals for Development: History, Prospects, and Costs," World Bank Policy Research Working Paper No. 2819 (2002).

23 Jan Vandermoortele and Rathin Roy, *Making Sense of MDG Costing* (New York: Bureau for Development Policy, UNDP, 2004).

24 For a detailed account see Sebastian Mallaby, *The World's Banker: Story of Failed States, Financial Crises, and the Wealth and Poverty of Nations* (New York: Penguin, 2004).

25 UN Millennium Project, *Investing in Development: A Practical Plan to Achieve the Millennium Development Goals* (London: Earthscan, 2005), 249.

26 Although the rich world governments have not pushed the point they could argue that poorer countries have not kept their part of the Monterrey bargain. There is little evidence that many recipient countries have significantly improved their governance or reduced corruption.

27 In a face-saving move a few friends helped Brown set up the much less ambitious International Finance Facility for Immunization.

28 Materials in this section are drawn from interviews with Guido Schmidt-Traub (September 17, 2007), Evelene Herfkens (September 19, 2007), Salil Shetty (September 19, 2007), Selim Jehan (September 17, 2007), Rathin Roy (September 17, 2007) and Sakiko Fukuda-Parr (June 29, 2007).

29 Annan, "Road Map."

30 UN Millennium Project, *Investing*. See this for more details on this section.

31 Interview, 19 July, 2007.

32 The Plan's informal influence – through task force discussions, people reading the documents, etc. – may have been greater than its formal impact on policies and budgets.

33 Sachs is an enigmatic figure. He has many supporters, indeed a group of professionals sometimes described as "disciples." He is the scientific/professional face of global poverty eradication making scores of presentations each year and his writings are widely circulated (in print and on the Internet). He is the leading figure in the United States demanding that the government increase its "stingy" aid levels. Conversely, he is a figure whom many of the people I have interviewed (in the UN, United States, bilateral aid agencies, academics, NGO staff) for this book went out of their way to criticize. Sometimes this was personal, for his ego and assertiveness, at other times it was strategic – he is seen as setting up MDG efforts for a fall by exaggerating the knowledge base on poverty reduction and underestimating the challenges of implementation.

34 Eveline Herfkens (September 19, 2007).

35 Kent Buse, Eva Ludi and Marcella Vigneri, *Beyond the Village: Sustaining and Scaling up the Millennium Villages* (London: ODI, 2008).

36 Interview Salil Shetty (September 19, 2007).

37 Interview, September 19, 2007.

38 But do note that Clive Gabay's work on GCAP in Malawi found the national network there very dependent on taking a lead from the UNDP.

39 Joseph E. Stiglitz, *Globalization and Its Discontents* (London: Penguin, 2002).

40 See Karin Christiansen and Ingle Holvard, "The PRSP Initiative: Multilateral Policy Change and the Role of Research," ODI Working Paper No. 216 (London: ODI, 2003) for a detailed discussion of these pressures and related issues.

41 Christiansen and Holvard, "The PRSP Initiative," 21–23.

42 A widely told joke at the Ministry of Finance in Kampala runs: "The World Bank saw what we were doing and wrote down a description of the PEAP process. They sent that back to DC where people changed the initials from PEAP to PRSP. Two years later other Bank staff visited us to teach us about the Bank's amazing new process – the PRSP" (interview, Margaret Kakande, March 28, 2007).

43 For a full account see chapter 9 of Mallaby, *The World's Banker*.

44 This was most evident to me in February 2002 at two meetings at the World Bank office in Dhaka. At the first a World Bank official described to me the great changes in Bank relations with the Government of Bangladesh because of the PRSP process. At the next meeting the senior economist negotiating a PRSC had a quite different position: ". . . they [the Government of Bangladesh] either agree to these three conditions and start to make changes now or they get nothing . . . you just can't trust them."

45 My colleague Sam Hickey has a different take on this – "With PRSPs, instead of the BWIs and donors telling developing countries what to do, developing countries now have to tell BWIs/donors what they want to hear."

46 Participatory processes (PPAs) and civil society consultations became de rigueur but these were often as an add-on. When Uganda's second PPA (UPPAP2) of 2001 found many Ugandans reporting that things were getting worse, Paul Collier, a World Bank Research Director, publicly stated that ". . . they are simply wrong" (ABCDE, Oslo, June 2002). Also see Oxfam, "From 'Donorship' to 'Ownership'," Oxfam Briefing Paper (Oxford: Oxfam, 2004); Jennie Richmond and Paul Ladd, "Ignoring the Experts: Poor Peoples' Exclusion from Poverty Reduction Strategies," Christian Aid Policy Brief (London: Christian Aid, 2001); Frances Stewart and Michael Wang, *Report on the Evaluation of Poverty Reduction Strategy Papers (PRSPs) and the Poverty Reduction and Growth Facility (PRGF)* (Washington, DC: IMF, 2004).

47 See Paul Cammack, "The Mother of All Governments: The World Bank's Matrix for Global Governance," in *Global Governance: Critical Perspectives*, ed. Rorden Wilkinson and Steve Hughes (New York: Routledge, 2002).

48 Geske Dijkstra, "The PRSP Approach and the Illusion of Improved Aid Effectiveness: Lessons from Bolivia, Honduras and Nicaragua," *Development Policy Review* 23, no. 4 (2005): 443–464.

49 David Craig and Douglas R. Porter, *Development beyond Neoliberalism?: The Poverty Reduction Paradigm* (London: Routledge, 2005), 88.

50 IMF Independent Evaluation Office, *Report on the Evaluation of Poverty Reduction Strategy Papers (PRSPs) and the Poverty Reduction and Growth Facility (PRGF)* (Washington, DC: IMF, 2004).

51 IMF Independent Evaluation Office, *Report*, 120.

52 IMF, 120.

53 Craig and Porter, *Development beyond Neoliberalism?* 93.

54 In Ghana, Malawi and Tanzania the governments had separate National Development Strategies for economic development running alongside PRSs. See David Peretz *Learning from Experience: Perspectives on Poverty Reduction Strategies from Four Developing Countries* (London: Commonwealth Secretariat, 2009).

55 CPRC, *Chronic Poverty Report 2008–09: Escaping Poverty Traps* (Manchester: CPRC, 2008), 32–35. See also Issac Shinyekwa and Samuel Hickey, "PRS Review: Uganda Case Study," Background Paper to the *Chronic Poverty Report 2008–09* (Manchester: CPRC, 2007), and other background papers to the Report, available from http://www.chronicpoverty.org/page/background-papers

56 Jeni Klugman, ed., *A Sourcebook for Poverty Reduction Strategies* (Washington, DC: World Bank, 2002).

57 Professor Barrientos is Professor of Poverty and Social Justice at the University of Manchester and Research Director of the Brooks World Poverty Institute.

58 Thérien, "Beyond the North-South Divide."

59 UN Millennium Project, *Investing*, 3.

60 Exceptions include Brazil and Chile where parties have had to compete over poverty reduction policies, and the United Kingdom where policy towards global poverty reduction is seen as an issue, but not a leading issue, for voters.

61 This is particularly evident in Italy which promised to double its aid budget to Africa at the Gleneagles meeting of the G7 in 2005. By 2010 it had reduced this budget by 6 percent from its 2005 level. While One, the charity led by Bono and Bob Geldof, called for Italy to be "kicked out" of the G7, in Italy the issue was barely noted (*The Guardian*, 25 May 2010, 23).

5   Strategic choices for global poverty eradication

"It is a tragic mix-up when the United States spends $500,000 for every
enemy soldier killed, and only $53 annually on the victims of poverty."

(Martin Luther King)

"Poverty is the most powerful weapon of mass destruction."

(Mohamed El Baradei)

The Millennium Declaration and the Millennium Development Goals (MDGs)
suggest there is a broad agreement that global poverty is a moral problem for
all of humanity and that "something must be done." However, such documents carefully avoid specifying how the goals should be achieved as there
are fierce debates about exactly what strategies should be chosen to tackle
global poverty and who should do it. Some of these debates still run along
the old, ideological fracture lines of capitalism versus socialism, or nowadays
capitalism versus anti-capitalism. But increasingly, policy debates about how
best to tackle global poverty are framed in the nuanced style of the "third
way" and seek to go "beyond left and right"[1] and identify "what works" in
different places at different times.

In this chapter the most important debates about strategies for global
poverty eradication are examined. The first section explores the choice of
national development strategy and the influences of multilateral institutions
over such choices. This is framed in terms of whether countries should pursue the orthodox neo-classical economic frameworks favored by the BWIs,
focused on achieving economic growth through economic liberalization
and trade, or the country-specific strategies with a greater role for the state
that UN agencies prefer. The second section examines international trade
policy, the operations of the WTO and the vexed debates around intellectual property rights. It also touches on the role of "fair trade" in generating

economic benefits and changing public attitudes. The third section analyses the arguments around foreign aid: is it essential for global poverty reduction or does it, as some critics argue, cause poverty? The next section moves beyond these historical pillars of debates about development and examines the idea that a focus on trade and aid policies fails to understand the nature of development: ". . . development is something largely determined by poor countries themselves . . ." This leads to a focus on what happens within poor countries and particularly in poorly governed or fragile states where so many poor people live. Rather than talking about aid and trade, do outsiders need to think about whether or not they can do anything to reduce conflict or build peace? The conclusion focuses on a common issue that underpins all of these strategic choices – the inability of the structures and processes of global governance to adapt to the problems and emerging power relations of the twenty-first century.

What is the best national strategy: orthodox or heterodox?

It is important to distinguish between two distinct forms of debate about choices of national strategy. These are linked but operate in very different ways. The first and most voluble form is public debate,[2] seeking to influence choice of strategy in individual countries and/or internationally. The second form is reserved for small groups of elite actors as, for example, when Ministers of Finance and Treasury officials meet with IMF and World Bank representatives to discuss their country's Medium Term Expenditure Framework, set macro-economic targets (such as maximum inflation rates) and consider budgetary allocations. Sometimes the public debates influence the elite discussions but at other times they seem to operate in parallel, as when the World Bank and IMF espouse "country ownership" of strategies and plans in public but privately tell the country what the policies will be.

Contemporary policy debates (what some call the "development discourse") have evolved out of, and often build on, decades of argument about development strategy. Historically, these debates were often more polarized than they are in the early twenty-first century. In the 1960s and 1970s the debate contrasted mixed economy, capitalist strategies with autarkic development based on radical delinking from the world economy. In the 1980s structural adjustment policies dominated but in the 1990s the debate contrasted this neo-liberal, economic growth-focused strategy with a mixed economy, human development strategy.[3] In the early twenty-first century the debates are more nuanced, with leading researchers and development agencies debating how growth can be made pro-poor (through market and state action), the relative prioritization of human development policies (which contribute most to well-being and which contribute most to future economic growth) and the best forms of service delivery (public or private or partnerships). This does not mean that everyone is "in the center" as some strategies, and the hybrid policies within them, are closer to a neo-liberal position, while other strategies are closer to a state-directed mixed economy position.

The position of the World Bank Research Department and the *World Development Report* has moved significantly closer to a UN position (UNDESA and *Human Development Reports*) since the mid-1990s with the recognition of the role of the state and the problems that inequality raises for tackling poverty.[4] However, this gradual shift of position in the Bank's research findings and policy recommendations was highly contested. For example, a widely reported paper by Dollar and Kraay argued that "growth is good for the poor" and attempted to ensure that policy prioritized economic liberalization.[5] Before it had been peer reviewed, the findings of this paper were reported in influential media such as *The Economist* and *Financial Times*[6] virtually as the First Law of Development Economics, even though internally other Bank researchers were questioning the robustness of the conclusions, the paper's methodology and the validity of the findings. Subsequently an independent evaluation of the Bank's research found that ". . . much of this line of research appears to have such deep flaws that at present, the results cannot be regarded as remotely reliable."[7] The Dollar and Kraay paper was criticized on a number of grounds, including that it utilized flawed statistical modeling; was based on unsafe data; drew conclusions that were not supported by the data; masked the large variation between countries in how much the poor share in growth; and drew results that were highly sensitive to changes in the sample of countries examined.[8]

In 2006 the highly respected economist Angus Deaton chaired an evaluation into the Bank's Research Department and the use to which research was put. His report worryingly pointed out that the Bank's research findings were not always reliable: the cross-country analyses that it used in the late 1990s and early 2000s were hard to interpret, particularly when trying to infer a direction for causality. Despite its understanding of these methodological flaws, the Bank's Research Department, Deaton's evaluation argued, used relatively new and untested research that supported the Bank's pro-globalization stance to ". . . proselytize on behalf of Bank policy, often without taking a balanced view of the evidence, and without expressing appropriate skepticism. Internal research that was favorable to Bank positions was given great prominence, and unfavorable research ignored."[9]

Perhaps the clearest evidence of these contests within the Bank shifting towards a position closer to the UN position comes from the 2005 World Bank Report, *Economic Growth in the 1990s: Learning from a Decade of Reform.* This focuses on growth policies, aimed at reducing poverty, and in essence writes-off the Washington Consensus strategy of the 1990s. As Dani Rodrik expresses it, "Occasionally, the reader has to remind himself that the book he is holding is not some radical manifesto, but a report prepared by the seat of orthodoxy in the universe of development policy."[10] The Report charts the dismal growth results of the policies recommended by the Bank and IMF in the 1990s and provides an explanation of why they failed. First, the focus on achieving efficiency gains (through privatization and liberalization) was not a means of stimulating dynamic growth processes; second, the Washington Consensus belief that macro-economic stability, a more outward orientation to trade and market-based incentives could only be achieved by policies to ". . . minimize fiscal deficits, minimize inflation, minimize tariffs, maximize privatization, maximize liberalization of finance"[11] was incorrect as these ". . . are just *some* of the ways in which these principles can be implemented." Third, the Report recognizes country heterogeneity – different contexts will require different policies. Finally, the Report found that countries might do better if they tackled a small number of binding constraints, and carefully learned from that experience, rather than leaping into implementing the ten elements of the Washington Consensus prescription all at the same time (see Table 5.1). The conclusions to be drawn from the 2005 Report are that country-specific and country-owned growth strategies need to be pursued;[12] something that brings the Bank, or at least its discourse, closer to UN-style (UNDESA, UNDP, UNCTAD) positions on a more heterodox economic approach to policy that involves both state and market.

Across the road from the World Bank, at the IMF there was agreement that the Washington Consensus policies of the 1990s had been disappointing but a quite different diagnosis of why this had happened. The IMF's 2005 review *Stabilization and Reform in Latin America*[13] concluded that structural adjustment had not succeeded because its reform package had not gone deep enough: the policy reforms of the original Washington Consensus needed to be augmented by a set of institutional reforms. One size would fit all; it just needed to be a bigger size than the original, what Rodrik has summarized as the "Augmented Washington Consensus" (Table 5.1).

This partial and public distinguishing of the policy positions of the Bank and IMF means that contemporary debates are less clearly structured than the "Washington Consensus versus anti-Washington Consensus" of the late twentieth century. The Bank's public discourse has moved closer to UN-type positions with its increased sectoral eclecticism (countries need to pursue

Table 5.1 The Washington Consensus and "Augmented" Washington Consensus

Original Washington Consensus	"Augmented" Washington Consensus – the previous ten items, plus:
Fiscal discipline	Corporate governance
Reorientation of public expenditures	Anti-corruption
Tax reform	Flexible labor markets
Financial liberalization	WTO agreements
Unified and competitive exchange rates	Financial codes and standards
Trade liberalization	"Prudent" capital-account opening
Openness to FDI	Non-intermediate exchange rate regimes
Privatization	Independent central banks/inflation targeting
Deregulation	Social safety nets
Secure property rights	Targeted poverty reduction

Source: Dani Rodrik, "Goodbye Washington Consensus, Hello Washington Confusion? A Review of the World Bank's Economic Growth in the 1990s: Learning from a Decade of Reform," *Journal of Economic Literature* 44, no. 4 (2006): 973–987.

growth, human development, social protection and better governance) and the recognition of country heterogeneity (different countries need different strategies and, strategies need to be domestically owned). But, there are still major debates about whether the Bank prioritizes macro-economic stability and economic growth to such a degree that expenditures on education, health and social protection are constrained – reducing progress towards the MDGs, constraining human development, increasing present-day suffering and reducing the potential of people to contribute to economic growth and social progress in the future. It can also be argued that the Bank automatically prefers the provision of services by private agencies, or public-private partnerships, regardless of differences in the quality of public provision in different countries. The Bank can point to its shift of expenditure into human development in the late 1990s, and its leap into "social protection and risk" in the 2000s to challenge such criticisms (Table 5.2).[14] It can also argue that it has gradually backed-off from its policy conditionalities about privatization, deregulation and other issues.[15]

The distinction between public debates about development strategy, by the World Bank and IMF and others, and the closed door discussions between the World Bank, IMF and borrowing country governments is important. We know that World Bank practice in the field differs, or at best lags behind, Bank research findings and policy declarations from Washington, DC.[16] In addition, we know that even in the heady days of both the Bank and IMF being wedded to full-blooded neo-liberalism there were significant differences between the two agencies over the speed and sequencing of economic

Table 5.2 Sectoral share of World Bank investments pre- and post-PRSPs

Thematic focus	Pre-PRSP adjustment lending (% of total)	Thematic focus of PRSPs (% of total)
Public sector governance	23	26
Human development	2	13
Finance and private sector development	40	19
Environment and natural resources	3	6
Economic management	17	0
Urban development	1	4
Trade and integration	5	4
Social protection and risk	5	21
Social development/gender	1	
Rural development	1	7
Rule of law	2	

Source: World Bank Operations Evaluation Department, "The Poverty Reduction Strategy Initiative: An Independent Evaluation of the World Bank's Support through 2003" (Washington, DC: World Bank, 2004), 40.

liberalization and deregulation.[17] Such differences are likely to be more common nowadays, given the different interpretations these agencies have of the 1990s policy reform experience, and so any belief that the Bank's policies will be better informed needs to be tempered by the recognition that in practice the IMF may be able to stall changes in strategy by its control over Medium Term Expenditure Frameworks[18] and key macro-economic parameters. Whether the efforts of Dani Rodrik and colleagues at Harvard to persuade the Bank and IMF ". . . to be skeptical of top-down, comprehensive, universal solutions . . . [and that] the requisite economic analysis . . . has to be done case by case," is a topic for empirical research.[19] It is much easier for institutions to change their policy statements than to change deeply held tenets of their organizational culture. The way in which the IMF caused severe teacher shortages in Malawi, Mozambique and Sierra Leone, and reduced prospects for the achievement of the education targets of the MDGs simply to achieve arbitrary public expenditure ceilings, illustrates what an obstacle the Fund remains to the evolution of country-specific development strategies (Box 5.1).

Trade policy: free trade, heterodox policies and fair trade

The consensus that has evolved around the centrality of economic growth to poverty reduction has not been matched by agreement on what this means for trade policy (and industrial policy). In the post-war period, the principal trade debate was between liberal trade policies versus more restrictive import substitution industrialization – the use of trade measures to protect industries that competed with imported products in an effort to bring about rapid industrialization and reduce dependence on imports. In the 1980s there was a significant shift away from import substitution towards greater trade liberalization, partly due to conditionality attached to World Bank and IMF loans. Nonetheless, the debate over whether free trade is the optimum policy for developing countries, as most orthodox neo-classical economists assert, continues. In particular, debate both within the WTO and within academic circles centers on the need for "policy space" or "development space" for developing countries in their trade relations.

For critics of the free trade orthodoxy, such as Robert Wade, "the 'development space' for diversification and upgrading policies in developing countries is being shrunk behind the rhetorical commitment to universal liberalization and privatization."[20] These critics argue that developing countries need to be able to use targeted trade protection to shelter infant industries while they build themselves up into a position in which they are able to compete on global markets.[21] In support of this, they point to the policies of those countries that have successfully industrialized, notably the

Box 5.1 How the IMF controls development strategy in poor countries

The Independent Evaluation Office of the IMF conducted an evaluation of the role and performance of the IMF in determining the volume and use of aid in low income sub-Saharan Africa over 1999–2005. It found that:

> A recurring theme of the evaluation concerned the disconnect in external perceptions between the IMF's rhetoric on aid and poverty reduction and what it actually did at country level . . . Underlying the theme of disconnect is a larger issue of attempted – but ultimately unsuccessful – institutional change . . . [with] . . . a staff professional culture strongly focused on macroeconomic stability . . . the IMF gravitated back to business as usual.

One of the results of this "business as usual" was the setting of arbitrary ceilings on public expenditure and the IMF "blocking" the use

(Box continued on next page)

of aid. In its carefully worded way this Report revealed how the IMF had publicly declared its commitment to more heterodox policies while continuing to push poor countries into orthodox, neo-classical policies. A related ActionAid study explored the consequences of this in detail and found that ". . . in Malawi, Mozambique and Sierra Leone . . . a major factor behind the chronic and severe shortage of teachers is that the International Monetary Fund (IMF) policies have required many poor countries to freeze or curtail teacher recruitment." When challenged by ActionAid, the IMF was not able to explain: "How are the [public expenditure] ceilings calculated? By whom? Are they too low as a result?"

Sources: Independent Evaluation of the IMF, *An Evaluation of the IMF and Aid to Sub-Saharan Africa* (Washington, DC: IMF, 2007), available at http://www. imf.org/external/np/ieo/2007/ssa/eng/index.htm; and ActionAid, *Confronting the Contradictions: The IMF, Wage Bills and the Case for Teachers*, April 2007, available at http://www.actionaid.org/main.aspx?PageID=581

newly industrialized countries of East Asia and before them the European and New World countries when they were catching up with Great Britain. All of these countries used a range of protective measures during their period of industrialization to protect their infant industries until they were competitive. Proponents of the policy space view argue that developing countries need to be able to repeat these successful policies, and that the WTO therefore needs to provide them the opportunity to raise tariffs if necessary. Those more in favor of free trade see the restriction WTO agreements place on trade policy as being one of the key benefits of WTO membership for developing countries, in that it prevents their governments from giving in to pressure from domestic interests for protection of inefficient industries.

The creation of the WTO with the completion of the Uruguay Round of trade negotiations extended multilateral trade regulation far beyond the area of industrial goods on which its predecessor, the GATT, was focused. Notably, the Uruguay Round was the first trade round to deal comprehensively with agriculture. Agriculture continues, however, to be the most difficult part of negotiations in the present Doha Round, creating difficulties for both developed and developing countries. The industrialized countries are unwilling to make substantial cuts to the subsidies that they pay to their farmers, despite the damage these subsidies do to farmers in developing countries by depressing world prices for agricultural products. A particular bone of contention has been the subsidies paid to cotton farmers by the United States, which have been estimated to depress world cotton prices by 26 percent.[22] These subsidies detrimentally affect cotton farmers in other countries, especially the "Cotton Four" of Burkina Faso, Benin, Chad and Mali (some of the poorest countries in the world), which have pushed this issue in the Doha Round, to little avail. Liberalization of agriculture has also been problematic for some developing countries that have large numbers of relatively inefficient, small scale farmers. Such countries, notably India, are wary of opening up their markets to cheap agricultural imports, fearful that this will devastate the livelihoods of peasant farmers reliant on producing food for local markets and politically destabilize rural areas. To protect food and livelihood security, in any Doha Round deal that eventually emerges developing countries will be allowed a certain number of "special products" that will be subject to smaller tariff cuts, and a "special safeguard mechanism" will be put in place that will allow the temporary raising of tariffs in the event of a surge in imports. The exact details of these have proven to be highly difficult to negotiate, however, as the farmer-agribusiness lobbies in many rich countries, especially the United States and France, are powerful political constituencies.

The Uruguay Round created other areas of contention between the developed and developing world, particularly in the area of intellectual property. The Agreement on Trade Related Intellectual Property Rights (TRIPs), signed as part of the Uruguay Round, made countries apply minimum standards of copyright and intellectual property protection. TRIPs subsequently received a great deal of criticism by NGOs and academics, particularly for raising the costs of AIDS drugs to poor countries which had previously been importing generic drugs. Such generic drugs are up to 90 percent cheaper than brand-name drugs,[23] but contravened TRIPs by failing to respect the patents held by the pharmaceutical companies that had first developed the drugs. With the implementation of TRIPs, developing countries had to pay the substantially higher prices for patented drugs. For those countries in Africa that are suffering from high rates of HIV/AIDS infection, the costs of providing anti-retroviral drugs suddenly became prohibitively expensive. Pressure from NGOs and developing countries led to an agreement reached at the 2003 WTO Ministerial Meeting in Cancun to make it easier for countries to import generic drugs to tackle health crises. However, this decision has been criticized for requiring an onerous and bureaucratic process to be completed before a compulsory license can be granted. Partly as a result of this, it was four years before the first case to make use of the provisions was completed.

TRIPs has also been criticized for its effect on developing countries' attempts to catch up technologically with the more advanced countries.

In previous eras, those countries attempting to catch up technologically have employed weak intellectual property rights to facilitate the adoption and copying of cutting-edge technology at low cost. As the Commission on Intellectual Property Rights set up by the UK's then Secretary for International Development Clare Short put it,

> Historically, now-developed countries used IP protection as a flexible instrument to help promote their industrialization. Discrimination against foreigners – by refusing them the right to IP protection or by charging higher fees – was common, as was the exclusion of entire sectors, such as food or pharmaceuticals, from patentability.[24]

TRIPs imposes a level of intellectual property protection that restricts the policy space developing countries have in this area, and thereby restricts their opportunity to copy successful industrialization strategies.

TRIPs is not the most restrictive agreement regulating intellectual property rights. A growing number of bilateral (between two countries) and plurilateral (involving a group of countries) free trade agreements have been signed, mostly between developing countries and either the EU or United States. These can be seen as win-win agreements forming a trade-off in which the developing countries seek guaranteed preferential market access to the world's largest markets, while the developed country gets stronger intellectual property rights protection and market access for exports of high technology, capital intensive goods. On the other hand, some commentators are concerned with this shift to bilateralism, seeing it as undermining the multilateral, non-discriminatory system embodied in the WTO and leading to a "spaghetti bowl" of competitive, preferential agreements.[25] It may be, however, that new bilateral and plurilateral deals will decline in number as countries become increasingly put-off by the amount of negotiating effort that such deals require, ultimately for little economic benefit. Developing countries are also increasingly being deterred by the high costs of such deals, for example in accepting stronger intellectual property protection and in opening their markets to subsidized agricultural products exported by the developed countries.

One response to the vast debates about the role of international trade in promoting economic growth, and the associated contribution to poverty reduction (see Chapter 2) has been the evolution of a campaign for fair trade[26] that directly seeks to ensure that poor people receive a higher price for the primary commodities they produce – especially coffee, tea and cocoa.

Campaigners for fair trade point to two beneficial results of their efforts. First, the incomes of some poor people are increased, with knock-on effects to the vibrancy of local economies. Second, fair trade provides a platform for raising the awareness of rich world consumers about poverty, and particularly about "working poverty," in poor countries and deepens their appreciation of the invisible global connections through which rich and poor interact.

These efforts are often treated condescendingly or criticized by orthodox economists who see such campaigners as naive do-gooders. They also have two main arguments. The first is that fair trade discourages diversification – "They get charity as long as they stay producing the crops that have locked them in poverty."[27] Second, they argue that fair trade will raise levels of production and this will reduce the prices for all the other producers. However, the conclusion of these critics that ". . . the fair-trade movement probably makes virtually no difference"[28] may be premature as: (i) some fair trade deals are moving to scale: Cadbury's shift to making all of its cocoa purchases fair trade will raise the incomes of primary producers for one-third of Ghana's main agricultural export;[29] (ii) the anti-fair trade economists do not recognize the contribution that fair trade ideas could make to norms in the rich world. The sorts of "unreciprocated" trade bargains espoused by Paul Collier to orient the WTO towards a genuine development round are more likely to be supported by countries in which there is a domestic political constituency that understands and promotes less nationalistic trade relations with poor countries. The fair trade campaign is the leading vehicle for such a moral shift.

Foreign aid: friend or foe?

The role of foreign aid, or more precisely ODA (see Box 5.2), continues to be the hottest media issue around global poverty. Positions can be diametrically opposed, with some writers and organizations seeing ODA as the easiest and most effective way of reducing poverty, while others believe aid to be the root cause of poverty.[30]

Aid flows started after World War II with the Marshall Plan – US support to rebuild Europe. As decolonization moved forward in the 1950s rich countries began aid programs in their former colonies. The scale of ODA increased substantially around that time as the Cold War unfolded and the United States and Union of Soviet Socialist Republics competed for allies. While the declared aim of aid was to promote development, then, as now, donor interests – commercial, geo-political and diplomatic – influenced aid volumes, the selection of recipients and uses. Carol Lancaster, building on David Lumsdaine's work, has shown that while the dominant motive for donors to start aid programs was self-interest, over time a "moral vision," promoted by civil society, begins to influence such activities.[31] Her case studies of Denmark, Germany, Japan and the United States show the ways in which civil societies, and their moral vision, differ from country to country. In Denmark the moral vision has almost become a national social norm but in Japan it has made much slower progress.

Contemporary debates focus on two closely related issues. The first is aid volumes and is concerned about whether the aggregate volume of ODA is sufficient to achieve the MDGs and whether specific countries are making a contribution proportional to their economic ability. The second is aid effectiveness. This used to be framed as "Does aid contribute to development?" (economic growth, industrialization, infrastructure), but since the MDGs it is increasingly framed as "Does aid reduce poverty?"[32] Aid volumes and aid effectiveness are related as in donor countries where the public believe aid is ineffective, and/or mis-used by recipients, aid volumes are likely to be constrained. In this section aid effectiveness is the focus (see Chapter 4 on "Doing Global Poverty Eradication" for a discussion of aid volumes).

The contesting sides on the aid effectiveness debate are easy to identify as leading writers have adopted diametrically opposed views, though, as shown below, it is the more nuanced analysts with less radical positions who offer the most useful advice. At one extreme are writers who argue that aid is effective and the main issue is maximizing aid volumes. These are led by Jeffrey Sachs, Senior Advisor to Kofi Annan and Ban Ki-moon, with his argument that the MDGs can be achieved: all that is needed is the money. According to Sachs the knowledge, technology and organizational capacity to reach the MDGs are available: if donors will just contribute more aid (US$121 billion in 2006 rising to US$189 billion in 2015) the world can meet the MDGs and proceed on to global poverty eradication. The philosopher

---

Box 5.2 Official development assistance

The Development Assistance Committee of the OECD defines official development assistance (ODA) as flows of resources that: go to low income or middle income countries; are primarily intended for development purposes (not military or export credits); and are highly concessional (having a grant element of at least 25 percent). Such flows may be bilateral, going from country to country, or multilateral, going from a country to an international agency and subsequently being transferred to a developing country or used to produce global public goods. For more details and full statistics see http://www.oecd.org

Peter Singer agrees. Basing his case on a moral argument rather than Sachs's economic analysis, Singer's "realistic approach" suggests that US taxpayers should, and could, give ". . . $471 billion a year for the world's poorest billion people."[33]

Towards the opposite extreme is Bill Easterly and his much-cited book *White Man's Burden*[34] (see also Chapter 2). While he does not argue that all foreign aid has failed, the datasets he presents and detailed case studies, such as that of the Congo, make it feel that way. He chides Sachs's over-optimism and points the finger at Gordon Brown: "Gordon Brown was silent about the other tragedy of the world's poor . . . the tragedy in which the West spent $2.3 trillion on foreign aid over the last five decades and still had not managed to get twelve-cent medicines to children to prevent half of all malaria deaths . . . to get three dollars to each new mother to prevent five million child deaths . . . that so much well-meaning compassion did not bring these results for needy people."[35] For Easterly, what is needed is much less aid, focused on a small number of interventions that have been proved to work and that assists "searchers" (private and social entrepreneurs) from developing countries to make incremental progress.

It is Dambisa Moyo who holds the extreme anti-aid position.[36] In *Dead Aid* she argues that ". . . [a]id remains at the heart of the development agenda despite . . . very compelling reasons to show that it perpetuates the cycle of poverty and derails sustainable economic growth." Aid corrupts African governments, encourages African elites and middle classes to pocket aid rather than run governments or businesses. From this perspective aid has not merely been ineffective, it has been destructive. Foreign aid should be stopped immediately, so that private finance and market forces can work their magic.[37]

These polar positions help us to identify the arguments for and against aid, but they say much less about how to use aid more effectively. Sachs's exaggeration of the state of knowledge of poverty reduction, in effect his claim that science now provides a cure for poverty and all that is needed is the money, provides a damagingly inaccurate assessment of levels of understanding – especially about how to deal with problems of governance and how to help institutions strengthen and evolve. Easterly's erudite cynicism, disparaging "planners" and praising "searchers," does not provide useful knowledge about how to do better that outweighs its damaging pessimism. And, although it is wonderful to have a young African woman deliberating on these issues (rather than the usual cohorts of aging white males),[38] Moyo's blanket dismissal of aid is no prescription for improving the lives of poor people in Africa. Foreign aid is not the cause of all Africa's problems; some aid, but not enough, is improving the prospects of Africa's poor (paying for them to attend school and be vaccinated); and, private finance and micro-finance are unlikely to meet the needs of poor African countries for investment in the coming decade.[39]

The arguments used to support the "aid works" and "aid does not work" positions are based on case studies of aid project and program performance; theoretical arguments; and econometric assessments of whether countries that have received more aid have experienced faster economic growth or poverty reduction. The first form of evidence depends on the selection of examples that are made: it can be rigged by selecting mainly favorable examples (an accusation leveled at Sachs) or mainly unfavorable examples (an accusation leveled at Moyo). The second set of arguments revolves around contrasting theoretical propositions. The aid optimists theorize that a "big push," through the infusion of ODA, will shock poor countries into economic growth and human development. The aid pessimists hypothesize that aid crowds out private sector investment, threatens macro-economic stability and may cause "Dutch disease."[40] The predictive capacity of these theories depends on the degree to which the assumptions that underpin them match, or do not match, empirical situations. The results of the econometric exercises depend on the models that are specified, the underlying assumptions and the availability and quality of data. As a result, Burnside and Dollar's claims that there is a robust positive relationship between aid and economic growth in countries with "good policies" have been refuted by subsequent analyses based on the same dataset and later datasets.[41] Econometricians conducting such exercises may need reminding that their sophisticated analyses provide evidence about, but do not "prove," aid-growth-poverty relationships.

The technical sophistication of attempts to prove that "aid works" or "aid fails" should not distract us from asking whether such exercises are futile. In practice, we know that aid does work (in some forms, in some places, at some times) and also that aid fails (in some forms, in some places, at some times). Knowing whether the average result of historical interventions is positive or negative is of limited contemporary policy relevance.[42] The knowledge that is required is about the selection of forms of aid that will work in specific countries at specific times and how to avoid ineffective or damaging aid allocations. Fortunately, many analysts of ODA have resisted the temptation of producing a headline for press releases and have produced detailed and thoughtful analyses of the complex, and sometimes contradictory, outcomes that foreign aid can produce.[43]

Roger Riddell's recent work provides a detailed review of what is known about good practice in aid policy and a radical, some would say utopian, proposal for a comprehensive restructuring of aid. The good practices include untying aid, using aid to put cash directly into the hands of poor people (especially in both humanitarian and development programs), making aid more predictable, implementing agreed reforms on donor coordination (such as the Paris Declaration) and reducing policy conditionality. Not only do donors need to carefully select their interventions but also ensure they learn more effectively from their experience.[44]

Riddell's radical proposal is for the centralization of most ODA into a single multilateral agency: an International Aid Office that would oversee a new International Development Aid Fund financed by compulsory contributions from each of the world's rich countries. This is thinking about global poverty reduction at the grandest scale but, as Chapter 3 revealed, such a proposal is politically infeasible in a multilateral system that found it hard to agree something as simple as the MDGs. It is also probably undesirable (just imagine the potential perverse consequences of such centralization).

Birdsall, Rodrik and Subramanian have also taken a measured look at aid effectiveness but reach different conclusions. While they list many of the achievements of aid, they caution that ". . . development is something largely determined by poor countries themselves, and that outsiders can play only a limited role . . . financial aid and the further opening of wealthy countries markets are tools with only a limited ability to trigger growth, especially in the poorest countries."[45] As a result they believe that aid should continue but that rich nations would achieve more if they focused on other policies – letting developing countries control their own policies, producing public goods that benefit poor people and countries and opening up labor markets.[46]

Perhaps, as Birdsall *et al.* argue, the greatest problem of a focus on aid effectiveness is that ". . . countries most in need of aid are often those least able to use it well."[47] In countries with the greatest need for aid, the commitment and the capacity of governments and leaders to use aid effectively is at its lowest. In such contexts – Afghanistan, DRC, Haiti, Somalia, and 50 to 60 others – providing ODA and using it effectively may be only a small part of a strategy for tackling extreme poverty. As Collier sums up: "Aid does have serious problems, and more especially serious limitations . . . but it is part of the solution rather than part of the problem. The challenge is to complement it with other actions."[48] The next section looks at what these might be.

Thinking outside of the "aid and trade" box: fragile states, conflict and migration

While the main issues for contemporary debate on tackling global poverty have been on the selection of development strategies, the role of foreign aid (and debt reduction) and reforming the world trade regime, an increasingly influential body of work indicates that these big issues may really be side issues. This counter-narrative argues that

... development is something largely determined by poor countries themselves, and that outsiders can play only a limited role ... financial aid and the further opening of wealthy countries markets are tools with only a limited ability to trigger growth, especially in the poorest countries. The tremendous amount of energy and political capital expended on these efforts in official circles threatens to crowd out attention to other ways in which rich countries could do less harm and more good.[49]

This challenges the cozy historical assumption that the concept of international development transferred to the concept of global poverty eradication: that most poor countries are relatively politically stable and have functioning, or at least partially functioning, governments. Much recent technical work[50] and even global agreements[51] fail to take account of the evidence that many extremely poor people are in countries with major governance problems, breakdowns in law and order, and/or countries experiencing or emerging from civil war. Such countries are often referred to as "fragile states."[52]

There are more than 50 fragile states and these account for around half of all the $2-a-day poor in developing countries. If one were to include weakly governed Indian states[53] in this category – Uttar Pradesh, Madhya Pradesh, Bihar, Orissa and others – then more than 50 percent of the world's $1.25-a-day poor world live in fragile states. In such contexts poverty rates are high and are likely to remain high. Where people are physically unsafe and property is insecure, physical and human capital is depleted (through violence, sabotage and closure of the education system), skilled labor migrates out so that economic growth stagnates or is negative and human capabilities decrease. A cycle of impoverishment occurs that pulls down economic and social conditions and degrades institutions so that recovery is less likely. These processes can be illustrated by the contrasting examples of Vietnam and Nicaragua: both came out of violent civil wars, were dependent on agriculture and received large amounts of aid. Vietnam's historical context provided an opportunity, seized by its leadership, to establish economic and political institutions supporting growth and poverty reduction. Nicaragua lacked such opportunities, and such visionary leadership, and is floundering in a low growth/persistent poverty trap.[54] Bangladesh provides an example in which even a "basket case" can be turned around and poverty tackled (Box 5.3).

In situations such as that of Nicaragua, increasing aid volumes and aid effectiveness,[55] or giving trade preferences, is unlikely to have a significant impact on poverty reduction (directly or through growth). What else could well-intentioned outsiders do to promote the political stability, improved social cohesion and better governance that might support growth and poverty reduction? The emerging literature provides a number of ideas: here I focus on three main proposals.[56]

First, rich countries could place a greater emphasis on peace-making and conflict prevention and resolution. This has several elements. The most obvious is reducing their arms sales to poor countries and strengthening the international controls over the sales of arms. More controversial, especially given the on-going experiences in Iraq and Afghanistan and the prospects of rich countries seeing their soldiers come home in coffins, is external military intervention. This can involve: (i) seeking to restore order by applying armed force to convince warring parties that they need to cease violent acts as the intervening force has greater military capacity than they

Box 5.3 From "basket case" to beacon of hope

At times accounts of development in poor countries read like tales of doom and gloom: setbacks occur, good leaders turn bad, crops fail, economies collapse and much worse. But, there are also experiences revealing that optimism about the possibility of rapid improvements is not unfounded. If one imagines a very poor country that has just emerged from a vicious civil war that has seen millions killed and horrendous atrocities; in which the industrial, transport and power infrastructure has been destroyed; that has just been hit by a natural disaster that has displaced millions and caused famine; and with an elite that is violently fractured and where assassinations occur – then prospects for poverty reduction seem negligible. But that has not been the case for Bangladesh.

Henry Kissinger may have described the country as a "basket case" in the mid-1970s – predicting a future of continuous food insecurity and hunger, dependence on food aid and humanitarian grants, frequent disasters that could not be managed, mass poverty and unemployment – but he was wrong. Since 1983–1984 the country's headcount poverty index has dropped from 52 percent to around 35 percent, the UN's Human Poverty Index (based on income poverty, illiteracy and health deprivations) has fallen from 61 percent to 41 percent in 2007–2008 and economic growth has been above 6 percent per annum for most of the last 15 years.

(Box continued on next page)

Life is still very hard for tens of millions of Bangladeshis but it continues to improve for many and Bangladesh is expected to achieve many of the MDG targets and to become a middle income (and middle human development) country after 2020.

At present several African countries can be portrayed as "basket cases." How they will escape this characterization and improve the lives of their people may be unclear at present, but the Bangladesh experience shows that the paralysis that can ensue from pessimism must be rejected. There is hope for what may appear to be the most hopeless cause.

have; (ii) deploying peacekeepers to maintain the post-conflict peace; and (iii) providing protection to heads of state against coups. All of these are likely to be highly problematic, but the costs of not intervening can be high – as with the more than half a million deaths in Rwanda when the world decided not to intervene.[57] If successful, such military intervention needs to be followed up by demobilization and disarmament, re-structuring and re-training national armies and, if all goes well, increasingly bringing the police and civil authorities back into the provision of services for law and order. The model for such interventions would not be big wars, as in Iraq, but smaller, intelligence-grounded, strategic actions as in the United Kingdom's Operation Palliser in Sierra Leone.

Second would be the rich countries of the world getting their own houses in order so that rich world business interests do not undermine political stability in poor countries and encourage corruption. This can be pursued by actively implementing laws to punish MNCs and MNC officials for making bribes in developing countries and by seizing the offshore bank accounts and properties of dictators and autocrats who siphon off public resources. The Extractive Industries Transparency Initiative provides a good example of how to reduce the harm that some rich world companies can do in poor countries and even Switzerland is now recognizing that providing banking services to despots is immoral.[58]

Third comes the issue of how to restructure international labor markets so that poor people and poor countries benefit more from the vast wage differentials between countries (the labor market is the one market that rich countries are keen not to see liberalized). If the rich world opened up the cross-border mobility of low skill labor only moderately then the annual earnings of poor country citizens would rise by more than US$51 billion and much of this would flow into remittances.[59] Bangladesh's poverty problems (deep poverty in a land-constrained country that will suffer greatly from climate change) could be solved at a stroke with reduced environmental pressures (due to out-migration), greater remittances, increased economic growth and improved public services (Box 5.4).

While political and commercial concerns about these proposals (the deaths of peacekeepers, lower profits for some MNCs and xenophobia about immigrants) may make them less appealing to pro-development lobbies in the rich world – "more aid" and "fair trade" are much easier arguments to make in Europe and even the United States and Japan – the positive examples that can be cited and opportunities to build rich world political constituencies to support these alternative policies might permit gradual progress. For example, HIV/AIDS sufferers in industrialized countries have supported cheaper anti-retroviral drugs for Africa and pharmaceutical companies have gradually changed their pricing policies (see above). In the future, those providing care services for the elderly infirm and the relatives of those needing such

---

Box 5.4 The impact of free international labor movement on Bangladesh

While there have been concerted efforts in the post-war period to liberalize trade and (to a lesser extent) capital, this has not been matched by attempts to free labor markets. Freeing labor markets, however, to allow more workers from developing countries to emigrate in search of work would have a huge impact on poverty. It is estimated that Bangladesh has around 3 percent of its population living abroad. These emigrants are today generating around US$12 billion in remittances each year. If this were to be increased to 10 percent of the population, the remittances generated would rise to about US$40 billion. This alone represents more than half Bangladesh's annual GNI in 2006, and 2,624% of Bangladesh's annual aid flows. Moreover, if the multiplier effect of this extra income is included, the increased national income is estimated to be around US$84 billion – more than Bangladesh's current GNI.

Source: Jonathon W. Moses, "Leaving Poverty Behind: A Radical Proposal for Developing Bangladesh," *Development Policy Review* 27, No. 4 (2009): 457–479.

services will see the advantages of freeing up the labor market for low cost/ moderate-skill care-workers from other countries.

Conclusion

The debates in this chapter may appear to be only partly related to each other. There is, however, an overarching issue that links them all – the inability of the structures and processes of global governance to adapt, or be adapted, to the problems and emerging power relations of the twenty-first century and to, at least partially, match grand promises about tackling global poverty with action. This inability to reform has been illustrated in several ways.

First, the emerging consensus that reducing global poverty requires country-owned and country-specific strategies and plans that draw on heterodox ideas about promoting inclusive economic growth and human development has been obstructed by the continued dominance of institutions, particularly the IMF, governed in accordance with the power relations of the mid-twentieth century and utilizing the analytical frameworks of the 1980s. Studies of the BWIs unanimously argue that their governance structures are fundamentally flawed but progress in reforming this has been negligible.

Second is the paradox of aid donors and agencies striving to achieve greater aid effectiveness and agreeing that for aid to be more effective it must be better coordinated and its volumes must be more predictable. But very few countries have been able to match their commitments to improved aid effectiveness with better practice. The pace of progress on aid coordination and predictability has been that of a snail.

Third, the declaration of the Doha trade negotiations as a "development round" has been followed by years of negotiation based on business as usual – expecting the poorest countries in the world to fully reciprocate any trade liberalization deals offered by rich countries (often in forms, such as TRIPs, that would impose high and long-term costs on poor countries).[60] Across Europe citizens have been shifting to "fair trade" products but their governments, and especially EU trade negotiators, have only gradually changed their positions.

Fourth is the continued under-resourcing of multilateral, military intervention to prevent conflict or make peace except when the conflicts have geo-political significance for rich nations (as with the wars in the former Yugoslavia and Iraq). Somalia and Rwanda were allowed to go to hell. Coalition troop numbers and military action in Afghanistan have been increased since 2008, but the original commitments to providing a substantial military force were made in 2003. The five-year "gap" may mean that Afghanistan will also go to hell. And, most OECD countries have avoided difficult domestic political debates and increased defense expenditures by sheltering under the wing of the US military. The hope that regional group-ings will be better able to resolve regional problems has made little progress. The AU peace-keeping force in Darfur has been under-resourced and AU and SADC efforts to return law and order to Zimbabwe maintained the status quo that has immiserized the country's population for many years.

The prospects for re-shaping the structures and processes of global govern-ance, so that they genuinely tackle global poverty, depend on the perspective taken. A pessimistic account argues that if global and regional structures and processes could not be made more effective during the "good times" (1990–2001) – the end of the Cold War, a single superpower available to take a lead, a sustained period of global growth and the new millennium creating an environment for new thinking and action – then it is unlikely to happen at the present time, as the world becomes multi-polar, the financial crisis plunges governments into unprecedented debt and the negative effects of climate change are already impacting. An alternative, more optimistic scenario, would argue that it is at times of crisis that human creativity comes to the forefront and technology and institutions advance. Could the emer-gence of global challenges that were unimaginable until very recently, such as climate change, lead to the transformation of international relations and the sharing of technologies? The next chapter examines the new challenges that will confront the idea and the practice of global poverty eradication in coming years.

Notes

1 For an analysis of the shift from seeing strategic social issues in polar terms see Anthony Giddens, *Beyond Left and Right: The Future of Radical Politics* (Cambridge: Polity Press, 1994). Barak Obama presents this as "uniting red and blue America."

2 This refers to academic institutions and journals/books and also the research work of development agencies and their reports (e.g. *World Development Reports* and *Human Development Reports*) and the media.

3 See Jean-Philippe Thérien, "Beyond the North-South Divide: The Two Tales of World Poverty," *Third World Quarterly* 20, no. 4 (1999): 723–742 and the discussion in Chapter 3.

4 See *World Development Report 1997* and *World Development Report 2006* respectively.

5 David Dollar and Aart Kraay, "Growth Is Good for the Poor," *Journal of Economic Growth* 7, no. 3 (2002): 195–225.

6 The Economist, "Growth is Good," *The Economist*, 355 no. 8172 (2000): 82; and Martin Wolf, "Kicking Down Growth's Ladder: Protesters Against the World Bank and the IMF are in Effect Seeking to Deny the Poor the Benefits of a Liberal World Economy," *Financial Times*, April 12, 2000.

7　Angus Deaton, Abhikit Vinayak Banerjee, Nora Lustig and Ken Rogoff, *An Evaluation of World Bank Research, 1998–2005* (Washington, DC: World Bank, 2006), 53.

8　Martin Ravallion, "Looking Beyond Averages in the Trade and Poverty Debate," World Bank Policy Research Working Paper 3461 (Washington, DC: World Bank, 2004); Malte Lübker, Graham Smith and John Weeks, "Growth and the Poor: A Comment on Dollar and Kraay," *Journal of International Development* 14, no. 5 (2002): 555–571; Richard Ashley, "Growth May Be Good for the Poor, but Decline Is Disastrous: On the Non-Robustness of the Dollar-Kraay Result," *International Review of Economics and Finance* 17, no. 2 (2008): 333–338; and François Bourguignon, "The Growth Elasticity of Poverty Reduction: Explaining Heterogeneity across Countries and Time Periods," in *Inequality and Growth*, ed. Theo S. Eicher and Stephen J. Turnovsky (Cambridge, Mass.: MIT Press, 2003).

9　Deaton *et al.*, *An Evaluation*, 6.

10　See Dani Rodrik, "Goodbye Washington Consensus, Hello Washington Confusion? A Review of the World Bank's Economic Growth in the 1990s: Learning from a Decade of Reform," *Journal of Economic Literature* 44, no. 4 (2006): 973–987 for a concise account of the *Learning from Reform* report and related documents.

11　World Bank, *Economic Growth in the 1990s: Learning from Reform* (Washington, DC: World Bank, 2005), 11.

12　Empirically this was not rocket science. The great success stories of the 1990s, in terms of both economic growth and poverty reduction, were China, India, Vietnam and other Asian countries. They may have all moved towards the market but this was *not* through wholesale privatization, abolishing industrial policy, removing all barriers to trade and prioritizing fiscal and financial discipline. Each of the star performers of the 1990s went in for gradual reform based on domestic economic and political analyses. See Ha-Joon Chang, *Bad Samaritans: Rich Nations, Poor Policies and the Threat to the Developing World* (London: Random House Business, 2007) for an elaboration.

13　Anoop Singh, Agnès Belaisch, Charles Collyns, Paula De Masi, Reva Krieger, Guy Meredith and Robert Rennhack, "Stabilization and Reform in Latin America: A Macroeconomic Perspective on the Experience since the Early 1990s," IMF Occasional Paper No. 238 (Washington, DC: IMF, 2005). See Rodrik, "Goodbye," for a review.

14　It is difficult to precisely examine changes in World Bank expenditure as the ways in which investments were categorized have changed over the 1995–2008 period.

15　Stefan Koeberle and Jan Walliser, "World Bank Conditionality: Trends, Lessons, and Good Practice Principles," in *Budget Support as More Effective Aid?: Recent Experiences and Emerging Lessons*, ed. Stefan Koeberle, Jan Walliser and Zoran Stavreski (Washington, DC: World Bank, 2006). It should be noted, however, that policy conditionalities may have been replaced by process conditionalities and that changes in Bank culture may be well behind Bank policy.

16　David Hulme, "Does the World Bank have a Learning Disability?" *Public Administration and Development* 14, no. 1 (1994): 93–97.

17　See Paul Mosley, Jane Harrigan and John F.J. Toye, *Aid and Power: The World Bank and Policy-based Lending* (London: Routledge, 1995).

18 The World Bank describes Medium Term Economic Frameworks as "a transparent planning and budget formulation process within which the Cabinet and central agencies establish credible contracts for allocating public resources to their strategic priorities while ensuring overall fiscal discipline. The process entails two main objectives: the first aims at setting fiscal targets, the second aims at allocating resources to strategic priorities within these targets." It fails to mention that if the "fiscal targets" do not match IMF parameters then the country will become ineligible for BWI loans and will be unable to access other international financial resources. See http://siteresources.worldbank.org/INTPEAM/Resources/MTEFprocess.doc

19 See Rodrik, "Goodbye," 986, 982.

20 Robert H. Wade, "What Strategies Are Viable for Developing Countries Today? The World Trade Organization and the Shrinking of 'Development Space'," *Review of International Political Economy* 10, no. 4 (2003): 622.

21 Wade, "What Strategies"; Chang, *Bad Samaritans*; Dani Rodrik, *The Global Governance of Trade as if Development Really Mattered* (New York: UNDP, 2001); and South Centre, "Policy Space for the Development of the South," TRADE Policy Brief No. 1 (Geneva: South Centre, 2005).

22 International Cotton Advisory Committee, *Production and Trade Policies Affecting the Cotton Industry* (Washington, DC: ICAC, 2002).

23 Oxfam, *Rigged Rules and Double Standards: Trade Globalisation and the Fight against Poverty* (Oxford: Oxfam, 2002), 213.

24 Commission on Intellectual Property Rights, *Integrating Intellectual Property Rights and Development Policy: Executive Summary* (London: DFID, 2002), 11.

25 Jagdish N. Bhagwati, *Termites in the Trading System: How Preferential Agreements Undermine Free Trade* (New York: Oxford University Press, 2008), 63.

26 See the Fair Trade Foundation (http://www.fairtrade.org.uk), Oxfam (http://www.maketradefair.org.uk) and Cafédirect (http://www.cafedirect.co.uk).

27 Paul Collier, *The Bottom Billion: Why the Poorest Countries are Failing and What Can Be Done About It* (Oxford: Oxford University Press, 2007), 163.

28 Martin Wolf, *Why Globalization Works* (New Haven, Conn.: Yale University Press, 2004), 206.

29 Stephanie Barrientos, Michael E. Conroy and Elaine Jones, "Northern Social Movements and Fair Trade", in Laura T. Raynolds, Douglas L. Murray and John Wilkinson (eds) *Fair Trade: the Challenges of Transforming Globalization*, (New York and Abingdon: Routledge, 2007).

30 Contrast the optimism of Jeffrey D. Sachs, *The End of Poverty: Economic Possibilities for Our Time* (New York: Penguin Press, 2005) with the pessimism of Dambisa Moyo, *Dead Aid: Why Aid Is Not Working and How There Is Another Way for Africa* (London: Allen Lane, 2009).

31 Carol Lancaster, *Foreign Aid: Diplomacy, Development, Domestic Politics*, (Chicago and London: University of Chicago Press, 2007) and David Halloran Lumsdaine, *Moral Vision in International Politics: The Foreign Aid Regime, 1949–1989* (Princeton, NJ: Princeton University Press, 1993).

32 Even more ambitiously some researchers have examined whether aid can contribute to the evolution of effective institutions in recipient countries. See Deborah Bräutigam and Steven Knack, "Foreign Aid, Institutions and Governance in Sub-Saharan Africa," *Economic Development and Cultural Change* 52, no. 2 (2004): 255–286.

33 Peter Singer, *The Life You Can Save: Acting Now to End World Poverty* (London: Picador, 2009), 165.

34 William Russell Easterly, *The White Man's Burden: Why the West's Efforts to Aid the Rest Have Done So Much Ill and So Little Good* (Oxford: Oxford University Press, 2006). This is a clever and entertaining book but Easterly does a disservice to efforts to improve the lives of poor people by his cynical, not skeptical, stance and the pessimism, not realism, that he preaches.

35 Easterly, *The White Man's Burden*, 4.

36 Moyo, *Dead Aid*.

37 Moyo's book has received much publicity but several reviewers have pointed out how unbalanced her arguments are and selective her use of data is.

38 Unfortunately I fall into this category.

39 In the present recession private finance for Africa has disappeared and micro-finance is best understood as a platform for poverty reduction, not a panacea – see David Hulme and Paul Mosley, *Finance against Poverty* (London: Routledge, 1996).

40 Dutch disease posits that a rapid inflow of foreign currency into a country leads to an increased exchange rate and the marginalization of manufacturing and, perhaps, agriculture.

41 Craig Burnside and David Dollar, "Aid, Policies and Growth," *American Economic Review* 90, no. 4 (2000): 847–868; William Russell Easterly, Ross Levine and David Foodman, "New Data, New Doubts: Revisiting 'Aid, Policies and Growth'," Working Paper No. 26 (Washington, DC: Center for Global Development, 2000); and Henrik Hansen and Finn Tarp, "Aid and Growth Regressions," *Journal of Development Economics* 64, no. 2 (2001): 547–570.

42 See Martin Ravallion, "Growth, Inequality and Poverty: Looking beyond Averages," *World Development* 29, no. 11 (2001): 1803–1815. An updated version of this paper was published in 2004 as a working paper. See Ravallion, "Looking beyond Averages."

43 Carl-Johan Dalgaard, Henrik Hansen and Finn Tarp, "On the Empirics of Foreign Aid and Growth," *The Economic Journal* 114, no. 496 (2004): 191–216; Finn Tarp and Peter Hjertholm, *Foreign Aid and Development: Lessons Learnt and Directions for the Future* (London: Routledge, 2000); and Howard White, "Challenges in Evaluating Development Effectiveness," IDS Working Paper No. 242 (Brighton, UK: IDS, 2005); Roger Riddell, *Does Foreign Aid Really Work?* (Oxford: Oxford University Press, 2007).

44 The recently established International Institute for Impact Evaluation (3iE) seeks to improve policy evaluation and share knowledge about methodologies and findings (http://www.3ieimpact.org).

45 Nancy Birdsall, Dani Rodrik and Arvind Subramanian, "How to Help Poor Countries," *Foreign Affairs* 84, no. 4 (2005): 136–152.

46 It should also be noted that future poverty reduction in India and China will not be dependent on aid as so little of their budgets comes from ODA.

47 Birdsall *et al.*, "How to Help Poor Countries."

48 Collier, *The Bottom Billion*, 123.

49 Birdsall *et al.*, "How to Help Poor Countries," 136.

50 For example, the Millennium Project Report (Sachs, *The End of Poverty*) allocates only a seven-page chapter, in its 264 pages, to "conflict."

51 The Millennium Declaration separated out its chapters on "peace" and on "development and poverty eradication." The IDGs and MDGs barely mentioned violent conflict, state fragility or weak governance.

52 A wide set of terms are used including the World Bank's "low-income countries under stress" (LICUS), DAC's "difficult partnerships" and the US government's "failed and failing states."

53 Each of these Indian states has a larger population than the average African country and displays characteristics of poor governance, a breakdown in law and order, violent movements, etc.

54 For detailed references see Birdsall *et al.*, "How to Help Poor Countries."

55 However, I agree with Collier (*The Bottom Billion*) that there may be some context-specific opportunities. These include well-designed technical assistance soon after conflict resolution (to enhance public sector management, establish electoral commissions, voter education and strengthen the media) and Africa's landlocked states could benefit from aid for long-term social protection and transport infrastructure.

56 The issue of reforming international agreements over intellectual property so that they are pro-poor has already been discussed above.

57 See Collier, *The Bottom Billion*, and Paul Collier, *Wars, Guns and Votes: Democracy in Dangerous Places* (London: Bodley Head, 2009) for detailed discussions.

58 Other suggestions include declaring some regimes "odious" and blocking MNCs from working with them, agreeing international standards and codes (democracy, budget transparency, cessation of violence and investment) and encouraging poor countries to remove trade barriers that damage the export potential of poor neighboring countries. See Birdsall *et al.*, "How to Help Poor Countries," and Collier, *The Bottom Billion.*

59 Terrie Walmsley and Alan Winters, "Relaxing the Restrictions on the Temporary Movement of Natural Persons: A Simulation Analysis," *Journal of Economic Integration* 20, no. 4 (2005): 688–726. Walmsley and Winters base their calculations on increasing the quota of migrants into developed countries to 3 percent of their workforce.

60 It should be noted, however, that the LDCs have more or less been assured a "round for free," i.e. they will not have to make reciprocal concessions. The only contribution they will have to make is to bind tariff levels. This was probably not the original plan among the rich countries, but they realized that they could not make significant demands on LDCs given that this is a "development round".

6 The future of global poverty

Emerging issues in an uncertain world

"Shanghai is a fitting location for a poverty conference but the rationale is diametrically opposite from the World Bank's [rationale] . . . Shanghai's top-down model and state-led urbanization programs are inherently anti-poor."

(Yasheng Huang, 2008)[1]

". . . are we doing as much for today's poor billions as we are seeking to do for tomorrow's vulnerable billions . . . are we doing as much to make poverty history as we are doing to stop climate chaos?"

(Mike Hulme 2009)[2]

Given the difficulties of estimating the scale and nature of poverty in the contemporary world – with the estimate for extreme poverty in 2000 being corrected from 1.2 billion to 1.7 billion in 2008 (see Table 4.1) – charting the future of global poverty needs to be approached with caution and humility. While the long-term trend for some factors may seem predictable (economic growth in Asia; continued urbanization; human population increasing but peaking, perhaps around 9 billion), other important factors can only be understood in terms of wide ranging scenarios (climate change, energy and food prices, conflict and security) and there are crucial issues that defy prediction (the future of capitalism, the use of weapons of mass destruction, new pandemic diseases and others).

The main prediction underpinning present-day thinking about global poverty is that it will steadily decline, both in income and human development deprivations, and that the prime analytical and policy issue is how to increase and/or maximize the speed of poverty reduction.[3] This prediction is based on a number of assumptions – that the Chinese and Indian economies will continue to grow; that this will ensure that recent poverty reduction trends will continue; that global capitalism will continue to generate wealth and will not "melt down" (as it nearly did in 2008); and that human creativity will produce technologies to raise productivity and deal with "new" problems that may arise. In the sub-structure of these assumptions are other assumptions – a belief that human organizational capacities and social norms will continue to gradually and imperfectly evolve in ways that support collective economic and social action – locally, nationally and globally.

The assumption that global poverty will continue to decline is reassuring and, given humanity's vast material capabilities, does not seem unreasonable. But a number of emerging issues seem likely to force a re-thinking of the processes that cause poverty and of the policies and actions that might most effectively tackle poverty. In this chapter it is only possible to examine a small number of the most important of these emerging geo-political, environmental and ideological issues – the rise of Asia and the restructuring of global material capabilities; the problem (or opportunity) of climate change; the urbanization of poverty; and, the evolution of international social norms (secular and religious).[4] The accuracy with which one can predict and/or build reasonable scenarios about each of these factors is highly questionable. Things get even more complicated when one recognizes that the individual dynamics of each of these important issues will have profound impacts on each of the other issues in iterative and hard to imagine ways. For example, Mike Hulme points out that the most profound impacts of climate change might not be direct but indirect as the idea of climate change leads to changes in human values and, perhaps, international social norms.[5] In this chapter we explore the most important of these factors and examine their implications.

The rise of Asia and the new geography of material capabilities

Projections of future global poverty reduction are based on the assumption that relatively high levels of global economic growth, and especially growth in China and India, will continue for several decades. Such growth would not only reduce global poverty: it would also re-structure the global political economy. After 40 years of Cold War bipolarity, the 1990s witnessed a sudden and dramatic shift to a uni-polar world with the United States as the only economic and military superpower. This uni-polar era looks as though it will be relatively short-lived as scenarios for the evolution of material capabilities (technological and organizational capabilities with productive and destructive potentials) in the twenty-first century have emerged.[6] These varying scenarios highlight the rise of Chindia (China and India), the BRICs (Brazil, Russia, India and China), BRICSAM (the BRICs plus South Africa and Mexico) and the Next 11[7] (countries that have the macro-economic stability, political maturity, openness and quality of education to become large middle income countries by 2050).

Whichever scenario one adopts economic growth in China and India is seen as the driving force behind the emerging geography of material capabilities. While this growth is by no means guaranteed it must be observed that much of it is a historical "bounce-back" and that even after their recent unprecedented spurts of growth neither country has yet reached the share of global GDP it commanded 200 years ago. In 1820 China and India produced 33 percent and 16 percent of global GDP respectively. By 2006 this had only returned to 17 percent and 6 percent.[8] Most scenarios assume that China's growth will outpace India's because: (i) it has done this for all except three of the last 30 years and its average growth rate is much higher than that of India; (ii) economically it is externally oriented; and (iii) they assume that Indian democracy will require political leaders and politicians to pursue populist policies that will reduce growth rates.[9] Whether or not this "China first, India second" scenario is correct, the twenty-first century seems set to be the Asian Century with many other coastal Asian "developing" countries following these two (Bangladesh, Indonesia, Malaysia, Sri Lanka, Thailand and Vietnam).

If one accepts the Chindia scenario then there are three main pathways through which global poverty will be impacted. The first is through the domestic impact of economic growth and, for levels of absolute poverty, this depends on the distribution of the benefits of growth within each country. Recent patterns have been highly unequal and substantial populations in both countries live in poverty in sub-Siberian Asia.[10] While aggregate $1.25-a-day poverty has dropped dramatically in China[11] there are wide regional disparities: Shanghai Province has achieved living standards similar to Portugal while Guizhou Province, among others, has indicators closer to Asia's poorest countries. In India there is an enormous contrast between states in the south and west and states in the north and east. This divide extends into urban areas with, for example, Mumbai having a vast middle class living alongside an equally large number of slum-dwellers (millions of whom are extremely poor despite calculations suggesting their incomes are above $1.25 a day[12]). Predicting the spread of benefits is difficult as it depends on aggregate growth rates, their employment impacts, population migration (still controlled in China) and state efforts to guide growth and public investment. If the *World Development Report 2009/10* is correct then poverty reduction will be greatest in dynamic city regions, so China and India's populations will have to continue to move on a vast scale to escape poverty. Whatever the details, if either country manages to spread the benefits of growth more effectively than at present, socially or geographically, then global poverty will reduce much more rapidly.

The second pathway derives from the economic impacts of China and India's growth on other countries. Already the demand of the Chinese economy for natural resources has led to China's commercial and political links with African countries deepening.[13] Analyses of this have been mixed. Some have been positive, applauding both the growth and the increased choice of geo-political relationships and sources of finance that this creates for Africa's leaders.[14] Others have been very negative, claiming that China's support for "bad" regimes (Robert Mugabe in Zimbabwe, Bashir Ahmed in Sudan and José Eduardo dos Santos in Angola) fosters bad governance in Africa, and that Chinese loans, and/or deals on future access to minerals and hydrocarbons, will create a new wave of highly indebted poor countries. India's profile in Africa has been lower but it is reported that it has a more sophisticated, "soft" strategy compared to China's: focusing on gaining control of ICTs and economic services and persuading Africans that the knowledge industries of the twenty-first century (research and development, higher education, health services) will be of highest quality and lowest price in India. Whatever these effects, it seems likely that Africa's terms of trade will improve with a continued rise in commodity prices in coming years. This improves the prospects for economic growth, which ran at almost 6 percent per annum 2000–2008, but the poverty reducing effects of this will depend on how benefits "trickle down." This is a worry as mineral and hydrocarbon exports usually produce highly concentrated gains, and associated increases in food prices impact badly on the poor and poorest. The specter of jobless growth shadows sub-Saharan Africa as evidenced by Angola's recent experience.

The third pathway is through the roles that China and India play in global public policy. This will take many forms, most of which have not yet clearly emerged. Both countries are expanding their foreign aid activities[15] with a focus on bilateral programs that relate to strategic commercial or geopolitical interests. If either country had the imagination and motivation, then they could attempt to play a leadership role in global poverty eradication at the UN, G20, WTO or other bases. This could be based on a strategy of increasing their international profile and/or on the "export" of their successful development models.[16] Recent experience suggests that this is not likely at the present time. In the Doha Trade Round China has continued to play its usual muted, non-confrontational role; India has attempted to position itself as the leader of a unified group of all developing countries, notably in the Hong Kong Ministerial Meeting of 2005. However, many other developing countries were highly skeptical of this and of the capacity or willingness of India to represent any country's interests but its own. In the UN and G20 the focus of both China and India has been largely based on short-term national self-interest.

Moving away from Asia, three other issues merit attention. First the prospects – the hope – that at least one of Africa's slumbering giants (Nigeria or South Africa[17]) will somehow get its economy growing. If either, or both, managed to achieve a high growth rate that would help to promote increased material capabilities across the continent, might provide an African economic model for emulation (of strategies, policies and institutions) and could transform the negative, but gradually improving, image of Africa so that both domestic and foreign investors see it in a more favorable light.

Second is the gradually emerging evidence that Latin America is becoming a hearth for the development and subsequent export of poverty reduction (and economic growth) models and policies. The success of cash transfers in Latin America, especially in Mexico (Oportunidades) and Brazil (Bolsa Familia) but also in other countries, has encouraged the export of these models to African and other poor countries.[18] While multilateral and bilateral aid agencies (the World Bank, DFID and Deutsche Gesellschaft für Technische Zusammenarbeit (GTZ) – Germany's development organization) have been part of these processes there is a Latin American intelligentsia and a regional dynamic behind this that reflects the strengthening of research and higher education capacities in the region. This is built on the region's long-established universities and research institutes which have been revitalized through economic growth. This might be a "one-off" but the placing of the UN's International Poverty Centre in Brazil, the establishment by the Government of Brazil of a Brazil-Africa Program, and the evolving networks of Latin American economists, social scientists and social activists engaged in global poverty knowledge creation introduce an additional ideational source.

Finally, there is the question of whether the United States will use its contemporary position of power to determine the moment at which the structures and processes of global governance are re-cast.[19] Arguably, from a national interest perspective and given that once global structures are designed they change relatively little over time, the United States might achieve long-term advantages by calling for the creation of a new or reformed set of global institutions while it remains the world's only superpower. If it delays 20 or 30 years, those negotiations would occur when the relative waning of US power is more evident and its bargaining strength and capacity to co-opt other countries is weaker than at present. The rise of Asia both creates a strong argument for reforming global institutions and might encourage the United States to move on this issue sooner rather than later.

Climate change and global poverty

Despite the continued manipulation of the media by US corporations and right wing lobby groups financing disinformation about the findings of research on climate change a consensus has emerged across the scientific community that global warming is underway and that anthropogenic activities (industrialization, transport, deforestation, agriculture and livestock rearing) are a significant, probably the major, cause. The IPCC's Fourth Assessment Report confirmed that the climate is rapidly changing. Between 1906 and 2005 the global average surface temperature is estimated to have increased by 0.74°C: between 2005 and 2100 this temperature could rise by 5.8°C. As the Director of the UK's Tyndall Centre on Climate Change, Kevin Anderson, puts it, ". . . we are in a different world" – with an increase of 2°C ensured by the existing CO_2 concentrations in the atmosphere regardless of whatever mitigation we achieve in the future.

This does not simply mean, as some popular newspapers suggest, that everywhere in the world will be a little warmer. It means that the patterns of global atmospheric and ocean flows will change and with that many different elements of the climate. In some places global warming will mean that temperatures may drop – it is complicated. Modeling some of these changes is possible with a reasonable degree of confidence as flows of air and water move further north or further south and/or speed up or slow down. But other changes are more difficult to predict as there are potentially catastrophic changes that will be triggered if hard to identify "thresholds" are exceeded (such as an accelerated melting of the Greenland Ice Sheet which would rapidly raise sea levels, by meters rather than centimeters, and close down the Gulf Stream).

These many interacting changes in flows will have multiple consequences for the global environment and will dramatically re-structure material capabilities around the world as some areas become less agriculturally and industrially productive while others gain. The three most significant changes for human populations are likely to be rises in sea level, changes in temperature and precipitation, and the increased frequency of extreme weather events.[20] The IPCC's Fourth Assessment Report estimated that by 2100 sea levels will probably rise from a minimum of 18cm to a maximum of 59cm. This will affect coastal settlements around the world, particularly those with large populations living in low lying areas. In Bangladesh, for instance, it has been estimated that between 6 and 8 million people will be displaced by 2050.[21] Changes in temperature and rainfall patterns will impact greatly on agriculture and health and seem likely to be especially negative in Africa and South Asia. Third, more frequent and changed patterns of extreme climatic events (cyclones, floods, droughts, etc.) are predicted. These impact immediately on livelihoods and suffering, with increased mortality and destruction of physical assets, and in the longer term may mean that some presently settled areas become unviable for human residence.

While the degrees of confidence around predicting the effects of climate change and the ensuing consequences for different parts of the world are modest, most scenarios indicate that poor people and poor countries will suffer most.[22] There are two main reasons for this. The first relates to pre-existing material capabilities. Wealthy people and countries have more resources to devote to adapting to climate change, and to invest in research and development on adaptation, than poorer people and countries. The second is geographical: all of the scenarios suggest that the parts of the world with the highest concentrations of poverty – sub-Saharan Africa and sub-Siberian Asia – will experience a greater share of the negative consequences of climate change than will the middle to high latitude regions (Europe, North America and Japan). The four principal impacts of these changes are examined below.

Agriculture

Climate change is predicted to lead to an aggregate reduction in agricultural productivity sufficient to raise agricultural produce prices by 2 to 20 percent over the short to medium term. This will impact most on the poor and poorest who spend a greater share of their income on food. But it gets worse. The negative impacts are likely to be concentrated in rain-fed agriculture and in tropical regions. In South Asia the prediction is that cereal yields will be down by 30 percent by 2050. Even more dramatically, in Chad, Ethiopia, Nigeria, Somalia, Sudan and Zimbabwe it is possible that growing cereal crops will be non-viable by 2080. Unless there are vast technological breakthroughs in agriculture, climate change seems certain to reduce both food security and economic growth in the world's poor countries.[23]

Water stress

Changes in rainfall patterns, especially in regions with weak infrastructure, will lead to increased water stress (less than 1,000 cubic meters of reasonable quality water per capita per annum) and associated problems of health, quality of life and opportunities for economic advancement. Estimates for Africa are of 75 to 250 million more people experiencing water stress by 2020 and 350 to 600 million by 2050. Water stress will also increase greatly in Latin America and South Asia. Some military scenarios warn of "water wars" between ethnic groups in sub-Saharan Africa and between states in the Middle East and North Africa. Given the close association of violent conflict with poverty this would be doubly problematic for scenarios of global poverty.

Coastal settlements

Rising sea levels and more frequent extreme weather events will mean that coastal regions experience higher levels of flooding, erosion and saline intrusion. A high proportion of the developing world's population is concentrated on the coast. These people are likely to experience both direct impacts on the quality of their lives and indirect impacts, through reduced economic prospects. A sea rise increase of 40 cm would displace 13 to 94 million people in Asia. In Africa, mega-cities are evolving on the coast – by 2015 there will be three cities of more than 8 million people on the coast as well as a cross-national megalopolis stretching from Accra to Port Harcourt of 50 million plus. Regular and severe flooding in low lying areas, where poor people's shacks are concentrated, will make social and economic progress more difficult and/or lead to large scale forced relocation. By 2050 several small island states in the Caribbean, and the Pacific and Indian Oceans, will be fully submerged and their entire populations displaced.

Health

Climate change will induce new patterns of morbidity and mortality. The overall balance seems likely to be negative especially in tropical and near-tropical regions. Most predictions indicate that problems such as heat stress, malaria, Chaga's disease, dengue fever, cholera and other water-borne diseases will increase. Higher temperatures and greater water stress raise the incidence of infections. Extreme events – cyclones, hurricanes, storm surges, floods and droughts – all impact negatively on health through drowning and injury, disease transmission and reduced resilience. Specific predictions include greatly increased levels of dengue fever (this already appears to be happening) and larger numbers of heat stress-related deaths in China and India. In Africa the predictions are of increased diarrhoeal disease and cholera and an extension of the range for malaria and arboviruses (dengue, Rift Valley, West Nile and other fevers). All of these problems will be compounded by food insecurity as poor nutrition exacerbates the effects of disease.

These negative predictions make the question of "what can be done" very pressing. Climate change re-shapes thinking about tackling global poverty in two particular ways. The first, and most obvious, is that the predicted impacts of climate change make the achievement of poverty reduction goals, such as the MDGs, more difficult and more costly. The second is that anthropogenic climate change represents a fundamental challenge to thinking about economic and human development. The historically rapid improvements in the human condition since around 1820 (see Chapter 1) have been closely associated with economic growth and that growth has been based on the exploitation of non-renewable energy sources – coal, oil and gas. Much, if not most, of the reduction in global poverty to date has involved strategies that raise CO_2 emissions – energy intensive industrialization and transportation processes, deforestation, energy intensive agriculture, cattle-rearing and energy profligate lifestyles. The recent reductions in poverty in China and India have centered on industrialization and urbanization with associated rises in the use of hydrocarbons and deforestation. Twenty years after the Brundtland Report and the launching of the idea of "sustainable development" our contemporary development model (be it "neo-liberal growth" or "growth with human development") is dependent on processes that massively increase CO_2 emissions and on the assumption that the real cost of adding CO_2 to the atmosphere is close to zero. Is it possible to reduce contemporary poverty without destroying the prospects of future generations? The glib answer to this is "green growth,"[24] which sounds very attractive but ignores the fact that, despite the odd billion dollars being invested here and there in green growth, such technologies are in their infancy. The wind farms of Europe and North America may be a start – but China and India's development plans for the next 25 years are centered on massively increasing the use of coal (and often dirty coal), gas and oil.

For analytical purposes two different approaches to re-shaping the world's energy profligate development model can be distinguished – reformist and radical.[25] The reformist approach is illustrated by the Stern Report[26] which adopted a welfare economics analysis of climate change to argue that from a social cost/benefit perspective immediate and sharp reductions in greenhouse gases were needed. Delaying such reductions would mean that much greater costs would be incurred in the future in terms of reduced gross world product and/or the scale of investment needed to moderate the effects of climate change. In essence, reformists view climate change as a consequence of a market failure: once this is corrected by charging for greenhouse gas emissions then economic growth and poverty reduction will continue but in forms that do not significantly emit greenhouse gases or raise temperatures.

While Stern has been criticized by other reformists for the high valuation he placed on carbon and his choice of discount rate, for radicals his work is absolutely flawed. As Clive Spash puts it: "The [Stern] authors maintain allegiance to an economic orthodoxy which perpetuates the dominant political myth that traditional economic growth can be both sustained and answer all our problems."[27] For radicals, the loss of species, the disappearance of glaciers, the flooding of coastal lands and increased human mortality represent losses which cannot be valued by market exchange and/or compensatory growth. Many radicals implicitly or explicitly adopt a rights-based analytical framework and thus: "Climate change, at least above a certain temperature rise, violates fundamental principles of sustainable development, intergenerational stewardship and fairness and therefore violates the inalienable rights of future generations."[28] Eco-anarchists and anti-capitalist environmentalists see the need for strategies that challenge market economics: rapid reductions in consumption by the rich, so that consumption of non-renewables and CO_2 emissions rapidly fall; the adoption of low consumption lifestyles around the world; and, a global society that provides for itself from local production systems. For some radicals "less is more": a low consumption lifestyle would permit development that does not generate the possibility of environmental catastrophe, increase levels of personal satisfaction and fulfillment and re-connects humanity with nature in a spiritual sense. This shades into "new wave" lifestyles and a non-utilitarian view of the environment that neo-classical economists see as irrational and many politicians see as unrealistic.

At a less abstract level the policy debate focuses on the ways in which mitigation (reducing CO_2 emissions so that climate change is not so rapid) and adaptation (changing present livelihoods so that people can better cope with climate change) form the basis for decision making. The Transatlantic Taskforce on Development argues that the links between climate change and global poverty can be understood diagrammatically (see Figure 6.1). Some of the MDGs, such as the health goals, can be achieved by coordinating poverty alleviation and climate change adaptation policies. Others, such as eradicating hunger, ensuring sustainable development and creating a global partnership, require a mix of poverty alleviation, adaptation and mitigation policies. The simplicity of the diagram hides the heated disagreements about mitigation and adaptation, two of which are especially significant: who

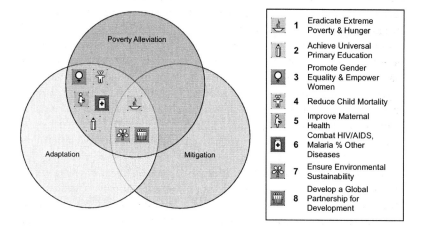

Figure 6.1 Climate change, global poverty and the MDGs

Source: The Transatlantic Taskforce on Development, *Toward a Brighter Future: A Transatlantic Call for Renewed Leadership and Partnerships in Global Development* (Washington, DC: The German Marshall Fund of the United States, 2009), 34.

should mitigate (i.e. reduce) their production of greenhouse gases and who should pay for the costs of adaptation?

Negotiations around these questions are always fraught, as shown by the United States refusing to sign up to the Kyoto Protocol in the 1990s, the maneuvering around the Bali climate meeting and the failure of the Copenhagen climate summit in 2009. The United States argues that it would be pointless for it to mitigate its carbon emissions (and potentially slow down its growth and suffer job losses) unless the emerging industrial powers, China and India, agree to dramatic reductions to their burgeoning emissions. China and India (and other emerging economies) point out that the world's present problems have been caused by the rich world (69 percent of anthropogenic emissions to date have been produced by the industrialized countries, while China, with 20 percent of the world's population, has contributed only 7.8 percent of CO_2 emissions[29]) and argue that this means the rich world has to do most of the mitigation. The idea of climate justice might provide a means of resolving this stumbling block, if different countries could agree on a common set of principles. Paul Baer, Tom Athanasiou, Sivan Kartha and Eric Kemp-Benedict have developed a "greenhouse development rights framework" that attempts this task.[30] They argue that if all individuals with a PPP income above US$20 are viewed as being responsible for global warming (the higher your income the more greenhouse gases you produce) and if one quantifies CO_2 emissions from 1990 (when global warming was identified) then equitable "national obligations" to mitigate and to fund adaptation policies can be computed. Such calculations are based on the numbers of a country's population with energy intensive lifestyles, so they include 80 million Indians and 350 million Chinese citizens (and they exclude millions of poor US citizens). On this basis the US would take on 33.1 percent of global mitigation targets, the EU 25.7 percent, China 5.5 percent and India 0.5 percent. All countries would contribute to mitigation, but the least developed countries, with 12 percent of world population, would be responsible for only 0.01 percent of mitigation targets as they have emitted so little CO_2. Similar forms of computation could share out national contributions to financing adaptation, estimated at between US$9 billion to $41 billion per annum by the World Bank.[31]

The elegance of such calculations does not yet seem to have won over climate change negotiators – especially those from the rich world. With almost 20 years of not fulfilling promises made at the "Earth Summit" at Rio in 1992 the continued likelihood of rhetoric not being matched by action seems strong. Pessimists, and that includes much of the popular and serious media, focus on what Mike Hulme[32] calls the "myth of Apocalypse" – predicting environmental collapse because our politicians and institutions appear to be incapable of "solving the problem." At the other extreme, optimists, of which there are relatively few, see in climate change (or more accurately the idea of climate change) the "myth of Jubilee . . . climate change provides the greatest opportunity to bring about justice and equality in the world."[33] They believe that the threat of climate change ". . . offers humanity the chance to do the right thing"[34] and provides a means for mobilizing a movement that will seek, and perhaps attain, global social justice. From this perspective, while in practical terms the existence of anthropogenic climate change makes global poverty reduction more difficult, the long-term case for global poverty eradication might be advanced by linking it to the idea of climate change. As global warming seems likely to stay higher up the international agenda than global poverty (because it impacts much more directly on the material and cultural interests of powerful countries and better-off people) it may be tactically most effective to promote policies for global poverty reduction through agreements about global warming. This would include increased funding for tropical agricultural research and health problems, constructing urban flood infrastructure, introducing global taxes on carbon and transferring low carbon energy technologies to developing countries without patent charges. All of these would help mitigate climate change, and assist poor people adapt to it, and at the same time directly reduce poverty. I return to this idea in the conclusion below.

The urbanization of poverty

Until recently the bulk of research on poverty, and most policy initiatives for poverty reduction, focused on rural poverty. There were good reasons for this: the numbers and proportions of the poor living in rural areas were much higher than in urban areas: economic and social indicators were almost universally lower for rural people than for urbanites in the developing world; and there were strong arguments that policies had an "urban bias" and that "rural poverty [is] unperceived."[35] Times have changed and this focus on rural poverty now has to be broadened – poverty is the issue and it must be understood and tackled across the rural-urban continuum (in villages, rural centers, towns, cities and hyper-cities).

The geography of human population and human suffering has and is changing. In the last few years humanity has gone past a tipping point with more than half of our population now living in towns, cities or megalopolises. Martin Ravallion, the world's most influential poverty measurer, estimates that on present trends more than half the of the world's extreme poor will live in urban areas by 2035.[36] Around two billion people will live in slums – overcrowded and unhealthy settlements with poor quality housing, inadequate access to safe water and sanitation, and insecure tenure. If David Satterthwaite is correct then the tipping point for the urbanization of poverty might come sooner. He argues persuasively that urban poverty is underestimated as poverty lines fail to take account of the higher costs – housing, transport, water, services for children – of meeting minimum needs in urban areas.[37] Urban living conditions are worse than the statistics suggest – as many who have wandered through an African or Asian slum would confirm.

While there are big problems with data "[s]lum populations are often deliberately and sometimes massively under-counted,"[38] evidence of the rapidly increasing scale and multi-dimensional nature of urban poverty is becoming more available. For example, in Maputo and Kinshasa around two-thirds of the population earn less than the extreme poverty line; two out of every five African slum-dwellers live in conditions that are "life-threatening."[39] The urban poor have low incomes but their poverty is much more than that: drinking contaminated water, having raw sewage in the open drain by one's house, breathing polluted air, being vulnerable to flash floods or landslips or street violence and much more. With 57 percent of urban Africans lacking basic sanitation the "flying toilet" (defecation into a plastic bag thrown out into the street) is a daily health hazard for tens of millions.

While the attention of those responsible for urban policy making is often captured by headlines about national capitals and/or the problems of emerging hyper-cities[40] (cities with more than 20 million residents) most urbanization occurs outside of these hotspots. Around three-quarters of the urban population increase in developing countries in coming decades will be in second-tier cities, towns and smaller urban units, where ". . . there is little or no planning to accommodate these people or provide them with services."[41] Indeed, analytically it may be best to think of the urban-rural continuum as in densely populated Asia it is already difficult to define what is urban and rural. Indeed, in Bangladesh researchers talk of "rurbanization" as rapidly growing rural towns are connected by roads with dense settlements on both sides.

While many factors are associated with this contemporary wave of urbanization, an influential UN Report argues that urban problems have been exacerbated by policies. "The primary direction of both national and international interventions during the last twenty years has actually increased urban poverty and slums, increased exclusion and inequality, and weakened urban elites in their efforts to use cities as engines of growth."[42] Structural adjustment programs created "disappearing peasantries" and "deagrarianization" across Africa, Asia and Latin America so that small farmers and laborers moved off the land.[43] In urban areas structural adjustment programs led to civil service downsizing, reduced numbers of formal sector jobs, dropping wage rates and reduced investment in infrastructure. The UN Report reaches a pessimistic conclusion: ". . . instead of being a focus for growth and prosperity, the cities have become a dumping ground for a surplus population working in unskilled, unprotected and low-wage informal service industries and trade."[44]

Any comforting notion that this contemporary burst of rapid and informal urbanization will progress through the sorts of historic stages that cities such as Manchester have seen (from the squalor of Engels' time to the improved conditions of late Victorian times)[45] needs challenging. As Mike Davis powerfully argues, the nature of contemporary urbanization[46] – centered on informal employment, markets, housing and services – is quite unlike earlier phases: ". . . at the end of the day, a majority of urban slum-dwellers are truly and radically homeless in the contemporary international economy."[47] The urban involution unfolding in his "planet of slums" sees a global informal working class slipping into ". . . spiraling labor self-exploitation . . . which continues, despite, rapidly diminishing returns, as long as any return or increment is produced."[48] In addition, the capacity of urban elites and middle classes to disconnect themselves from the broader processes of urbanization – through gated communities, independent water and power supplies, private transport, schools and hospitals, and security services – weakens the political pressure on such groups to take action. This suggests that strategies to tackle urban poverty through anti-poverty programs and support for informal micro-entrepreneurs will be ineffective. Radical changes in national and international development strategies will be required to provide infrastructure, decent work and reasonable living conditions for hundreds of millions of slum-dwellers.

In the long-term the issues raised above point to the need to support the political mobilization of the urban poor alongside slum-dwellers more broadly, so that they can start to demand policy change. These changes will challenge elites and middle classes in rich and poor countries as they will include policies to distribute incomes and assets (particularly land), nationally and internationally, more equitably. Shorter-term, this highlighting of urban poverty might be seen to suggest that the resources available for poverty reduction should be shifted away from rural problems to urban problems. Such thinking must be forcefully resisted. The recognition of the burgeoning issue of urban poverty needs to be used to (i) reform the ways in which the ". . . existing envelope of urban resources is allocated,"[49] and (ii) argue for a dramatic increase in the resources available for tackling global poverty across the rural-urban continuum.

Changing international social norms

The earlier sections of this chapter focused on changes in material capabilities as they shift towards Asia and are re-shaped by climate change; and, on institutional changes as we move to an urbanized world. This final section focuses more on ideas and the dramatic ways in which ideational change can impact on attitudes and practices around the world. It examines global poverty eradication from an international norms perspective: more specifically it asks could a norm evolve that views "the existence of extreme poverty in an affluent world as morally unacceptable"[50] – a norm that would make people around the world demand that poverty eradication genuinely be made a global priority? The power emanating from control over material capabilities shapes individual, corporate and country behaviors but so do normative concepts and values as Martha Finnemore and Kathryn Sikkink have eloquently argued.[51] Institutions play a central role in promoting and contesting ideas and encouraging or discouraging changes in social norms.[52]

When international norms change, what is seen by most people as "just the way the world is" can become absolutely unacceptable. For example, in 1800 most British people thought that slavery was unavoidable and for many it was unobjectionable. It had always been happening somewhere, it was central to the economy and particularly to the merchants and shippers of the booming cities of Liverpool and Bristol. Many believed it was probably good for the slaves as they would be materially more secure and might gain eternal salvation through conversion to Christianity. By 1850 anyone holding these views in the UK would have been viewed as unreasonable and probably immoral. In 1820 you could be a slave trader and a pillar of the local church: by 1840 you would not be welcome in that church if you did not believe that slavery was an offence against man and God. Over the nineteenth century this norm diffused across Europe and to North America and during the twentieth century every state in the world has declared slavery to be both immoral and illegal. Similar radical but gradual moral shifts can be traced over international norms about votes for women, laws about the conduct of war and apartheid and racial segregation.

Finnemore and Sikkink argue that the progression of international norms follows a three-stage life cycle: "norm emergence" in which a norm begins to receive domestic and international attention that (if successful) culminates in a "tipping point" – when a critical mass of states adopt the norm; this is followed by "norm cascade" when the norm diffuses across the broader international community; and finally "internalization" when the norm changes behaviors across many countries. There is no guarantee that any norm will proceed smoothly along this life cycle: their progress can stall and/or reversals can occur.

It can be argued that the creation of the MDGs has significantly raised the possibility of global poverty eradication becoming an international norm. Over the 1990s a global norm began to emerge and agreement on the IDGs by OECD countries and later on the MDGs, in 2001 and 2002 at the UN General Assembly and the Monterrey Consensus, took this past its tipping point. It cascaded internationally with most states signing non-binding agreements that they would pursue the MDGs. However, the internalization of the norm has been disappointing as the rhetoric of commitment to MDG achievement has not been matched by equivalent action – the allocation of more resources, the reform of multilateral institutions and the preparation of national plans based on need rather than a neo-classical economic notion of affordability. It may be that the Monterrey Consensus of March 2002 marked the high point of global poverty eradication as a norm. However, I am a little more optimistic and believe that the processes of internalization are still unfolding.[53] For example, in 2004 the 12 new member states of the EU had to agree that on accession they would set up a public agency for international development and agree a target for foreign aid in pursuit of the MDGs.[54] The commitment of many new member states to this norm may be weak but this requirement indicates that the unacceptability of extreme poverty is being internalized as a regional norm across the EU – if you want to be part of the EU club you have to publicly agree to be part of plans to eradicate global poverty and start to take some actions. That is relatively rapid progress, in comparative terms, in the life cycle of an international norm.

This leads Sakiko Fukuda-Parr and me to encourage proponents of global poverty eradication to not only think of the international agenda in instrumental terms (goals, resources and plans) but also to see it as an arena for the promotion of new values and changed norms. As well as asking "How do we achieve the MDGs?" we also need to ask "Are the MDGs an effective vehicle for diffusing and internalizing global poverty eradication as an international norm?" Perhaps the recent waning of interest in the MDGs means that they need to be changed and/or re-vitalized or perhaps they need abandoning and another vehicle needs to be brought to the fore. There are innumerable positions on this, but three can be identified that are analytically useful.

The first possibility focuses on changing the concept: moving from the basic needs and results-based management concepts that underpin the MDGs to a vehicle derived from other concepts. A front runner among alternatives is the concept of human rights, as passionately argued by Irene Khan and Thomas Pogge,[55] and perhaps the "right to development" which was formally agreed at the UN General Assembly in 1986. This recognized "an inalienable human right, of which every human being and all peoples are entitled to participate in, contribute to and enjoy economic, social, cultural and political development in which all human rights and freedoms can be fully realized." Conceptually, being a "right" has great advantages as this entails that the obligations of duty holders need to be identified and that forms of leverage over those who should take action can be designed and perhaps applied. However, this idea continues to meet substantial resistance both technically and politically. Technically it is challenged by neo-classical economists as the indivisibility of rights is viewed as making them inoperable for budgeting and planning purposes – how can you set budgets when all the goals have the same status so there is no hierarchy of priorities? Politically it has faced opposition as the world's rich countries believe that the developing countries would try to use the 1986 UN declaration to create an international obligation for high income countries to provide ODA. That is, that foreign aid levels, and perhaps uses, would not be at the discretion of the donor country but would be set internationally. In addition, China and some South-east Asian states have been concerned about human rights frameworks imposing "Western values" on them. The MDGs handled these tensions through the Goal 8 compromise of "global partnership"[56] – countries should negotiate shared responsibilities and mutual commitments to global poverty eradication, but they would not be internationally required to meet specific obligations.

From the opposite end of the spectrum, thinking pragmatically rather than philosophically, it could be argued that the MDGs are just too complicated for the sound bite culture of the twenty-first century. Would it not be better to strip the concept down to a really simple and attention-demanding focus? Why not concentrate on the most basic need and right of humans – the right to life? Perhaps a simple focus on reducing child mortality would muster agreement from almost all societies, can be easily communicated to citizens and could become an international social norm that could be rapidly internalized. It would capture much of the content of the MDGs (increased income and reduced hunger, gender equality, reduced child mortality, reproductive health for all, improved health services) in a simple form that is media friendly – "Stop preventable child deaths now." These two extremes – a fully fledged human rights position versus an attention-grabbing headline – illustrate the choices facing proponents of global poverty eradication as in the run up to the 2015 deadline they ask themselves "What comes after the MDGs?"

A second approach would be to stick with the MDG message but try to drive forward its public recognition and acceptance through more effective leadership. The MDGs have lacked an identifiable face to lodge them in the public mind and challenge attitudes and behaviors. Kofi Annan, the previous Secretary-General of the UN, though held in high regard by many observers of the international scene, was an international civil servant and not an international celebrity like Tony Blair, Bill Clinton or Nelson Mandela. His successor, Ban Ki-Moon, lacks charisma and appears much less committed to the pursuit of the MDGs. Behind the scenes, as with the mounting of the UN's high level event on the MDGs in 2008, Gordon Brown took on the role of global cheerleader for poverty eradication but he lacks the international profile and "pulling power" of Tony Blair. The hope would have to be for a charismatic leader, preferably from a developing country, to advance the

MDGs, or some alternative vehicle for global poverty eradication. My dream ticket is President Lula of Brazil, who steps down from office at the end of 2010. He has delivered economic growth, reduced poverty and reduced inequality in Brazil, has a powerful personal presence and is widely respected by national leaders in both the developing and developed worlds.

A third possible way by which global poverty eradication might advance as an international norm would be if a religion, or a coalition of religious groups, took it forward. The Enlightenment assumption that religion would retreat with the advance of modernity appears to have faltered, as in most parts of the world religion has remained an important social force or is returning. Islam has experienced a grand resurgence and its 1.2 billion adherents are clearly a social and political force to be reckoned with. Although Islam is commonly analyzed from a "clash of civilizations" view or with a focus on extremism and fundamentalism, Islamic social thought, and the Koran, take strong positions on poverty and on the obligation of those who are better off to help the poor. This might provide a resource that could influence the values of hundreds of millions of Muslims.[57]

Like Islam, Hinduism (in India) has experienced a resurgence that has both religious and political dimensions and has been associated with fundamentalist positions and increased communal tension. Fascinatingly, the secular Congress Party's recent commitment to nationwide social protection for the poor (the National Rural Employment Guarantee and the Unorganized Sectors Acts) evolved partly out of the need for a populist response to challenge the influence of the BJP (a Hindu-based political party) over the Hindu poor. The challenge of religious populism led to the Congress Party responding by launching populist anti-poverty schemes that have helped keep it in power and that appear to be helping to reduce poverty.

The Christian revival of the last two decades has been led by the Pentecostals and other Evangelicals.[58] They have swept across sub-Saharan Africa and Latin America in recent times and are winning converts in their tens of millions. While most of the focus of these expanding denominations has been religious conversion rather than pastoral concerns there is some evidence that they are now taking more interest in poverty and the poor. The Micah Challenge, initially spearheaded by the World Evangelical Alliance, now runs active campaigns in support of the MDGs in 39 countries. It directly links Christianity to poverty reduction through the production of "MDG prayer guides" and focusing services on the need for Christians to take action to reduce poverty around the world through both personal charity and political action (i.e. demanding that governments meet their MDG obligations).

Katherine Marshall, a former vice president of the World Bank, argues that ". . . the poverty-equity-faith nexus is more central to international politics and global governance challenges more broadly, than is generally recognized."[59] She points out that large numbers of development NGOs have religious bases (World Vision, Catholic Relief Services, Caritas, Islamic Relief, Jewish World Service, the Aga Khan Network and many others) and/or draw on members from religious communities. She cites the recent evolution of global interfaith organizations focused on development and poverty – the World Conference for Religions and Peace, the Parliament of World Religions, the United Religions Initiative, alongside the long-standing World Council of Churches. There are also more difficult to categorize "movements" – such as the Community of Sant'Egidio, the Gulen movement, Risho Kossei Kei and the Brahma Kumari movement – that are combining religious and developmental work. Marshall also points out the links between religion and international affairs that national and global leaders – Madeline Albright, Bill Clinton and Tony Blair – have reported in their work. One could add George Bush (with the setting up of the Millennium Challenge Account), Gordon Brown, Bono and many others to this list.

Marshall does not present religion as a magic bullet for tackling poverty or for shifting international norms towards a greater concern for the poor. Many different forces are shaping religious structures, thought and action, and there are several "minefields" that question what religion could contribute: isn't religion socially divisive; doesn't religion oppose modernization and change; aren't religions controlled by the wealthy and powerful, and will they not therefore resist changes to the status quo? What Marshall does argue is that in a world that appears to be returning to religion, in its many different faiths and forms, systematic thinking about how faith could be used as a tool to foster poverty eradication could be highly productive. The World Bank has engaged with faith communities in pursuit of the MDGs; UNFPA has engaged with faith leaders on reproductive health; and, UNICEF works closely with faith-inspired organizations around the world to promote child welfare. Religion may be a double-edged sword, but given its contemporary expansion (especially in the poorest parts of the world), its capacity to change human behavior and the declarations of most religions towards alleviating poverty, it may have a significant role to play in changing attitudes and behaviors to promote poverty eradication locally, nationally and internationally.

The directions that international social norms will take in the twenty-first century cannot be predicted, but it is possible for organizations and individuals, especially leaders, to exercise personal agency and seek to influence those directions. Proponents of global poverty eradication would do well to bear this in mind and to search out opportunities to advance it as a social norm: surely in an affluent world, with an average annual per capita product of PPP$10,500, extreme poverty and children dying for want of access to $1 of medicine must be regarded as morally unacceptable. If democracy, in its many different and imperfect forms, continues to be the most common system for national governance, then many governments will have incentives to respond to changes in public attitudes. Effectively promoting global poverty eradication as an international norm would raise the prospects of rich countries matching their promises about global poverty with action (tackling climate change, making trade fair, increasing aid and aid effectiveness and reducing the trade in arms) and of the elites and middle classes of poorer countries taking more interest in extreme poverty in their own countries.

Conclusion

While the World Bank's predictions for extreme income poverty are that globally this will continue to gradually decline in the medium and long term – once a recovery from the fuel, food and credit crunches of 2008 and 2009 has occurred – there are no grounds for complacency. Geo-politically and environmentally we are moving into a different world. Ultra-pessimists advise that climate change will not simply impoverish humanity but will produce an apocalypse that will annihilate it. At the other extreme, ultra-optimists believe climate change may be the event that pushes humanity into a deep social solidarity: this will foster compassion and create an egalitarian and sustainable future for all. Somewhere between these positions the prospects for long-term global poverty eradication are challenged by the likely impacts of climate change in the poorest parts of the world. At the present time, the future support that this grand goal will muster from the international community seems far from secure, with aid levels reducing and negotiations about mitigating climate change, meeting the costs of adaptation and reforming international trade staggering from meeting to meeting without any enforceable agreements in sight.

The continued economic rise of China and India, which is probable but by no means guaranteed, may re-write geo-politics but in itself seems unlikely to re-write "the rules of the game" of international relations: that the material, commercial and security interests of the most powerful countries and corporations determine what is on the agenda and how it is addressed. Whether the rise of Asia could re-define capitalism as "Asian culture . . . honed by centuries of hard experience . . ."[60] fosters a more prudent form of global economic activity, remains to be seen. Could better-argued secular moral rationalism; or a resurgence of religious belief; or better "marketing" of global poverty eradication to politicians and publics; or a combination of these factors lead to a shift in international social norms so that the existence of poverty becomes morally unacceptable across the world?

The central focus of this book – the invention of the idea of global poverty eradication – has moved some of these social forces a small way towards actions that have helped improve the lives of some poor people. But, often concern about global poverty looks like the flotsam and jetsam of international relations: it bobs up and down in the water but is barely noticed by the vast ships passing by. Finding ways of using the idea of global poverty eradication – and more effective vehicles for promoting an international norm to end poverty – may be as important as directly challenging institutions and confronting those who control material capabilities.

Notes

1 Yasheng Huang, *Capitalism with Chinese Characteristics: Entrepreneurship and the State* (New York: Cambridge University Press, 2008).
2 Mike Hulme, *Why We Disagree about Climate Change: Understanding Controversy, Inaction and Opportunity* (Cambridge: Cambridge University Press, 2009), 265.
3 Since 2008 confidence in this assumption has faltered with the food price spike and global financial crisis. However, Chen and Ravallion (http://www.voxeu.org (May 22, 2009)) believe that after an increase in $1.25-a-day poverty in 2009 and 2010 of 73 million people ". . . the aggregate poverty rate is still expected to fall over time."
4 Other crucial issues include: food availability and prices, increased longevity and the aging of world population, and technological changes (ICTs, energy, GM foods).
5 Hulme, *Why We Disagree* and see later sections of this chapter.
6 All of these scenarios are based on predictions of economic and demographic growth. Military analysts argue that the US dominance in military terms (technological and intelligence capabilities) will continue for decades after US economic power moves into a second position against China.
7 This idea was developed by Goldman Sachs. The 11 countries are Bangladesh, Egypt, Indonesia, Iran, South Korea, Mexico, Nigeria, Pakistan, the Philippines, Turkey and Vietnam.
8 Angus Maddison, *The World Economy: A Millennial Perspective* (Paris: Development Centre of the Organisation for Economic Co-operation and Development, 2001).
9 All these scenarios focus on aggregate economic growth rates and make no adjustments for "pro-poor" growth performance.
10 See Chapter 1.
11 I have my suspicions about these figures. Clearly poverty reduction has been epic but the official data on income/expenditure lacks independent validation and the PPP assumptions are heroic. The scale of rural protests, state controls on urban migration and the collapse of health services for low income households warrant concern. Also see Huang, *Capitalism with Chinese Characteristics*.
12 The lack of urban PPPs and the greater costs of living in cities mean that figures on the global urban poor are underestimated (see later in this chapter).
13 Fascinatingly, this also extends into social links. At Victoria Falls in Zimbabwe in late 2009 I found myself the only European in a hotel booked up with more than 100 Chinese tourists.
14 See Dambisa Moyo, *Dead Aid: Why Aid is Not Working and How There is Another Way for Africa* (London: Allen Lane, 2009); and Carlos Oya, "Greater

Africa-China Economic Cooperation: Will This Widen 'Policy Space'?" Development Viewpoint No. 4 (London: SOAS, 2008).

15 India has been systematic and has set up the Indian International Development Agency with around US$1 billion of aid in 2007 – see David Hulme, "Imagining Inclusive Globalisation: Chronic Poverty and What India Can Do About It," Export-Import Bank of India Annual Public Lecture, Mumbai (April 20, 2007). Sinologists report that Chinese aid programmes are spread around many different ministries and that the scale and scope of activity is unclear (David Sumbough, personal communication, January 30, 2008).

16 Do note that both countries have pursued unorthodox macro-economic and industrial policies and that IMF influence over policies in poorer countries would block the implementation of Chinese- or Indian-type strategies.

17 East Africa is attempting to revive the East African Community which has a population of more than 126 million people. DRC has a large population and fabulous natural resources but there are few optimists on its future.

18 Joe Hanlon, Armando Barrientos and David Hulme, *Just Give Money to the Poor* (West Hartford, Conn.: Kumarian Press, 2010).

19 Assuming the EU remains incapable of presenting itself as a global power.

20 There will be many other consequences such as reduced biodiversity and loss of valued landscapes.

21 Government of Bangladesh, "Bangladesh Climate Change Strategy and Action Plan 2008" (Ministry of Environment and Forests, Dhaka, 2008), available at http://www.moef.gov.bd/moef.pdf

22 The figures that follow are extracted from IPCC, *Summary for Policymakers: Working Group II Climate Change 2007 – Climate Change Impacts, Adaptation and Vulnerability* (Geneva: IPCC, 2007); and Anthony Nyong, "Climate Change Impacts in the Developing World: Implications for Sustainable Development," in *Climate Change and Global Poverty*, ed. Lael Brainard, Abigail Jones and Nigel Purvis (Washington, DC: Brookings Institution, 2009), 43–64.

23 The experience in middle and high latitudes, where the richer countries are located, may be the reverse with higher temperatures leading to higher yields.

24 For a discussion see Abigail Jones, Vinca LaFleur and Nigel Purvis, "Double Jeopardy: What Climate Crisis Means for the Poor', in *Climate Change and Global Poverty*, ed. Lael Brainard, Abigail Jones and Nigel Purvis (Washington, DC: Brookings Institution, 2009).

25 The examples of reformist and radical approaches presented here are drawn from Hulme, *Why We Disagree*.

26 Nicholas Stern, *The Economics of Climate Change* (Cambridge: Cambridge University Press, 2006).

27 Clive Spash, "The Economics of Climate Change Impacts a la Stern: Novel and Nuanced or Rhetorically Restricted?" *Ecological Economics* 63, no. 4 (2007): 706–713.

28 Eric Neumayer, "A Missed Opportunity: The Stern Review on Climate Change Fails to Tackle the Issue of Non-substitutable Loss of Natural Capital," *Global Environmental Change* 17, no. 3 (2007): 297–301.

29 World Development Movement, *Blame it on China: The International Politics of Climate Change* (London: World Development Movement, 2007), 5.

30 Paul Baer, Tom Athanasiou, Sivan Kartha and Eric Kemp-Benedict, *The Greenhouse Development Rights Framework: The Right to Development in*

a *Climate Constrained World*, 2nd edn. (Berlin: Heinrich Böll Foundation, Christian Aid, EcoEquity and the Stockholm Environment Institute).

31 For a list of the different estimates see Brainard *et al.*, *Climate Change*, 184.

32 See Hulme, *Why We Disagree* for an excellent discussion of the ways in which climate change feeds into contemporary discourses.

33 Christine Stewart, Canada's former Environment Minister speaking in 2007, quoted in Hulme, *Why We Disagree*, 354.

34 James Garvey, *The Ethics of Climate Change: Right and Wrong in a Warming World* (New York: Continuum International Publishing, 2008).

35 See Michael Lipton, *Why Poor People Stay Poor: Urban Bias in World Development* (London: Temple Smith, 1977) and Robert Chambers, *Rural Development: Putting the Last First* (London: Longman, 1983).

36 Martin Ravallion, *On the Urbanization of Poverty* (Washington, DC: World Bank, 2001).

37 David Satterthwaite, "The Under-estimation of Urban Poverty in Low and Middle-income Nations," Poverty Reduction in Urban Areas Series Working Paper No. 14 (London: International Institute for Environment and Development, 2004).

38 Mike Davis, "Planet of Slums: Urban Involution and the Informed Proletariat," *New Left Review* 26 (2004): 14.

39 Davis, "Planet of Slums," 13, 16.

40 By 2025 these will include Jakarta (24.9 million), Dhaka (25 million), Karachi (26.5 million), Mumbai (33 million) and the Abidjan-Ibadan region (70 million).

41 UN-Habitat, *The Challenge of the Slums: Global Report on Human Settlements 2003* (London: UN Habitat, 2003), 3.

42 UN-Habitat, *The Challenge*, 6.

43 Deborah Bryceson, Cristobal Kay and Jos Mooij, eds., *Disappearing Peasantries? Rural Labour in Africa, Asia and Latin America* (London: Intermediate Technology Publications, 2000).

44 UN-Habitat, *The Challenge*, 10.

45 This is not to argue that by late Victorian times Manchester was a utopia, but over the middle of the nineteenth century the earnings, living conditions and social indicators of many of Manchester's working class improved significantly.

46 However, I would distinguish between the urbanization-with-growth contexts (Shanghai, Guangjou, Bangalore, Hyderabad, Kuala Lumpur, etc.) and urbanization-without-growth contexts of Northern India, Pakistan, sub-Saharan African countries and others. Davis's generalizations are not as relevant to the former.

47 Davis, "Planet of Slums," 26.

48 Davis, 29.

49 Marie Ruel, Lawrence Haddad and James Garrett, "Some Urban Facts of Life: Implications for Research and Policy," *World Development* 27, no. 11 (1999): 1934.

50 For a fuller discussion of this issue see Sakiko Fukuda-Parr and David Hulme, "International Norm Dynamics and 'the End of Poverty': Understanding the Millennium Development Goals (MDGs)," BWPI Working Paper No. 96 (Manchester: BWPI, University of Manchester, 2009).

51 Martha Finnemore and Kathryn Sikkink, "International Norm Dynamics and Political Change," *International Organization* 52, no. 4 (1998): 887–917.

52 Richard Jolly, Louis Emmerij and Thomas G. Weiss, *UN Ideas that Changed the World* (Indiana: Indiana University Press, 2009).

53 Fukuda-Parr and Hulme, "International Norm Dynamics."

54 Also see Chapter 7 and Box 7.1.

55 Thomas Pogge, *World Poverty and Human Rights: Cosmopolitan Responsibilities and Reforms* (Cambridge: Polity, 2008); and Irene Khan, *The Unheard Truth: Poverty and Human Rights* (London: W.W. Norton and Company, 2009).

56 Laure-Helene Piron, "The Right to Development: A Review of the Current State of the Debate for DFID" (London: ODI, 2002), report available at http://www.odi.org.uk

57 It would have to be observed, however, that the Koran, and many interpretations of it, present poverty as something that is to be largely remedied by charity. The responsibilities of Islamic states to improve the well-being of the poor (at home or in other countries) do not seem to figure prominently in contemporary debates, and Islamic countries, and countries with large numbers of Muslims do not seem to have played much of a role in UN debates about poverty eradication (other than challenging reproductive health rights).

58 The long-established churches, Anglicanism and Roman Catholicism, have been losing membership in recent times.

59 Katherine Marshall, "Governance and Inequality: Reflections on Faith Dimensions," in *Global Governance, Poverty and Inequality*, ed. Jennifer Clapp and Rorden Wilkinson (London: Routledge, 2010), 297.

60 See Kishore Mahbubani, "Lessons for the West from Asian Capitalism," *Financial Times*, May 15, 2009.

7 Why don't we care about ending poverty?

In this chapter the partial advance of the idea of "ending poverty," and the progress achieved over the last 25 years, are analyzed through the lens of Robert Cox's critical political economy. Subsequently it is argued that, alongside judgments about the economic and social improvements occurring in the lives of poor people, an assessment of whether the promotion of the idea of global poverty has impacted on international norms is needed. Have the activities and initiatives associated with "ending poverty" – UN declarations, the International Development Goals (IDGs), the Millennium Development Goals (MDGs), debt forgiveness, Finance for Development (FFD), PRSPs and PRSs – raised the prospects for the establishment of an international social norm that finds the existence of extreme poverty in an affluent world morally unacceptable?

Understanding efforts to end poverty: ideas, institutions and material capabilities

The placing of the idea of global poverty eradication on the international agenda in the 1990s was not the result of some natural moral progression. Nor was it accidental. It arose out of the interaction of social forces within the historic structure of that era as individuals, groups, organizations, networks, nations and associations of nations pursued their goals and collaborated and/ or contested with each other. Most of these actors pursued what they believed to be in their self-interest – the creation of an account showing that the spread of capitalism would benefit all of the world's people (and so economic globalization should continue); policies and programs that might reduce flows of illegal immigrants from poorer countries into richer countries; programs that would discourage the recruitment of young men into "terrorist" organizations; images of compassion that improved a country's or organization's standing in international circles; stabilized aid flows so that aid agencies did not have to downsize; and many other self-interested reasons. But this was also tempered by compassion and informed by varying moral visions of the world that many actors sought to live in and to bequeath to future generations – a genuine desire to improve the lives of very poor people; a belief that social and economic inequality had to be reduced; a commitment to reducing the impact of climate change on poorer people and stopping humanity from destroying the earth; religious beliefs and other moral sentiments. Part of this moral vision (to use David Lumsdaine's idea) focused on extreme poverty and was favored by an historic moment, the new millennium, which created an opportunity to push this issue up the international agenda.

To explain the processes surrounding the evolution and advance of the idea of global poverty eradication, and its institutionalization (in the MDGs, PRSs, $1-a-day poverty measures, Global Monitoring Reports, the US's Millennium Challenge Account and other mechanisms) this section explores the historical structure that underpinned its evolution. It looks at the interactions of the different forces (material capabilities, ideas and institutions) that supported, opposed and shaped the idea and its practice. These interactions are complex and multi-directional. As an example, while the idea of human development has many sources its roots lay in debates between the academic world and UN agencies – with Paul Streeten, Amartya Sen, Mahbub-ul-Haq and many others. An institution, the UNDP, literally institutionalized the idea of human development by publishing an annual *Human Development Report* and establishing a Human Development Report Office. By creating the Human Development Index it launched a measure for economists and econometricians, the high priests of scientific work on development and poverty, which helped to steer some of them away from their obsession with economic growth. These initiatives greatly raised the level of academic and policy interest in the idea, encouraging further conceptual elaborations and influencing the UN conferences and summits of the 1990s. This led to the re-allocation of material capabilities, the increased resourcing of efforts for human development and, once the MDGs were agreed, these resources impact on the UNDP which established a Millennium Project, to make a global plan for a human development approach to poverty eradication, and a Millennium Campaign, to raise public awareness around the world about the need to "end poverty." To understand the promises that have been broken, and the progress that has been made, we must examine this constant interaction of ideas, institutions and material capabilities.

Ideas

As discussed in earlier chapters, many ideas informed and contested "what" global poverty was and "how" it could be tackled. The previously dominant overarching framework for world development, neo-liberal capitalism (summarized in the Washington Consensus), was being strongly challenged. Although powerful voices (at the IMF, World Bank and in the "freshwater" universities of the United States) argued that it was still the only way forward, the failure of structural adjustment policies to rapidly promote growth and welfare improvements in poor countries, allied to the evidence that these policies directly immiserized the urban poor and others, meant the technical case for structural adjustment was now much weaker than in the 1980s. On the other side of the ideological spectrum, structuralist and Marxist academics and social activists were looking for radical alternatives to capitalism[1] but there was no clearly articulated alternative. Critics of neo-liberalism could explain what they did not want but struggled to construct a clear specification for a radical alternative. As a result the formulation of what ending poverty meant and how this could be pursued was partly the outcome of a fragmented conversation between moderate critics of neo-liberalism, loosely grouped around the idea of "human development," and non-fundamentalist neo-liberals, drifting towards a post-Washington Consensus.

The idea of re-framing international development as global poverty eradication, rather than neo-liberal growth, gradually emerged over the 1990s. The moral case for focusing on the poor and poorest had long been known. The negative effects of structural adjustment programs had meant that the World Bank had been forced to pursue "social dimensions" and social fund initiatives from the late 1980s onwards. In essence these were direct poverty reduction programs so the Bank had some recent experience of poverty reduction. The pressure for policy change from critics of structural adjustment, allied to the need that the Bank's new president, James Wolfensohn, perceived to transform the Bank's image,[2] made poverty reduction a politically attractive goal for the Bank. As Collier and Dercon[3] write:

> [T]he choice of absolute poverty was essentially a political solution to a range of political problems . . . the World Bank . . . needed an objective that signaled it 'cared' . . . there was a clear need for some reasonably specific and measurable objective to assess agency performance . . . further, poverty reduction offered an objective that could be embraced by the entire pantheon of development agencies and so offered the prospect of coordination that had otherwise proved illusive . . . a focus on 'the poor' offered the possibility of a compromise with this [the Left] critical lobby.

But how would poverty reduction (note that Collier and Dercon avoid eradication) be conceptualized? This was where the idea of human development came in. The idea had provided general support for UN conferences and associated declarations throughout the 1990s. While it has many variants, and has a wide breadth of supporters rather than a coherent epistemic community, it promoted two specific theoretical strands that became underpinnings for efforts to tackle global poverty. These particularly shaped the MDGs. First, it advanced the case that development strategies needed to directly pursue the goals of development, and not just the means (economic growth). Human development provided an overarching conceptual framework for arguing that education and health improvements, gender equality and other goals were not only good in their own right but were essential components of the pursuit of a dynamic vision of the good life. Social goals should not play second fiddle to economic goals; they had to be pursued on an equal footing.

Second, when the conveners of the UN Social Summit, the OECD's DAC and the UN Secretariat drew up lists of goals they could explicitly or implicitly argue that a list was needed as development and poverty reduction were multi-dimensional. Lists of goals were not mere "shopping lists" reflecting a failure to analyze problems and select priorities (a criticism that had partly undermined UN promoted "basic needs" strategies in the 1980s). Rather, multiple goals were essential for any rigorously thought-out poverty reduction effort. While the processes behind the placing of items on such lists involved complex interactions – involving ideas, empirical evidence, political interests and personal values – human development provided a well-reasoned case for multi-dimensional lists. In the background were the works of Nobel Laureate Amartya Sen. His name, along with others, could be cited in an iconic fashion to show that a deep theoretical resource lay behind such lists.[4]

But human development needed to reach an accommodation with ideas about economic growth if it was going to be acceptable to those interests that dominated decision-making in the most powerful institutions and controlled the world's material capabilities. The idea that economic growth was essential for global poverty reduction, alongside the self-interest of the countries, corporations and people doing well out of capitalist development, meant that the MDGs had not merely to include but had to be headed by the goal of reducing income poverty (i.e. raising incomes through growth). Importantly, the MDGs identified goals but did not specify the strategy that would be followed to pursue such goals. Should poverty reduction strategies be growth-led or human development-led? This would have required an agreement between the different sets of institutions and interests championing these choices. Such an agreement was infeasible and so the goals were as far as the specification went. The policy choices would be battled over, ideationally and politically, in the field – with PRSPs, MTEFs and other devices.

The idea of human development was not just challenged by those with material interests in maintaining the status quo. Other institutions also contested the emerging super-norm of the MDGs. The very strong human development case for reproductive health was challenged by the Vatican and a handful of conservative Islamic states. As a result, the International Conference on Population and Development's reproductive health goal disappeared during secret negotiations to finalize the MDGs in 2000 and 2001 (Box 7.1).

The ideational adjunct to human development, in terms of the MDGs and plans to achieve the MDGs, was results-based management (RBM). This did not directly contribute to the content of global goals and strategies but it did determine the form they took. This reflected the interests of the rich, aid donor countries and especially their politicians and senior public servants who wanted to be able to explain to their publics that aid would not be wasted because best practice management tools would ensure effectiveness. The common sense nature and linearity of RBM made it attractive – set targets, monitor achievement and reward staff on the basis of performance. For the aid-financed programs of the DAC membership, World Bank and UN it was particularly attractive. The widely reported underperformance of aid in earlier years would not occur in the future as RBM methods would ensure high levels of performance.

RBM influenced the idea of global poverty eradication in three main ways. First, it determined the structure of the MDGs and explains why they are

Box 7.1 Ideas and institutions: the case of reproductive health

The institutional interactions and contestations around the idea of reproductive health are particularly revealing. In the early 1990s the women's movement, and particularly networks such as the International Women's Health Coalition, made enormous progress in developing and popularizing the idea of sexual and reproductive health rights. By accepting a compromise at the very heated UN International Conference on Population and Development in Cairo in 1994 (they dropped the terms "sexual" and "rights") they managed to shift the population paradigm from "population control" to "reproductive health." However, in the negotiations before the Millennium Declaration they were out-maneuvered by the Holy See.[1] It forged an alliance with a small group of conservative Islamic states and used this to persuade the G77 to block reproductive health

(Box continued on next page)

as a goal. In the final negotiations around the MDGs, reproductive health was the only goal on the DAC's IDG list that was thrown out.[2] These complex and multi-layered institutional interactions, often conducted in secret, permitted a group of less than 1,000 celibate, elderly males (the official residents of the Vatican) to reduce the access of 3 billion women to reproductive health services.

Source: David Hulme, "Politics, Ethics and the Millennium Development Goals: The Case of Reproductive Health," Brooks World Poverty Institute Working Paper No. 104 (Manchester: University of Manchester Press, 2009).

Notes

1 The Holy See was, and remains, concerned that reproductive health services may offer women access to abortion services.

2 See David Hulme, "Politics, Ethics and the Millennium Development Goals: The Case of Reproductive Health," Brooks World Poverty Institute Working Paper No. 104 (Manchester: University of Manchester, 2009) for a discussion. Note that in 2005 the General Assembly agreed that reproductive health could be an MDG target (i.e. sub-goal).

a nested hierarchy of goals, targets and indicators focused on time-bound "outcomes." RBM theory argues that goals must be SMART – stretching, measurable, achievable, realistic and time-bound – and this thinking was applied to the goals emerging from UN conferences and DAC analyses. Second, it shaped the specification of goals. While determining what is "achievable" is not an exact science, one sees this tenet in operation with the $1-a-day poverty target. At the World Summit for Social Development in Copenhagen 1995 this was set as "eradicating" extreme poverty. RBM thinking about this target reduced it to the stretching but feasible "halve" extreme poverty by 2015.[5] Third, the idea of RBM meant that the pursuit of global poverty eradication was focused on measurables: this meant that politically contentious goals, such as human rights and participation, could be avoided on the technical grounds that they were difficult to measure. These issues could be placed in the introductions and conclusions of key documents, but not in the lists that were to guide resource allocation and plans of action. As a result the variety of human development that lay behind the Millennium vision of ending poverty was more "meeting basic needs" than "promoting human rights." As with human development, political interests moderated the full application of RBM, as with the under-specification of Goal 8.[6]

Power relations took precedence over ideas so Goal 8 has only one quantitative target and no dates for achievement. The rich countries, which were most keen to see RBM applied to development goals, were too smart (and too powerful) to have SMART thinking applied to goals about which their performance might be monitored.

Institutions

A vast number and range of institutions have shaped, and continue to shape, thinking and action (or lack of action) on global poverty. These range from the UN General Assembly and UN specialized agencies, to the G8 and G20, the OECD's DAC, the World Bank and IMF, to bilateral development agencies, the finance ministries of developing countries to social movements, the Holy See, NGOs, think-tanks and epistemic communities. Often these institutions form formal and/or informal networks and coalitions, such as Jubilee 2000, in pursuit of their aims.

The UN has been central to the re-framing of international development as global poverty eradication through the conferences and summits of the early 1990s, the formulation of the Millennium Declaration and MDGs (1998–2001) and subsequent plans for MDG implementation. This has involved the UN General Assembly, the UN Secretariat, the UNDP and other specialized agencies. Early on the UN's main contribution was as a convening power, pulling together international conferences and world summits and persuading member states to negotiate and agree socially progressive declarations. Some parts of the UN made major efforts and contributions. UNDP played a central ideational role by promoting the concept of human development, as an alternative to neo-liberal growth, throughout the 1990s. UNICEF operated highly effectively: it re-launched UN summitry, steered child development to the heart of poverty eradication (and the MDGs) and, pursuing a human rights approach, achieved the Convention on the Rights of the Child.[7]

However, the UN Secretariat was often walking a tight rope, tasked with brokering agreements between its members, and other groups, that had very different interests and ideas about what improving the human condition meant and how global poverty reduction might be achieved. As pointed out above, the Secretariat had to focus on "what should be achieved" but not on "how it should be achieved." The latter would have led to disagreements that it was judged best to delay until the idea of human development had made progress. The Secretariat brokered the "final" MDG deal in 2001 with the incorporation of Goal 8 into the MDGs – what rich countries should do. This made MDG implementation plans feasible but also created an Achilles heel – the weak specification of Goal 8 targets meant that the world's most powerful countries could continue with business as usual.

Within the broader UN system, but at the opposite end in terms of its contribution to focusing on global poverty eradication, is the IMF. While it participated in key activities, such as being one of the four members of the technical committee that finalized the MDG goals, and has re-named its key products (e.g. the Poverty Reduction and Growth Facility) there is little evidence that its actions or culture have been impacted by the shift of focus to poverty eradication. The IMF has been reluctant to shift from its neo-liberal, "Chicago" analysis and to embrace the broader set of goals in the MDGs (that go beyond economic stability and economic growth). Interviews with IMF staff revealed that "we mention the MDGs in the introduction of reports but they don't change anything" and "the MDGs are European social policy and the IMF does not do European social policy."[8] The IMF has been able to give an impression of being part of global agreements on poverty eradication without making any significant changes in its thinking or practice.

The preference of international institutions specializing in public finance to avoid the human development content of the global goals (MDGs) may be systemic. When negotiating Nigeria's debt relief deal with the Paris Club in October 2005 the country's Finance Minister, Dr Ngozi Okonjo-Iweala, remembered Kofi Annan as saying that a country could only be considered sustainable if it could finance the MDGs: ". . . we were told not to mention the word 'MDGs,' that it was not a concern of the Paris Club."[9] Neo-liberal arguments – that education and health expenditures are consumption expenditures that need to be capped so that public expenditure is kept low and state activity is rolled back – still have power for those who oversee the management of developing country debt.

The World Bank has played a major role in thinking and action about global poverty eradication. The work of its Research Department in developing the idea of $1-a-day poverty helped persuade many rich world politicians that global poverty counted (because apparently precise figures could be produced about it). The design of PRSPs was closely associated with the Bank. While it is not possible to classify the Bank's practice of poverty eradication as easily as it is that of the IMF it is clear that Bank rhetoric – about participatory assessments of poverty, shifting to country ownership of PRSPs and a greater focus on social development – moved well ahead of its actions. In particular, during the early 2000s parts of the Bank's Research Department mounted a powerful campaign to prove that economic liberalization always led to poverty reduction. This supported a continuation of the neo-liberal policies of the 1980s and 1990s and, although this was eventually discredited, it weakened attempts to broaden the focus of PRSPs beyond market-based economic policies.

Civil society groups (social movements, NGOs, faith groups and others) were an influential force in the promotion of the idea of global poverty eradication and in its specification. Their profile and capacity had risen greatly since the end of the Cold War and they gained access to UN events and became powerful advocates for a range of international norms aimed at reducing human deprivation and inequality and promoting human rights. Many of these groups aspired to promote an agreement around an alternative development that did not merely reject neo-liberalism but was actively post-capitalist.[10] However, they were bitterly disappointed about the "third way" configuration of the final MDGs, with social goals listed below the economic goal of raising incomes. They were also dismayed that the major responsibilities for implementing poverty eradication were left to the IMF and World Bank, without their governance processes being reformed.

The types of institution that might have been able to advance ideas that would have forced change on the IMF and World Bank – a powerful social movement for poverty eradication or a coherent epistemic community promoting human development or human rights – did not emerge at the millennium moment. The progress made with the idea of human development was the result of shifting networks and coalitions of actors and did not produce a robust institutional support for the idea. The idea of human development made progress, but still it fell between two stools. It did not lead to the emergence of a self-fueling social movement that could consistently place human development on the political agenda when decisions were being taken.

As pointed out in Chapter 3, the closest it came to this was with time-limited campaigns mounted by coalitions of NGOs and faith-based organizations such as Jubilee 2000, Make Poverty History and ONE. There are several reasons for this – poverty may be just too broad a concept for effective social mobilization and the specification of poverty reduction in the MDGs meant that it was hard to see "who was the enemy"; poverty and/or poverty eradication does not provide an identity for effective activism; and, the poor/non-poor division inherent in the idea of absolute poverty makes it difficult to create social solidarity and stalls the evolution of a leadership cadre.[11]

Nor did an epistemic community emerge (in academia, the professions and the media) that could agree on a tightly defined analytical and causal framework that could capture and dominate decision-making in key organizations, as had the neo-liberal epistemic community at the IMF, World Bank, US Treasury and ministries of finance around the world.[12] Those who wish to see the idea of human development genuinely shape policies and resource allocations post-2015 may need to put less time and effort into refining the minutiae of the concept and more time and effort into thinking through how to institutionalize the idea more fully. However, human development might be a concept that does not lend itself easily to form the base for an epistemic community. It is broad, it recognizes the need for deliberation and debate (and thus eschews the type of elite domination that made the neo-liberal epistemic community so powerful) and it is multi-disciplinary. The prospects for human development creating a tight-knit epistemic community that might wrest control of technical advice on public policy in the most powerful organizations away from neo-classical economists, often with a neo-liberal orientation, do not seem good. Perhaps the best hope is that in the United States (not only the world's greatest economic and military power but also its greatest intellectual power) the "saltwater economists" of New England and California can challenge the hegemony that the "freshwater economists" of Chicago have enjoyed in the social sciences in the US and in key economic institutions.

Material capabilities

Material capabilities (technological and organizational capabilities with productive and destructive potentials) lay at the heart of the idea of ending poverty. Humanity now has the material capabilities to dramatically reduce or eradicate extreme poverty across the world and a re-distribution of a small part of these capabilities would permit the poor to meet their needs for basic goods and services. In practice, reforming access to material capabilities has proved very difficult. The units that might re-write "the rules of the game" for access to and use of material capabilities – primarily national governments and associations of governments – have been prepared to reach general agreement on the need for change but key members and groups of members oppose specific changes (such as increasing their aid budgets or reforming the governance of the BWIs). This is partly because of active opposition to changes because of national self-interest[13] and partly due to a more passive lack of interest in global poverty reduction. For most high and middle income countries, and their governments and citizens, global poverty (poverty in other countries) is neither a high priority nor a pressing public issue. There are more pressing global issues – security, climate change, conflict, trade, energy supplies – or global poverty is judged to be of little political significance by those who hold power at the national level.[14] For the leaders of most low income countries national poverty reduction is only one of several goals, and other goals – national security, staying in power, amassing personal wealth, religious goals – are often much more pressing. As a result, most heads of government and national political leaders find it easy to agree that global poverty must be reduced but few have the personal commitment, or come under sufficient political pressure, to move beyond rhetoric and commit significant political or material resources to this end.

So, while material capabilities in the aggregate create the opportunity for global poverty eradication it is the contemporary distribution of those capabilities that sets the limits on achieving this goal. While material capabilities are spread around the world, the concentration of capabilities in the United States, the world's only superpower (economically and technologically), means that it has been, and remains, in a unique position to shape the evolution of goals and plans for tackling global poverty (as with all other global goals and problems).[15] It has appeared to be deeply ambivalent about how to respond to the challenge of global poverty.[16] At times it has supported the processes, as in 2002 when George W. Bush spoke enthusiastically[17] at the Monterrey Finance for Development Summit and announced massive increases in US foreign aid.[18] At other times it has appeared to oppose international efforts, as in 2005 when John Bolton (the then US Ambassador to the UN) sought to have the terms "Millennium Development Goals" and "poverty" removed from the "Millennium plus Five" General Assembly Declaration. Despite this ambivalence the United States is central to most efforts and activities to end poverty: directly, through its vast resources and influence over institutions such as the IMF, World Bank and G7/8; and indirectly, as every other actor (governments, multilateral and bilateral agencies, social movements, NGOs, activists, celebrities) in the process asks "What is the US position on this?" Their actions, for better or for worse, are partly conditioned by what they think the US position is or will be.[19]

The power of the United States, deriving from its material capabilities, has had many impacts on the evolution of efforts to tackle extreme poverty. Most significantly, the framing of global goals and plans of action had to be done in a way that ensured the United States would be a part of global efforts – this set limits on how radical they could be. While the ideas behind the UN conferences and summits (and later the IDGs and MDGs) dismissed the thinking and prescriptions of the "Washington Consensus" they could not imagine challenging the idea or practice of free market, global capitalism as the basis for the improvement of the human condition. It is no accident that MDG Goal 1/Target 1 is personal income growth. How this goal will be achieved – by rapidly opening up an economy and encouraging Foreign Direct Investment or through industrial policy to guide the establishment of infant industries – was not specified as that would have led to argument and the blocking of an agreement. Similarly, the MDGs' focus on reducing extreme absolute poverty (economically and socially) was acceptable to the United States (and many of its allies and business interests more generally). Had the IDGs or MDGs focused on reducing economic and social inequality more broadly the global goal setting process may have stalled.[20] The MDGs had to remain open on whether or not inequality was a bad thing as the United States, and other powerful countries and interest groups, would have actively opposed a more assertive stance on inequality and/or re-distribution. While philosophers in New England might bemoan the lack of ambition of the MDGs[21] politicians in Washington, DC knew where the line on global aspirations needed to be set. Growth with absolute poverty reduction was fine but growth with re-distribution would be a step too far.

US ambivalence made it easier for other powerful nations[22] to be similarly ambivalent. The exceptions to this ambivalence have been a small number of European countries which have energetically promoted increased finance and stronger action for global poverty eradication. These like-minded countries – Denmark, the Netherlands, Norway and Sweden – were joined by the United Kingdom in 1997. The efforts of these countries have helped push the EU into agreeing to significantly increase foreign aid budgets and have impacted on wider multilateral processes. Indeed, it can be argued that the norm of "ending poverty" has been institutionalized in the EU, particularly through the vehicle of the MDGs.[23] However, the institutionalization of the MDGs as a nascent norm in the EU does not mean that it is playing a leading role internationally. International development, and thus global poverty eradication, is a foreign policy item that EU countries deal with at the national level. As a result the message that the EU provides to the world about tackling global poverty is incoherent – as with so many of its foreign policy positions.

While a number of countries have made major efforts to promote the idea and practice of global poverty eradication, the United Kingdom stands out for the global leadership role it has unilaterally taken on. It played a lead role in mobilizing international support for DAC's IDGs, the precursors of the MDGs;[24] it hosted a "child MDGs" mini-summit in 2001 that helped to keep the global goals agenda in the public eye; it energetically encouraged countries to commit to the Monterrey Consensus and proposed an International Finance Facility; it used its chairing of the G8 and presidency of the EU, both in 2005, to re-ignite plans to achieve the MDGs and assist Africa; and, most recently it has worked behind the scenes at the UN to promote the MDGs, by leading the 2008 "Call to Action" at the UN General Assembly.[25] While the personal moral commitment of the UK's political leaders to global poverty reduction should not be doubted, domestic political considerations have meant that giving global poverty eradication a high profile has been a good move politically for New Labour.[26]

Why should allies like the United States and the United Kingdom – who could agree to invade Iraq – have such different perspectives on tackling global poverty? The United States appears to be a reluctant partner in this project; the United Kingdom takes on a leadership role and places global poverty on the international agenda whenever possible. The reasons are several but mainly relate to their differing positions in the global political economy and to domestic political processes. The United States, an inward-looking global superpower that is suspicious of the UN, may be prepared to participate in the rhetoric of "global poverty must be tackled" but sees little benefit in taking on leadership for such a difficult task. If it did it might be expected to contribute a lot more finance to that task – something that would not be politically popular domestically.[27] By contrast, an outward-looking former superpower with deep ties to many former colonies and powerful civil society groups promoting global poverty eradication finds the leadership role very attractive.[28] Such a role raises its international standing and plays well domestically in relation to public opinion and voting behaviors.[29]

But how can one explain the lack of interest that many of the world's poorest countries have often shown to efforts to tackle global poverty and especially MDG formulation and implementation processes?[30] This might seem strange but it can be relatively easily understood. First, on the basis of past experience, most developing countries believe that they will achieve the "best deals" at a national level through bilateral negotiations with trading partners (in the past the United States, EU and Union of Soviet Socialist Republics but more recently China and India) and aid donors rather than through UN processes. Their relationships with the IMF and World Bank, over loan conditionalities and PRS approval, are much more important at least in the short and medium term than those at the General Assembly. Global agreements at the UN are a public good that are unlikely to deliver significant additional resources and/or more favorable treatment to individual nations in the near future. In addition, many poor countries were ambivalent about the "new" ideas being introduced by multilateral action around the new millennium. They did not want to fall out with powerful institutions over matters of detail, but most developing countries already had national plans (so did they need PRSPs?), national poverty measures (so did they need $1-a-day poverty measures?) and often national goals (so did they need the MDGs?). All of these things might be new and interesting for rich countries but for poor countries these issues of domestic public policy and the sudden interest of rich countries in them could be a challenge to sovereignty.

During the period of MDG formulation (1998–2001), the main interest of developing countries focused not on economic and social goals and new planning processes but on the need for goals for rich countries (more aid, more debt relief and fairer trade). Developing countries, and notably India, were concerned that the goals set in *2000: A Better World for All* (a joint IMF, OECD, UN, World Bank document) made no commitments about rich country contributions to global poverty reduction. Statements about rich world contributions were subsequently drafted into the Millennium Declaration and eventually developed into Goal 8 of the MDGs. In terms of the developing country "voice" in the formulation of global goals, the biggest disappointment relates to the issue of reproductive health where the G77 blocked progress because of an "unholy alliance" between the Holy See and a handful of conservative Muslim countries (see Box 7.1 above).

Ten years of global poverty eradication: what has been achieved?

Assessing what has been achieved by all of the efforts for global poverty eradication described in this book is a complex statistical task that generates several annual reports and many statistics. Table 7.1 provides a summary of MDG performance to 2009 and identifies the impacts of the recent "triple crisis" on the MDGs. The accuracy of this information varies from indicator to indicator because of the poor quality of much of the underlying data[31] and problems of estimation. Assessing how recent efforts to end poverty (MDGs, FFD, PRSPs, etc.) have contributed to these changes in levels of human development is even more difficult, as this would require isolating the contribution of each mechanism from that of other factors (such as economic growth in Asia, global warming, the war in the DRC, patterns of rainfall in Asia and Africa or the global financial collapse of 2008). Such assessments also vary with the perspective that is taken: should we assume that anything less than 100 percent achievement for all eight MDG goals is failure or does partial achievement represent significant progress? Does China's over-achievement in reducing extreme income poverty, and other targets, partially compensate for underperformance in other parts of the world? Or, given doubts about the data and time lags between policy change and outcome change, should the focus be on process changes and trying to identify whether or not a step change occurred in international and national efforts to reduce poverty around 2000?

What has been achieved?: MDG performance

The most recent data[32] provide grounds for being deeply impressed with poverty reduction achievements since 1990 and deeply alarmed by the recent reversal of progress and its impacts on poor people. On the positive side, the period since 1990 has witnessed the reduction of income/consumption poverty at historically unprecedented rates. Using the "new" global poverty line of $1.25-a-day and the 2005 PPPs then by 2010 the MDG Goal 1/Target 1 commitment to halving extreme poverty will have been achieved – five years earlier than targeted. Projections indicate that by 2015, $1.25-a-day poverty will have dropped from 41.7 percent of humanity in 1990 to 15.1 percent. As a headline figure this is a 64 percent reduction in extreme poverty

Table 7.1 Progress with the MDGs and impacts of the financial crisis on the MDGs

MDG	Status in 2009	Impact of the fuel, food, and financial crisis 2008–2009
1. Halve extreme poverty	Globally on track because of China but unlikely to be met in sub-Saharan Africa	• 200 million more people fall into extreme poverty in 2005–2008 • 44 million people permanently damaged by malnutrition • Increase in hungry from 850 million (2007) to 960 million (2009)
2. Universal primary education	Close to target but will probably not be achieved in sub-Saharan Africa and South Asia	• Unknown number of children will be withdrawn from school and will not complete primary school
3. Gender equality	Likely to be achieved at primary and secondary school level but other targets are lagging	• Crises likely to impact particularly negatively on poor female-headed households and women more generally
4. Reduce child mortality by three-quarters	Significant reductions in all regions but three-quarters of countries "off target"	• 200,000 to 400,000 additional child deaths per annum – most are easily preventable
5. Reduce maternal mortality by two-thirds	Least progress of all the MDGs with 500,000 pregnancy-related deaths per annum. Very problematic in sub-Saharan Africa and South Asia	• Almost certain to increase mortality rates
6. Combat HIV/AIDS, malaria and other diseases	Most countries face difficulties in meeting targets. HIV/AIDS a particular problem and worst in sub-Saharan Africa	• Increased infection rates predicted
7. Environmental sustainability	Access to water target likely to be met but sanitation is lagging. Limited progress with CO_2 emissions and deforestation	• Mixed impacts

(*continued on next page*)

Table 7.1 (Continued)

MDG	Status in 2009	Impact of the fuel, food, and financial crisis 2008–2009
8. Develop a global partnership	No evidence of a step change in relationships. • Aid at 1990 levels in 2008 • Trade talks stalled • Climate change – limited progress	• Aid levels likely to reduce from 2009 • UNGA 2010 MDG review likely to be sidelined by domestic political concerns of member states

Sources: World Bank, *Global Monitoring Report: A Development Emergency* (Washington, DC: World Bank, 2009), and author.

in 25 years: not quite the "eradication" target declared at the World Summit on Social Development at Copenhagen in 1995, but much better than the "halving" target of the IDGs and MDGs. Two qualifications to this good news need to be borne in mind, however. First, much of this achievement has been concentrated in China. Progress in sub-Saharan Africa, and to a lesser degree in South Asia, has been much weaker. Second, there are big questions about how much of this extraordinary achievement can be attributed to international action to tackle global poverty. Autonomous policy change in China in the late 1970s and 1980s – land and agrarian reform and the opening up of the economy to international trade – may be responsible for much of the achievement in income poverty reduction.[33]

On the negative side, the ". . . triple jeopardy of fuel, food and financial crises . . . [pose] serious threats to their [poor countries] hard won gains in boosting economic growth and achieving progress towards the Millennium Development Goals."[34] The impacts of the recent crisis in terms of human development are likely to be appalling. Around 200 million people have slid back into extreme poverty between 2005 and 2008; preventable infant deaths have increased by 200,000 to 400,000 each year;[35] an estimated 44 million people will suffer permanent damage (physiological or cognitive) caused by malnutrition; and the number of those experiencing hunger is rapidly increasing (from 850 million in 2007 to 960 million by 2008 and probably over 1 billion by late 2009). In effect, sub-prime mortgages and mortgage derivatives have been responsible for their own mini-holocaust.

Moving beyond the boom or bust headline claims that can be made about global poverty reduction then, there are complex patterns of MDG achievement in different regions and countries and for different goals.[36] These are outlined below.

In 2000 the Millennium Declaration recognized Africa's "special needs." Unfortunately, this special status is still justified. This is the region of the world where MDG progress has been most limited and, even if one accepts that the MDG specification makes Africa's achievements appear worse than they are,[37] progress has been unsatisfactory. Between 1990 and 2005 extreme poverty has been well below the trend needed to "halve" poverty (from 57.6 percent in 1990 to 50.9 percent in 2005) and only a 36 percent reduction is estimated by 2015. This is clearly disappointing: but it must be noted that this is a decline – poverty has reduced in sub-Saharan Africa despite the impression from the media that "things are getting worse." Social development achievements are also disappointing: there has been only limited progress on universal primary education; gender equality in primary and secondary education has moved slowly (from 79 percent in 1990 to 86 percent in 2000); child mortality has declined but is at much higher levels than other regions (146 deaths per 1,000 births in 2006 compared to South Asia's 78 deaths per 1,000 births); maternal mortality has barely changed (from 920 deaths per 100,000 pregnancies in 1990 to 900 per 100,000 in 2005) and is almost at twice South Asia's rate; the region has encountered great difficulty in achieving HIV/AIDS reduction targets; and, there has been little progress on water supply and sanitation. The picture is not uniform across the continent, and there are outstanding examples of progress. For example, several sub-Saharan countries have made significant strides in tackling the incidence of malaria. Rwanda has increased the proportion of children under five sleeping under insecticide-treated bed nets from 4 percent in 2000 to 56 percent in 2008. Countries that have achieved high coverage of malaria interventions, notably Rwanda, Eritrea, Zanzibar and Sao Tome and Principe, have seen declines of more than 50 percent in severe malaria cases and deaths in health facilities.[38] Clearly, significant progress is being made in certain areas but Africa still merits special attention.

The goal of achieving universal primary education is likely to come close to achievement in 2015 but sub-Saharan Africa and South Asia will lag. A key concern about this goal is whether the progress on the numbers of children in schools has impacted negatively on educational quality.

There is substantial achievement in terms of gender equality at primary school level but less at secondary school level as substantial male:female gaps remain in sub-Saharan Africa and South Asia. Work-related indicators (labor force participation, occupational levels and wages) continue to reveal significant gender gaps.

Child mortality has fallen in all regions and is on target to reduce by three-quarters (1990–2015) in East Asia, Latin America and the Middle East and North Africa. Progress in sub-Saharan Africa has been limited and easily preventable deaths remain high.

Maternal mortality is the goal for which progress has been most limited. Each year more than 500,000 women die from pregnancy-related health problems. Sub-Saharan Africa (900 deaths per 100,000 live births) and South Asia (500 deaths per 100,000 live births) remain especially problematic. Most countries and regions face difficulties achieving HIV/AIDS targets. This is an exceptionally severe problem in sub-Saharan Africa. Halting the incidence of malaria and TB also remains a challenge.

In terms of environmental sustainability, the target on access to water is likely to be met globally and in many countries. However, the sanitation target has made more limited progress especially in sub-Saharan Africa and South Asia. Global CO_2 emissions have increased since 1990 and deforestation rates remain high.

The lack of quantitative targets for the goal of developing a global partnership means it cannot be judged against specific measures. However, with aid at similar levels to 1990, the Doha Trade Round stalled, and slow progress on the mitigation of climate change it seems reasonable to state that the rich world has broken its promises. The main developing country contribution – NEPAD and the Africa peer review process – has also stalled.

What has been achieved?: Is ending poverty an international norm?

Moving beyond the counting of MDG achievements and under-achievements to the grander level of international relations, it can be argued that recent efforts at global poverty eradication have failed to institutionalize poverty eradication as a global priority. The build-up to the Millennium Summit created a once in a lifetime, perhaps once in a century, opportunity to engineer a transformation in the relative prioritization that the international community, in all its guises (G7/8, G20, G77, OECD, UN, etc.), allocates to global poverty. Had this been achieved then a series of major policy changes (trade, aid, debt) and institutional changes (most obviously in the Security Council and governance of the IFIs but also in the quality of domestic governance in poor countries) would be evident. This potential, but unlikely, transformation did not occur, and so the pursuit of global poverty reduction has had to return to a long-term strategy of gradualist, progressive change.

From this gradualist perspective it is possible to draw up a short list of ways in which efforts to tackle global poverty, and particularly the MDGs and MDG-related initiatives, have contributed, positively and negatively, to processes that seem likely to foster global poverty reduction (Table 7.2). Such a stock-taking can guide action towards building on success and working out how to tackle the negative impacts of the processes that the MDG exercise has fostered.

Balancing out whether these contributions are positive or negative overall is a judgment that often comes down to asking whether the MDG glass is "half full or half empty." From my perspective it is both. One cannot help but

Table 7.2 Have the MDGs (and associated activities) contributed to more effective poverty reduction?

Positive indicators
- The MDGs have increased pressure for data and there has been a great increase in the amount of data collected on human development in poorer countries. There are also significant efforts to improve the quality of data. More and better data increase opportunities for evidence-based policy making.
- The MDGs have increased the number of opportunities for politicians and activists to publicly address the issue of global poverty and have created a "hook" for the media to publish/present materials. This has increased the awareness of people in rich countries about global poverty. In the United Kingdom and some other parts of Europe this has helped raise the political profile of global poverty and impact on public opinion and political party policies.
- In the EU, and especially the United Kingdom, the pursuit of the MDGs has supported increases in foreign aid. This aid is better targeted on poverty reduction than in the past. In the United States the MDGs led directly to the increase in aid associated with the Millennium Challenge Account and also helped expand budgets for HIV/AIDS initiatives.
- The processes leading up to the MDGs helped to ensure that the Doha round of trade talks was declared a "development round".

Negative indicators
- There is little evidence that the MDGs have influenced the domestic plans of developing countries and/or PRSs (which remain under the influence of the BWIs).
- There is a danger that reports (by right wing think-tanks and the media) of "MDG failure" (even in developing countries where conditions are gradually improving) will lead to public disillusionment in the United States and other countries and foster disengagement with the issue of global poverty eradication.
- The MDGs tend to lead to an exaggerated focus on the role of foreign aid in global poverty reduction and a consequent neglect of other issues (such as quality of domestic governance).
- In most countries national leaders have not been held accountable for the promises they have made about the MDGs. This may create an ingrained practice of leaders making big promises about global poverty reduction and then conducting business as usual ("everyone gets away with it").
- The processes of negotiation at Doha run against the commitment in MDG 8 for there to be a "global partnership" for poverty reduction.

be deeply disappointed that the heady declarations of New York (2000, 2005 and 2008), Monterrey (2002), Gleneagles (2005) and others have not been matched by budgets and policy changes. For most national leaders speeches about the MDGs or FFD are nice rhetoric but promises of increased aid or pro-development negotiating stances at Doha can be left behind once the speech has been delivered.

But, counter-balancing this negative view is evidence that in some parts of the world public norms have changed and that recent efforts to tackle global poverty have helped this process. Most clearly this is the case in the United Kingdom where all three political parties appear committed to foreign policy positions that are supportive of global poverty reduction. This may be partly because they think it is the moral thing to do, but it is also because they believe that public opinion in the United Kingdom now supports the meta-goal of global poverty eradication and that that parties could lose votes if they do not take the MDGs, levels of foreign aid and global poverty more seriously. In some democracies, it appears that constantly "talking the talk" eventually brings pressure on leaders and political parties to start "walking the walk" (see Box 7.2).

While, logically, much of the contemporary effort to reduce poverty and achieve the MDGs focuses on short-term, practical actions, this needs to be accompanied by strategic analysis. When thinking longer term about how to tackle global poverty, and what should come after the MDGs, two particular challenges need to be addressed.

First, the strategic compromises of the 1990s meant that tackling global poverty was framed from a basic needs perspective – meeting the minimum human development needs of the poorest people. This may remain the "best" frame for improving the lives of the disadvantaged, but there are other frames that could be considered. For example, would the broader approach of reducing economic and social inequality within and between countries be a more effective means of promoting progressive policy reform and re-shaping the imaginations of the better-off about how they might assist local and distant strangers improve their lives? The historic structure of the 1990s generated the global meta-goal of "basic needs for the poorest." When the MDGs "end" in 2015 could the historic structure of the twenty-first century (with its focus on security, terrorism and climate change) be influenced or manipulated to support more of a "one world"[39] meta-goal that views the acceptance of high levels of social and economic inequality within and between countries as the underlying cause of most international problems?

Second, the material capabilities surrounding the identification of goals and mechanisms for tackling poverty were of the late twentieth century and dominated by the United States and its OECD allies. The world of 2015 will be quite different with China's economic and technological capacity rapidly converging on the United States', with India, Brazil and Russia (perhaps) expanding, and with the "Next 11" becoming increasingly significant economically and politically. By 2015 the first question informing national policy debates will no longer be, "What is the US position on this?" It will be the more complex: "What is the US and Chinese and Indian and EU (and perhaps Brazilian and South African and . . .) position on this?" The future

Box 7.2 Norm dynamics and "ending poverty" in the EU

The impacts of international efforts to promote global poverty eradication on policy and behavior vary from country to country and region to region. In rich countries their most significant impact appears to have been in the EU. Here there has been a positive dynamic between domestic and international norms,[1] and alongside this a partial regional norms internalization process has been initiated. The enthusiasm of the like-minded EU countries for the IDGs (Denmark, Sweden, Finland and the Netherlands) was bolstered by the arrival of New Labour in the United Kingdom in 1997 and the formation of the Utstein Group. Thus, an influential group of EU member states came in powerfully behind the IDGs and subsequently the MDGs, with particularly strong support from the UK Chancellor, Gordon Brown, who effectively lobbied EU finance ministers to commit themselves to increasing financial flows to poorer countries at Monterrey. The British premier, Tony Blair, became highly involved in promoting the MDGs and this took the debates to national heads. As a result of these and other efforts, the EU committed itself to achieving quantitative and time-bound targets to increase aid (and other targets) in its member states. The creation of this regional norm has meant that even new members of the EU, many with only limited domestic political constituencies supporting development and global poverty reduction, now have to pursue aid targets. EU countries which joined the Union before 2002 have committed to reach ODA targets of 0.56 percent of GNI by 2010 and 0.7 percent by 2015. Countries which joined the EU after 2002 have committed to increase ODA to at least 0.17 percent of GNI by 2010 and 0.33 percent by 2015.[2] The MDGs have been used by influential European norm entrepreneurs to create regional enforcement mechanisms (formal EU agreements) that are much stronger than the wider international enforcement mechanisms.

The MDGs are also being used to re-engineer public norms in countries with little development experience through public action. The EU, in conjunction with the UNDP, has run a series of events

(Box continued on next page)

based on the MDGs for the parliamentarians of EU new member states. These force a debate on the MDGs in the parliament and generally lead to the government and opposition stating that they will pursue the MDGs. Personal involvement in these initiatives revealed that these "MDG events" introduced many politicians to "development" and "global poverty reduction" for the first time and created powerful opportunities for domestic NGOs and lobbyists to meet politicians and ministers and achieve progressive policy statements about pursuing the MDGs in public.

1 Margaret E. Keck and Kathryn Sikkink, *Activists beyond Borders: Advocacy Networks in International Politics* (Ithaca, NY: Cornell University Press, 1998).
2 Council of the European Union, 2005.

of how the world imagines international development or global poverty reduction will depend less on the elites and publics of the United States and Western Europe and more on those in the emerging powers. Longer-term, changing the ideas of the man on the street in Nanjing, Bangalore, Sao Paulo, Dubai, Jakarta and Istanbul may become as important as lobbying in Washington, DC and New York. Identifying strategies to shape social norms in the future in the emerging economies of the world is a priority task for those trying to tackle global poverty today.

Conclusion

One cannot predict the future but one can have hope. My hope about the efforts of the late twentieth and early twenty-first centuries to tackle global poverty is that, over the *longue durée*, they will be seen as one significant element in a longer-term process of international norm change that led to the existence of extreme poverty, in an affluent world, being seen as morally unacceptable. This may seem unlikely . . . but then so did abolishing slavery, ending apartheid and giving the vote to women.

Notes

1 In both its neo-liberal and more middle-of-the-road, mixed economy varieties.
2 Sebastian Mallaby, *The World's Banker: Story of Failed States, Financial Crises, and the Wealth and Poverty of Nations* (New York: Penguin, 2004).

3 Paul Collier and Stefan Dercon, "The Complementarities of Poverty Reduction, Equity and Growth: A Perspective on the World Development Report 2006," *Economic Development and Cultural Change* 55, no. 1 (2006): 223–236.

4 In a similar way promoters of structural adjustment had cited Hayek as their icon.

5 In addition, the IDGs targeted halving the *proportion*, rather than the absolute number, of people living in extreme poverty. When expected population growth is taken into account, achieving a 50 percent reduction in the proportion of people in extreme poverty equates to only an approximate 19 percent reduction in the number of people in extreme poverty. The target is therefore considerably less ambitious than it might at first appear. See Thomas Pogge, "The First United Nations Millennium Development Goal: A Cause for Celebration?" *Journal of Human Development and Capabilities* 5, no. 3 (2004): 377–397.

6 See Sakiko Fukuda-Parr, "Millennium Development Goal 8: Indicators for International Human Rights Obligations?," *Human Rights Quarterly* 28, no. 4 (2006): 966–997.

7 UNICEF was highly effective and used different concepts at different times to pursue its mission. It pursued the basic needs approach to child welfare at UN summits and IDG/MDG processes while it pursued a human rights approach through other UN modalities.

8 Senior Social Development Advisor (July 2006) and Senior Economist, Africa Division (August 2006).

9 Ngozi Okonjo-Iweal, "Fifty Years of Orderly Sovereign Debt Restructuring," Proceedings of the International Policy Forum, June 14, 2006 (Paris: Paris Club, 2006), 56–57.

10 See Anthony J. Bebbington, Sam Hickey and Diana C. Mitlin, eds., *Can NGOs Make a Difference? The Challenge of Development Alternatives* (London: Zed Books, 2008).

11 See Chapter 3 for a discussion of these issues.

12 Whether the Human Development and Capabilities Association (HDCA) formed in 2004 can shape its membership into an epistemic community remains to be seen.

13 Commonly such active opposition comes from special interest groups within a polity, for example farmers and advocates of tax minimisation.

14 The most obvious example of this is Russia. While the original seven members of the G8 regularly put global poverty and/or Africa on the G8 agenda the Russian position on this has been "no comment."

15 Gunnar Myrdal, in *The Challenge of World Poverty: A World Anti-Poverty Program in Outline* (London: Penguin, 1970), states: ". . . the United States is such a very important country. The policies it pursues are of overwhelming interest to the entire world. In a sense we are all involved in American politics" (17).

16 Pre-9/11 the Bush administration may have considered engagement with the activities generated by the Millennium Declaration. However, post-9/11 the administration reconsidered the role of soft power in its international relations and was careful not to be seen as opposing efforts at global poverty reduction (except for John Bolton). However, the Bush administration believed that poverty reduction would be achieved by trade and that poor countries needed to take the lead.

17 "We meet at a moment of new hope and age-old struggle, the battle against world poverty . . . We fight against poverty because hope is an answer to terror. We fight

against poverty because opportunity is a fundamental right to human dignity. We fight against poverty because faith requires it and conscience demands it. And we fight against poverty with a growing conviction that major progress is within our reach." President George Bush, Monterrey, Mexico, March 22, 2002.

18 Bush increased US ODA more than any US president since Roosevelt. See Carol Lancaster, *George Bush's Foreign Aid: Transformation or Chaos?* (Washington, DC: Brookings Institution Press, 2008).

19 This impacts in different ways. Many rich countries were ambivalent to the MDGs and their implementation and US ambivalence meant that they could remain comfortable in their ambivalence. The United Kingdom took a committed position and put considerable efforts into attempting to get the Bush administration to give the MDGs a higher profile in its international relations. Reportedly, reproductive health returned to the MDGs because of the desire of a wide grouping of Muslim countries to annoy George Bush and his conservative Christian supporters.

20 The exception to this is Goal 3 promoting gender equality but that relates only to equality within nations, not between countries or across the world's population.

21 Thomas Pogge, *World Poverty and Human Rights: Cosmopolitan Responsibilities and Reforms* (Cambridge: Polity, 2008).

22 Including China, India and Brazil.

23 Sakiko Fukuda-Parr and David Hulme, "International Norm Dynamics and 'the End of Poverty': Understanding the Millennium Development Goals (MDGs)," BWPI Working Paper No. 96 (Manchester: BWPI, University of Manchester, 2009).

24 David Hulme, "Global Poverty Reduction and the Millennium Development Goals: A Short History of the World's Biggest Promise," Brooks World Poverty Institute Working Paper 100 (Manchester: University of Manchester, 2009).

25 Prime Minister Gordon Brown put large amounts of time into ensuring this event was mounted. Staff at the Cabinet Office and DFID joke that all their colleagues at the UN had to do was remove the UK logos and put in the UN logo as all the documents were drafted in London.

26 See David Hulme, "The Making of the Millennium Development Goals: Human Development Meets Results-Based Management in an Imperfect World," in *Global Governance, Poverty and Inequality*, ed. Jennifer Clapp and Rorden Wilkinson (London: Routledge, 2010); and Peter Burnell, "Britain's New Government, New White Paper, New Aid? Eliminating World Poverty: A Challenge for the 21st Century," *Third World Quarterly* 19, no. 4 (1998): 787–802.

27 As pointed out earlier, President Bush massively increased US ODA. However, much of this related to the wars in Afghanistan and Iraq (especially massive debt forgiveness for Iraq). Other increases in aid were to activities that are popular with US political constituencies (such as humanitarian support after the 2004 Asian tsunami and HIV/AIDS ARV provision) or which were crafted to ensure high performance – the Millennium Challenge Account (see Vasudha Chhotray and David Hulme, "Contrasting Visions for Aid and Governance in the 21st Century: The White House Millennium Challenge Account and DFID's Drivers of Change," *World Development* 37, no. 1 (2008): 36–49).

28 Public opinion in the United Kingdom had become sympathetic with the ideas of aid and international development through the highly effective work of the country's major NGOs (Oxfam, SCF, ActionAid, Christian Aid, CAFOD, etc.)

in the 1980s and 1990s. The Jubilee 2000 Campaign generated enormous public support for debt forgiveness and a better deal for poor countries and people.

29 See Burnell, "Britain's New Government."

30 Except when these relate to promises of increasing aid volumes.

31 These problems include: data on fragile states, where poverty levels are high and volatile, is often not available; statistics on China are very important in terms of their contribution to target achievement but there are questions about whether this data is reliable; and data on some indicators, such as maternal mortality and decent work, is highly dubious.

32 World Bank, *Global Monitoring Report: A Development Emergency* (Washington, DC: World Bank, 2009).

33 In addition, there is a strong argument that much of the poverty reduction reported in the 1990s may actually have occurred in the 1980s. See Yasheng Huang, *Capitalism with Chinese Characteristics: Entrepreneurship and the State* (Cambridge: Cambridge University Press, 2008).

34 World Bank, *Global*, 1.

35 This suggests 1.4 million to 2.8 million additional infant deaths between 2009 and 2015.

36 Here only the major points can be covered. See World Bank, *Global* (and other years) for statistical details and analysis.

37 William Easterly, "How the Millenium Development Goals are Unfair to Africa," *World Development* 37, no. 1 (2009): 26–35.

38 UN, *The Millennium Development Goals Report 2009* (New York: UN, 2009), 36.

39 Peter Singer, *One World: The Ethics of Globalization* (New Haven, Conn.: Yale University Press, 2002).

8 Moving forward on global poverty
Can we care?

"I guess basically one wants to feel that one's life has been more than just consuming products and generating garbage. I think that one likes to look back and say that one's done the best one can to make this a better place for others."

(Peter Singer)[1]

"So while academics seek problems and criticize, practitioners seek opportunities and act. Academics look for what has gone wrong, practitioners for what might go right . . . practitioners have a sense, too, that their actions or non-actions make a difference."

(Robert Chambers)[2]

In *Rural Development: Putting the Last First*, Robert Chambers writes of the contrast between "negative academics," who are rewarded for the quality of their criticisms and elaborations of why efforts to improve the human condition fail, and "positive practitioners," who strive to assist the efforts of poor people in difficult contexts. While one must recognize that critical pessimism can help re-shape thought and action, and over-optimism can waste resources and on occasion may be dangerous, in this final chapter I step back from academic analysis and adopt a practical perspective – what can be done to help poor people improve their prospects and the prospects of their children?

When people who are not poor try to help those who are poor there is a strong chance that they will neglect the agency of the poor. This needs to be watched against at all times. Most of the practical and academic work I have done over my career has been at the micro-level – from teaching in rural schools in Papua New Guinea to researching community conservation in Uganda to designing micro-finance and ultra-poor programs in Bangladesh. The work for this book has been the first systematic work I have done about global poverty and looking at what can be done to change structures of global governance and international social norms. The contrast between this micro and macro work has made it clear to me that most poverty reduction is done by poor people – strategizing about educating their children, thinking about whether to migrate to a town or city in an attempt to win a job in a factory, changing the crops they plant, expanding their micro-enterprises, helping poor friends and neighbors cope with a crisis, working 14 hours a day rather than 12 hours . . . and a million other actions.

Those of us outside of the "poor world" – elites and middle classes in rich countries *but increasingly* elites and middle classes in developing countries – need to recognize this but we can also actively support the efforts of poor people. Poor people have not chosen the contexts within which they strive to improve their lives and the lives of their children – unfair trade regimes, social discrimination, resource scarcity, limited or no access to technology and finance, bad governance and the many other factors discussed in this book. But, we can try to improve those conditions (by demanding trade reform, providing more predictable and effective aid, mitigating climate change, making technology available and other actions) so that the poor can achieve more. We need to encourage our leaders and public institutions to match their promises with resources and action. We need to show "we do care," practically and strategically, about assisting the poor and poorest to improve their lives.

Poverty reduction is not a gift that the better-off give to the poor but a form of social solidarity through which the better-off support the efforts of poor people more effectively. We share a common humanity and live in "one world."[3] Foreign aid and policy reform are only a part of the task of global poverty eradication. The key issue is accelerating the speed of progressive social change by identifying effective strategies and tactics to establish the unacceptability of extreme poverty in an affluent world as an international social norm. Central to these efforts are creating and promoting ideas that change attitudes, norms, policies and behaviors in ways that create the economic, social and political space for poor people to improve their lives and their prospects in the ways that they seek – ideas matter.

There are two risks in trying to "be practical" in this conclusion – the risk of sounding as though I am preaching and the risk of making the contribution that any individual can make to global poverty eradication sound so miniscule that personal angst displaces practical action.[4] The first is a personal risk that someone in a privileged position such as mine can cope with – there are worse things than being criticized for moralizing. The second risk needs careful consideration, the sort of analysis that Susan Neiman produces in *Moral Clarity: A Guide for Grown-Up Idealists.*[5] One of her findings has particular relevance for this book: "We may need great deeds for inspiration, but they should not distract us from good ones. Most of these are banal – acts that can be broken down into steps that are so easy to carry out that they're hard to recognize for what they are."[6] The suggestions for personal action at the end of this chapter identify many small steps.

Where are we? The context for personal action

The last 200 years have seen an extraordinary transformation in the human condition – incomes have risen at staggering rates (particularly for elites and middle classes), life expectancy and health status have greatly improved and extreme poverty and insecurity is no longer the norm for the majority of people. These improvements accelerated in the 1980s (with land reform in China) and the 1990s (with partial economic liberalization in India). Over the last 20 years economic progress has occurred at an unprecedented rate and hundreds of millions have been lifted out of income poverty, especially in Asia. Alongside this levels of human development (health status, life expectancy, literacy, the status of women and others) have improved, often dramatically.

In historical terms poverty may be at low levels (at least proportionately if not in terms of absolute figures) but humanity's extraordinary wealth and command over resources is at levels that were unimaginable to previous generations. Such unprecedented progress has impacted on the human imagination and led increasingly to the recognition that poverty is in no sense a natural condition: in an affluent world people are poor because of the ways in which we – our local, national and international societies – organize things. With 2.5 billion people living on less than $2 a day and almost one billion people going hungry each night, present-day levels of poverty are appalling. In the 1990s such thinking helped fuel the idea that global poverty could be eradicated and this laid the basis for the world's biggest promises – the Millennium Declaration and the Millennium Development Goals.

Unfortunately, the opportunity created by the "Millennium Moment" for a truly concerted international effort to reduce poverty around the world between 2000 and 2015 appears to have passed. Such an effort was always only an outside possibility for reasons that have been examined in detail in earlier chapters. Here I provide only a summary – a blunt summary (see Chapter 7 for a full analysis of why extreme poverty persists in an affluent world).

First, poverty persists because those of us doing well – powerful countries, corporations, political and economic elites, professionals, middle class folk in rich and poor countries – simply "don't care" or "don't care enough." We place a low priority or no priority on the welfare of the "distant needy" while maintaining, or increasing, our control over resources, technology and organizational capacities in ways that advance our present and future access to assets, goods and services. While global wealth has been increasing rapidly, so has global inequality:[7] the recent benefits of global growth have been concentrated in particular regions, countries, social classes and individuals. The precise motivations for such a lack of concern are hard to pin down but it is clearly not "lack of information," as could be claimed at earlier times. For some – the Mugabe regime in Zimbabwe, the military junta in Burma, people traffickers across Europe, many bankers in New York and London, the Russian government – pure selfishness and greed explain that it is not "we don't care" but "we don't give a damn."

For others, a much larger group than the former, "we don't care enough" seems more appropriate. This position might describe the Bush administration in the US (dramatically increasing the US aid budget while demanding that UN declarations remove the term "poverty");[8] the EU (committing itself to binding aid targets but being unable to tackle anti-poor subsidies to its farmers); compassionate corporations (starting to check out conditions in their supply chains but maintaining vast carbon footprints); probably you and me (recycling paper, plastic and bottles to lower our CO_2 emissions but not yet prepared to give up vacations that involve airplane flights). At a global level, the values held by humanity (mixes of self-interest and compassion that emphasize the former), our social norms, the ideas we pursue (economic growth, increased income, more goods) and the institutions we shape (governments, corporations, multilateral organizations) continue to ensure that a minority of people have privileged access to the world's resources and technology – and that we can maintain that privilege in the future.

Second are the unbalanced contests about the ideas that shape thinking about development and poverty, and action for, poverty eradication. Debate about such important issues is a healthy thing – and disagreements are essential to reduce the prospects of a dominant orthodoxy emerging, that meets the needs of only a particular sub-set of humanity. Such debates are always likely to favor the better-off, as it is they who finance and shape knowledge-creating institutions such as schools, universities and think-tanks. A major problem in recent times is the way in which the most powerful institutions for promoting ideas about poverty and development have been prepared to (i) dissimulate about their policies and practices, and (ii) produce inaccurate findings about the impacts of the policies they favor. On the first item and as an example, the World Bank and IMF have publicly claimed that to make poverty reduction policies effective national plans must be nationally "owned." There is substantial evidence to support this finding as when governments do not "own" policies we know that there are many ways in which they can avoid policy implementation – as the Bank and IMF found out with structural adjustment conditionalities 20 years ago. However, throughout the 2000s the BWIs have sought to control the content of PRSPs and PRSs in aid dependent countries to such a degree that the idea of "national ownership" became to be seen as a joke in the finance ministries of many countries. While overtly the World Bank and IMF claim to have learned the lessons of the 1980s and 1990s this is not yet evident in their behavior.

On the second item, the production and active dissemination of inaccurate findings and the Deaton Review of World Bank research conclusion that ". . . the Bank proselytized and selected new work in major policy speeches, without appropriate caveats on its reliability" are truly alarming. Although only a few of the Bank's Research Department staff were guilty of data mining so as to show that trade liberalization was always good for the poor,[9] their work significantly influenced policy around the world.[10] If this continues then the Bank will have the capacity to prove that its favored policies work . . . even when they don't! The debates between academic economists in the US "freshwater" and "saltwater" universities may seem a long way from Kinshasa and Kathmandu but, given the influence of the US economics discipline over BWI ideas, these debates have a considerable (specialists on the DRC and Nepal might say ridiculous) influence on World Bank and IMF policy advice and action in all countries.

The third factor explaining the limited action and progress on global poverty eradication in the last ten years concerns the institutional framework. Formally, multilateral institutions designed to meet the problems of the mid-twentieth century provide the lead on global poverty reduction. The UN struggles on but it has not been reformed to make it more effective. Its General Assembly continues to make big promises without having to match these with resources and/or corresponding policy changes by its members. UN agencies remain poorly coordinated and their effectiveness may be reducing.[11] While there is a consensus that the governance structures of both the World Bank and IMF are inappropriate (arguably illegitimate) for the twenty-first century – with both institutions dominated by US and Western European members and thinking shaped by US-trained neo-classical economists – change has been slow. The initial response to the 2009 Zedillo Commission on World Bank reform by the President of the World Bank, Robert Zoellick, about changing the size and structure of the Bank's board and choosing presidents without regard to nationality, has not been encouraging.[12] He agrees that reform is needed but makes no reference to membership or procedures for the selection of his successor. Zedillo notes that "[o]nly national leaders can break the gridlock on reform of the World Bank Group" – but, will the G20 take up this challenge? The evolution of the G8 into the G20 in 2009 – recognizing that actions to limit the damage of the global financial crisis would be ineffective if China, India, the African continent and the Islamic world were not party to discussions – might be viewed as progressive change. But the rules of the game at the G20 remain unchanged (leaders push for national self-interest from a short-term perspective) and its initial deliberations suggest that the widening of membership has not led to any significant improvement in its concern for the world's poor people. At the same time the informal, non-state institutions that might re-shape action for poverty eradication have made only limited progress. While those NGOs, civil society groups, faiths and coalitions that promote public awareness and concern about global poverty have developed a capacity to produce reasonably effective campaigns (such as Jubilee 2000 and Make Poverty History) a fully fledged social movement demanding global poverty eradication, which one might have imagined around 2000, now seems unlikely to emerge. At the elite end of the spectrum, attempts to create an epistemic community that could challenge the power of the cabal of neo-classical economists prescribing growth through liberalization as the panacea for poverty have made only limited progress. The idea of human development has helped many individuals and agencies elaborate alternative visions and policies but its influence now may be stalling. It has not captured the intellectual heights within any powerful academic discipline or the institutions that dominate policy (such as the World Bank, IMF or ministries of finance).

What should be done?

As argued in earlier chapters, hope for re-kindling concerted action against global poverty has to lie in more gradualist institutional changes seeking to change international social norms. The efforts of the late 1990s and 2000s to make global poverty a genuinely international issue – through debt cancellation campaigns, advances in poverty measurement, agreeing the MDGs, promoting PRSPs, debating innovative finance mechanisms – targeted at UN meetings and at G8 and EU summits, have led to increased public recognition of the problem of extreme poverty in an affluent world. Finding multiple strategies to advance this social norm – through new campaigns, lobbying strategic events, links to religions, re-shaping school curricula, supporting leaders, working with celebrities and other devices – seems the best way of thinking about future action. While the advance of an epistemic community would require a conceptual focusing of exactly what global poverty eradication means, its advance as a social norm can pick and choose from different concepts, depending on the audience and the context. At times narrow concepts, such as $1-a-day measures, may be useful for challenging public attitudes. At other times broader concepts, such as poverty as an abrogation of human rights, may be needed to re-shape public thinking. A sudden "breakthrough," such as a new Millennium Declaration, seems unlikely. Instead the slow accretion of the understanding (and its diffusion) among those who are doing well, that extreme poverty in an affluent world is morally unacceptable, is the way forward.

Disappointments with overall achievements in global poverty eradication over the last ten years do not mean that nothing has been achieved – debt cancellation has been unprecedented, aid flows have been stabilized (if not increased), the EU has made its new members commit to the MDGs and foreign aid, and countries such as Ghana, Rwanda, Mozambique, Tanzania and others have improved their capacity to plan and program poverty reduction. Global poverty is now on the international agenda, which it was not in the 1990s. But it is a sub-item compared to the issues that genuinely have the attention of those with power and influence at the global level – terrorism, climate change, trade and growth, access to natural resources, energy security and financial stability. The grand promises national leaders made in 2000 and 2001 have made a little difference but they have not been honored: nor have leaders been held accountable for this.

Those seeking to improve the position and prospects of the world's poorest people will need to think both practically and strategically. Practically, with an eye on the short term, they must strive for incremental improvements in policies and resourcing for poverty reduction – increases in aid, more effective aid, making trade a little fairer, implementing anti-corruption measures, strengthening social protection policies and improving social services in poorer countries and so forth. With an eye on the longer term and the grander goal, they must strategize on how to advance poverty eradication as a global social norm – through promoting ideas, gaining media and political attention, lobbying politicians, encouraging norm entrepreneurs and many other strategies. Their hope – our hope – must be that in the not too distant future extreme poverty in an affluent world will be seen as morally unacceptable by the vast majority of world citizens and in all societies, as occurred for earlier generations with slavery, apartheid and not letting women vote.

In the rich and "emerging" countries a focus on global poverty (measurement, awareness, analysis) and global poverty eradication (global goals, policies, finances and institutional reform) will continue to be useful. In developing countries this global focus has much less relevance. The priority must be on the national level (measurement, diagnostic analysis, national goals and national policies and domestic institutional reform). Governments and activists in poorer countries, and poorer people, need national goals to pursue (not generic global goals), improved estimates of poverty by national agencies (not more accurate $1.25-a-day measures in Washington, DC), better domestic revenue mobilization (more important than foreign aid), reformed service delivery agencies (as well as reformed global institutions) and national poverty eradication strategies. The relative lack of interest that developing countries had in the MDGs and similar global poverty ideas around 2000 reflects that global poverty is of less interest to developing countries than it is for rich countries. This was not due to a lack of understanding but recognition by developing countries that their most effective contribution to poverty reduction is at the national level or below.

What should be done . . . by agencies and leaders?

As this book has shown, there are vast debates about all aspects of tackling global poverty and magic bullets are hard to find. But perhaps a little advice can be offered to those with leadership roles or who define agency positions. Although these roles vary with who you are and where you are, the key point to make is the need to think both practically (what can be done to reduce poverty for some people in the near future) and strategically (what can be done to create an international system that will prioritize human welfare over the longer term)? Anything that a leader or agency does, or advises others to do, should be "tested" to ensure that practical and strategic choices reinforce each other.

Practically, the following actions can be recommended.

- Maintain the pressure on rich country governments to honor their MDG, Finance for Development and other commitments – make political parties and leaders accountable for the promises made to end poverty.
- Continue to push for reform to the UN, World Bank and IMF. (In the short term this means stopping the Zedillo Report on the Bank from being shelved.)
- Maintain the pressure on developing countries to improve domestic governance and plan and implement national strategies focused on poverty reduction. This will mean helping national governments to develop and strengthen their own approaches to national planning as they move away from BWI-controlled PRSs.
- Encourage the institutionalization of social protection programs for the poor and poorest in all countries.[13]
- Prioritize programs and policies that will provide food security for poor households through increased agricultural productivity and improved access to food.

Strategically leaders and agencies could:

- Look for ways of linking poverty reduction initiatives to more favored global issues and, especially in rich countries, to climate change. Try to poverty-proof other policies (anti-poor programs like bio-fuel subsidies must be avoided) and/or have them framed in ways that are pro-poor (e.g. understanding responses to climate change as climate justice).

- Ensure that their activities, directly and/or indirectly, promote global poverty eradication as an international norm by raising public awareness and mobilizing support.
- Use different conceptualizations of poverty reduction (in different contexts) to reinforce prospects for poverty reduction. Aid-financed activity may progress best with a basic needs approach but re-shaping public attitudes in rich countries could focus on reducing inequality or promoting human rights.
- Think very carefully about whether the long-term interests of the poor are best represented as a "development emergency"[14] requiring global charity or as a structural problem requiring institutional reforms and new thinking. Global poverty demands urgent action but framing global poverty as an emergency may grab media headlines but weaken public understanding of the issue.

What should be done . . . by me?

The people who read this book will be elite and middle class people – mainly from rich countries but also, hopefully, from low and middle income countries. You have busy lives to lead (earning an income, studying at university, raising children, caring for aging parents) and many pressures (job insecurity, mortgage payments, and school and university fees). But you also know that you are connected to global poverty – from the labels on the food and clothes you buy, newspaper reports about the metals in your mobile phone (almost certainly from mines in the DRC), the illegal migrants who deliver your pizza and your carbon footprint (helping to flood Bangladesh while adding to climate variability in Africa). You can't solve the problem of global poverty but you too can act practically and think strategically, making small steps that can make a difference.

In practical terms you could:

- Make contributions to a development NGO (ideally one that you pick carefully on the basis of evidence about its performance and that you contribute to regularly). You could consider becoming a volunteer promoting awareness or raising funds.
- Buy fair trade products and letting retailers know this is your preference.
- Ask your local councilors, elected representatives and others about their views (and political party policies) about development. Let them know that global poverty is a domestic policy issue for you.

- Find ways of reducing your personal carbon footprint – start small and gradually add on new ways of emitting less CO_2.
- Ask your pension fund, bank, insurance company or investment manager whether they have a policy on ethical investment. If they do, could it be improved? If they do not, why not?
- Read around the topic and share your opinions with others. Is there more you could do to help the poor and poorest?[15]

More strategically you might:

- Think about your personal views on related issues. If you support a political party that opposes immigration then that will reduce flows of income and wealth to poorer countries and poorer people. Is that fair?
- Think about whether you support multilateralism and agencies such as the UN when talking with others. The UN has many problems and it is easy to criticize it, but that may mean it needs strengthening rather than weakening;
- Use your personal networks – social groups, church, mosque, and friends – to discuss ideas about "what should be done" to reduce global poverty.
- Could you become an activist? Join a local NGO group, join a "debt forgiveness" march or pursue an idea with friends (see Box 8.1 for an example).

Box 8.1 Local action and global poverty: fair trade towns and cities

Twenty years ago a small group of Oxfam supporters in the village of Garstang (Lancashire, UK) talked about what they could do to help contribute to Oxfam's campaign on "fair trade." One idea was to persuade the schools and businesses at which they worked to use fair trade products. That was relatively easy, so then they decided to persuade all of their local schools, hospitals, shops, cafes and pubs to use and stock fair trade tea, coffee and chocolate. This did not merely mean that fair trade sales went up – it also meant that local schools started to include fair trade and global poverty as issues in their curricula and the local media began to run occasional articles about poverty and trade. It took several years to persuade all of their local institutions to switch to fair trade goods, but when that was achieved they declared Garstang the world's first "Fair Trade Town."

(Box continued on next page)

What next? They decided to encourage other towns with Oxfam member groups to switch to fair trade products and started off a campaign. Fifteen years on there are now more than 500 fair trade towns in 17 countries and fair trade cities (Chicago may be the first in the United States) are on the drawing-board. At a conservative estimate this group has introduced more than half a million people into using fair trade products and thinking about the links between trade and poverty. In October 2009 this group launched the Fair Trade Way, a six-day walking trail from Garstang to Keswick using fair trade overnight stops each night. Their plan is to eventually have a Fair Trade Trail, linking Lands End to John a Groats, via fair trade towns that cross the UK. This won't be something they design – it will be other local activists taking the idea forward. Their practical action, increasing demand for fair trade products, has contributed to strategic change – promoting an international social norm to end poverty.

Concluding words

Historically, the evidence indicates that the human condition is improving and that poverty is reducing, in proportional terms. But, levels of poverty and the associated reduction in human flourishing remain high and the absolute numbers involved have increased in recent years. Feeling angst about this has little value; action is needed. In the short term this means the practical actions described above. In the longer term it means becoming part of a process that is contributing to moves towards a tipping point in international social norms – a point at which there is genuine recognition across the people of rich and poor countries that extreme poverty in such an affluent world is morally unacceptable. Progress may seem slow . . . but that was the case for the abolition of slavery, attaining votes for women and ending apartheid. Poverty can be eradicated, if enough people take enough small steps to do so.

Notes

1　Peter Singer, *The Life You Can Save: Acting Now to End World Poverty* (New York: Picador, 2009).
2　Robert Chambers, *Rural Development: Putting the Last First* (London: Longman, 1983), 30–35.
3　Peter Singer, *One World: The Ethics of Globalization* (New Haven: Yale University Press, 2002).
4　Interestingly, the idea that "there is very little I can do" is not limited to "ordinary people." In researching this book I have had African Ministers of Finance and heads of aid agencies express the opinion that they have very little influence over the ways in which their economies or agencies behave. But, we should not confuse little influence with *no* influence.
5　Susan Neiman, *Moral Clarity: A Guide for Grown-Up Idealists* (London: Bodley Head, 2009).
6　Neiman, *Moral Clarity*, 434.
7　Branko Milanovic, *Worlds Apart: Measuring International and Global Inequality* (Princeton, NJ: Woodstock: Princeton University Press, 2005).
8　While there was great hope that President Obama might strengthen the US position on tackling global poverty, optimism is waning. It took a full year after his election for the appointment of a head to USAID, the country's main aid agency. During this period USAID staff reported that this greatly hampered efforts to argue the case for global poverty reduction in foreign policy discussions in Washington, DC. USAID just did not seem important enough to merit the President's attention.
9　On the work of Dollar and Kraay arguing that trade-liberalizing countries had faster poverty reduction than other countries, the Deaton Report concluded: "Much of this line of research appears to have such deep flaws that, at present, the results cannot be regarded as remotely reliable." Dollar is now head of the Bank's office in China.
10　I remember DFID economists telling me that this meant that poverty reduction was almost purely about trade policies after they had read this finding – so they did not need to focus on human development so much. They assumed that because this was World Bank research its quality was assured.
11　Indeed, the UNDP which led the UN's promotion of human development in the 1990s appears to have stalled.
12　Lawrence MacDonald, "Zedillo Commission Offers G-20 a Blueprint for Fixing the World Bank (But Will Zoellick Be a Gorbachev or Brezhnev?)," Center for Global Development, Views from the Center, October 29, 2009.
13　Joseph Hanlon, Armando Barrientos and David Hulme, *Just Give Money to the Poor: The Development Revolution from the Global South* (West Hartford, Conn.: Kumarian Press, 2010).
14　Ban Ki-Moon and Gordon Brown have both used this term at the G20, but it frames MDG achievement as a mega-humanitarian activity.
15　For example, Singer, *The Life*, or Irene Khan, *The Unheard Truth: Poverty and Human Rights* (London: W.W. Norton and Co., 2009).

Appendix 1
The Millennium Development Goals

Goal 1: Eradicate extreme poverty and hunger

Target 1.A   Halve, between 1990 and 2015, the proportion of people whose income is less than one dollar a day

Target 1.B   Achieve full and productive employment and decent work for all, including women and young people

Target 1.C   Halve, between 1990 and 2015, the proportion of people who suffer from hunger

Goal 2: Achieve universal primary education

Target 2.A   Ensure that, by 2015, children everywhere, boys and girls alike, will be able to complete a full course of primary schooling

Goal 3: Promote gender equality and empower women

Target 3.A   Eliminate gender disparity in primary and secondary education, preferably by 2005, and in all levels of education no later than 2015

Goal 4: Reduce child mortality

Target 4.A   Reduce by two-thirds, between 1990 and 2015, the under-five mortality rate

Goal 5: Improve maternal health

Target 5.A   Reduce by three quarters, between 1990 and 2015, the maternal mortality ratio

Target 5.B   Achieve, by 2015, universal access to reproductive health

Goal 6: Combat HIV/AIDS, malaria and other diseases

Target 6.A   Have halted by 2015 and begun to reverse the spread of HIV/AIDS

Target 6.B   Achieve, by 2010, universal access to treatment for HIV/AIDS for all those who need it

Target 6.C   Have halted by 2015 and begun to reverse the incidence of malaria and other major diseases

Goal 7: Ensure environmental sustainability

Target 7.A   Integrate the principles of sustainable development into country policies and programs and reverse the loss of environmental resources

Target 7.B   Reduce biodiversity loss, achieving, by 2010, a significant reduction in the rate of loss

Target 7.C   Halve, by 2015, the proportion of people without sustainable access to safe drinking water and basic sanitation

Target 7.D   By 2020, to have achieved a significant improvement in the lives of at least 100 million slum dwellers

Goal 8: Develop a global partnership for development

Target 8.A   Develop further an open, rule-based, predictable, non-discriminatory trading and financial system. Includes a commitment to good governance, development and poverty reduction – both nationally and internationally

Target 8.B   Address the special needs of the least developed countries. Includes: tariff and quota free access for the least developed countries' exports; enhanced program of debt relief for heavily indebted poor countries (HIPC) and cancellation of official bilateral debt; and more generous ODA for countries committed to poverty reduction

Target 8.C   Address the special needs of landlocked developing countries and small island developing States (through the Program of Action for the Sustainable Development of Small Island Developing States and the outcome of the twenty-second special session of the General Assembly)

Target 8.D   Deal comprehensively with the debt problems of developing countries through national and international measures in order to make debt sustainable in the long term

Target 8.E   In cooperation with pharmaceutical companies, provide access to affordable essential drugs in developing countries

Target 8.F   In cooperation with the private sector, make available the benefits of new technologies, especially information and communications

Source: The UN Millennium Project, www.unmillenniumproject.org/goals/index.htm, accessed 25 November 2009.

Select annotated bibliography

Kofi A. Annan, *We the Peoples: The Role of the United Nations in the 21st Century* (New York: United Nations Department of Public Information, 2000). Sets out the vision Kofi Annan had for the role of the UN at the time of the Millennium Summit. This document formed the basis of the creation of the MDGs.

Paul Collier, *The Bottom Billion: Why the Poorest Countries are Failing and What Can be Done About It* (Oxford: Oxford University Press, 2007). Collier argues that the central issue for development policy is assisting the "bottom billion" – the world's extreme poor who live mainly in sub-Saharan Africa. He identifies four traps that keep poor countries poor and develops a set of proposals for how these traps might be overcome.

William Russell Easterly, *The White Man's Burden: Why the West's Efforts to Aid the Rest Have Done So Much Ill and So Little Good* (Oxford: Oxford University Press, 2006). A critical examination of aid and the development "project." Though Easterly's analysis may be too cynical about the role aid has played in poverty reduction, this remains an important and influential book.

Richard Jolly, Louis Emmerij, Dharam Ghai, and Frédéric Lapeyre, *UN Contributions to Development Thinking and Practice* (Bloomington, Ind.: Indiana University Press, 2004). The UN has been, and is likely to remain, central to the area of global poverty eradication, particularly through the generation of the ideas that underpin development. This book reviews the UN's contributions.

Angus Maddison, *The World Economy: A Millennial Perspective* (Paris: Development Centre of the Organisation for Economic Co-operation and Development, 2001). This authoritative study of human social and economic progress over the last 2,000 years is essential reading for those seeking an analysis of and data on the human condition over the centuries.

Gunnar Myrdal, *The Challenge of World Poverty: A World Anti-Poverty Program in Outline* (London: Penguin, 1970). The idea of eradicating global poverty has a longer history than the MDGs. Gunnar Myrdal's analysis is an excellent early contribution to the field and many of his ideas remain pertinent.

Thomas Pogge, *World Poverty and Human Rights: Cosmopolitan Responsibilities and Reforms* (Cambridge: Polity, 2008). The human rights approach to development and poverty eradication is currently marginalized but growing in influence. The moral philosopher Thomas Pogge gives an important contribution to this area.

Jeffrey D. Sachs, *The End of Poverty: Economic Possibilities for Our Time* (New York: Penguin Press, 2005). Though Sachs is a controversial figure and his analysis of ending poverty is sometimes seen as simplistic, his thinking is highly influential. This book sets out his vision of how the MDGs can be achieved and poverty eradicated.

Amartya Kumar Sen, *Development as Freedom* (New York: Knopf, 1999). Sen provided much of the intellectual underpinning for the human development approach which ultimately fed through to the MDGs. This volume builds on his earlier work and provides an introduction to some of his more technical work.

Peter Singer, *The Life You Can Save: Acting Now to End World Poverty* (London: Picador, 2009). This book is an impassioned plea for people to act now to reduce poverty, written by a leading moral philosopher.

Joseph E. Stiglitz, *Globalization and Its Discontents* (London: Penguin, 2002). Stiglitz was pushed out of his position as chief economist of the World Bank due to his criticisms of the Washington Consensus. This book, published shortly afterwards, is a devastating critique of the role the IMF played in these flawed policies, particularly in the Asian financial crisis of 1997.

The United Nations, *The Millennium Development Goals Report 2009* (New York: UN, 2009). The UN provides an annual report on progress towards achieving the MDGs. These give excellent overviews of where development is advancing and lagging.

Index